Moral Tradition and Individuality

Moral Tradition and Individuality

John Kekes

PRINCETON UNIVERSITY PRESS

PRINCETON, NEW JERSEY

Copyright © 1989 by Princeton University Press
Published by Princeton University Press, 41 William Street,
Princeton, New Jersey 08540
In the United Kingdom: Princeton University Press, Guildford, Surrey

Library of Congress Cataloging-in-Publication Data

Kekes, John.
    Moral tradition and individuality / John Kekes.
        p.   cm.
    Bibliography: p.
    Includes index.
    ISBN 0-691-07813-0
    1. Ethics. 2. Individuality. 3. Satisfaction. 4. Tradition (Philosophy) I. Title.
BJ1531.K28   1989
171'.3—dc19   88-32519
                                                                             CIP

This book has been composed in Baskerville

Clothbound editions of Princeton University Press books
are printed on acid-free paper, and binding materials are
chosen for strength and durability. Paperbacks, although satisfactory
for personal collections, are not usually suitable for library rebinding

Printed in the United States of America by Princeton University Press,
Princeton, New Jersey

For J.Y.K.

Contents

Acknowledgments

IN COMPLETING this book, I received much help from fellow scholars who, in conversation or in writing, gave me the benefit of their comments and criticisms. Listed alphabetically, they are Max Black, John Calabro, Josiah Gould, Anthony Hartle, James Kellenberger, Konstantin Kolenda, Joel Kupperman, Berel Lang, Wallace Matson, Lynne McFall, Stephen Nathanson, Nicholas Rescher, and Bonnie Steinbock. I am very grateful to them for taking time and energy away from their own work to help me to do mine.

I owe a different sort of debt to Sanford Thatcher, my editor at Princeton University Press. Over the years, I have enjoyed his sympathy and encouragement for the sort of work this book represents. I am grateful for his understanding and help.

I am grateful to the Earhart Foundation for a fellowship that enabled me to continue to work on the book. Part of the book was completed in the hospitable setting of the Rockefeller Foundation's Study and Conference Center in Bellagio, Italy. For granting me a period of residency, I thank the Rockefeller Foundation and Roberto and Gianna Celli, whose direction of Villa Serbelloni makes it as close to a scholar's heaven as one is likely to find in our imperfect world.

The State University of New York at Albany and its College of Humanities and Fine Arts have been generous in granting me several leaves of absence necessary for working on the book. I gratefully acknowledge their support.

Several chapters of the book originated as journal articles. "Objectivity and Horror in Morality," *Philosophy and Literature* 12(1988), is used in chapter 1; " 'Ought Implies Can' and Two Kinds of Morality," *Philosophical Quarterly* 34(1984), is used in chapter 2; "Civility and Society," *History of Philosophy Quarterly* 1(1984), is used in chapter 3; "The Great Guide of Human Life," *Philosophy and Literature* 8(1984), is used in chapter 4; "Moral Intuition," *American Philosophical Quarterly* 23(1986), is used in chapter 5; "Understanding Evil," *American Philosophical Quarterly* 25(1988), is used in chapter 6; "What Makes Lives Good?" *Philosophy and Phenomenological Research* 48(1988), is used in chapter 10; and "Constancy and Purity," *Mind* 92(1983), is used in chapter 12. I am grateful to the editors and publishers of these journals for allowing me to incorporate in the book often substantial parts of the material they published.

I dedicate this book, as all the others, to my wife with gratitude for the help, both philosophical and private, she has given toward making it possible.

Moral Tradition and Individuality

Introduction

> We are considering no trivial subject, but how . . . [one] should live.
>
> —Plato[1]

MORAL PHILOSOPHERS have traditionally addressed the educated public of their societies on the central question of morality: how to live well. I follow this tradition both in my choice of subject and intended audience. The idea I propose to develop is that good lives depend on doing what we want. However, no sooner is this said than it must be qualified, for we may want to do vicious, destructive, stupid, or incompatible things, and they, of course, do not lead to good lives. Thus, we should do what we want to do but only within the bounds of reason. Yet this qualification is just a qualification. The presumption is in favor of our doing what we want. Doing that is natural; consequently, justification is required, not for the activity, but for interfering with it. Of course, the presumption can be overruled, interference can be justified, and doing what is natural does not necessarily lead to good lives. A large part of my concern is to spell out what restrictions on our pursuit of good lives are reasonable in contemporary Western circumstances.

The goodness of lives may be thought to depend either on the personal satisfaction they provide or on the moral merit they possess. I shall call lives good only if they are both personally satisfying and have moral merit. Thinking of good lives in this way requires understanding the complicated relation between their good-making components. The possibility I shall explore is that in good lives there is no conflict between personal satisfaction and moral merit because they coincide. Indeed, lives are good, according to my view, partly because of the coincidence of these aspects.

Correspondingly, the goodness of lives can be judged subjectively and objectively. The former assumes that we are the ultimate judges of the satisfactoriness of our lives, while the latter is committed to there being moral standards for judging lives independently of their satisfactoriness. Again, my view is a combination of these. Good lives require that we should find them personally satisfying. But this sub-

[1] Plato, *Republic*, 352d.

jective judgment must be backed by the objective judgment that the lives have merit, because they conform to independent moral standards.

Thus understood, good lives are not hard to find, for many people around us live them. They choose a way of life, work hard at it, often in the face of adversity, and they like what they are achieving. One form their lives can take is participation in an institutionalized activity they value and whose standards they make their own. Achievement here consists in continuing the activity, being favorably judged by its standards, enjoying the esteem of fellow participants and outsiders who benefit from it, and thus having a justified sense of worth. The lives of teachers, physicians, novelists, judges, soldiers, actors, craftsmen, athletes, and architects may occasion this sort of satisfaction and appreciation. But participation in an institutionalized activity is not necessary for enjoying life and for receiving the justified high regard of others. Mothers and explorers, philanthropists and amateurs, inventors and housewives, entrepreneurs and handymen may also live full lives; live with verve, relish, and enthusiasm; greatly benefit others; and be fittingly admired.

At the same time, in contemporary Western societies, there is also a deep and serious disquiet about good lives. People reflecting on the conduct of their affairs, because they are naturally thoughtful, or because disappointment or boredom prompts them, wonder about the point of it all, about what would be an improvement of their lot, about why and how they should face adversity. In this situation, moral philosophers ought to be able to give reasonable answers, and that is what I try to do here.

My answer, that good lives depend on doing what we reasonably want to do, does not mean that we should merely pursue pleasure. Good lives may involve doing our duty at great cost to ourselves, enduring much hardship in the service of a cause, or making sacrifices for people we love. We satisfy a want if we achieve its object, but that need not be pleasure. Nor need the object concern us directly, since we may want to benefit, punish, help, or resist others. Thus, the satisfaction of a want need not be selfish either.

Yet, good lives do not require satisfying all of our wants, for many of them are superficial; good lives require only that we should satisfy our important wants. Doing so, however, is still not sufficient because our important wants are frequently incompatible. The achievement of long-term goals routinely requires the frustration of short-term ones, and long-term wants often conflict with each other. These tensions can be resolved by establishing priorities among our important wants. Yet even if we succeed in satisfying the most important of our hierarchically ordered wants, our lives may still not be good. For we aim to satisfy our wants because we believe that the result will contribute to a good life; but we may be mistaken: the marriage, career, or position we seek may turn to ashes. The satisfaction of our most important wants is compatible with our own estimate that we have failed to achieve good lives. So an additional condition of good lives is that the satisfaction of the most important of our hierarchically ordered wants must occur in the context of lives we have good reason to value, and we do value, for both their personal satisfaction and moral merit.

This way of looking at the matter makes evident the significance of the qualification that we should be guided by good reasons. Among the many reasons guiding us, the conventions of the moral tradition of our society have primary importance. Thus, at the core of good lives lies the need to maintain a balance between moral tradition and individuality. Individuals endeavor to live good lives, and their moral tradition guides their endeavors by defining possible forms good lives can take and limiting permissible ways of trying to achieve them. The balance is successfully maintained if the traditional guidance actually fosters good lives and if individuals appreciate their tradition for it.

My view of the ideal relation between moral tradition and individuality is, therefore, one of reciprocal enhancement and limitation. The justification of a moral tradition must include that it improves its participants' chances of living good lives. Consequently, a reasonable moral tradition is not an uncomfortable suit we may put on for the sake of propriety but a repository and a safeguard of the ideals of good lives that have stood the test of time. Nor is the aspiration to develop our individuality a search for unfettered lives. It is rather a search for forms of life that suit our characters and circumstances, forms that civilize the raw energy behind our diverse wants. So my view involves neither the justification of individualism, at the expense of moral tradition, nor the justification of moral tradition, on the grounds that it curtails the excesses of individualism. My view is that good lives require balancing the claims of moral tradition and individuality and that, if things go well, both make essential and equally important contributions to good lives.

I shall refer to my view as *eudaimonism*. I use this foreign and technical term because it has no simple English equivalent and because it identifies a moral tradition to which my view belongs. The original Greek, *eudaimonia*, denotes the state of human flourishing, the state in which people are living well. This state is close enough to what I mean by *good life* to justify the employment of the term, eudaimonism, for my purposes. What exactly I understand by eudaimonism will appear as the argument unfolds. But as an initial indication, I can characterize it as a combination of Aristotelian objectivism, Humean concentration on custom and feeling, and Millian emphasis on individuals and their experiments in living.

Of course, there are other versions of eudaimonism, other moral traditions, and other conceptions of good lives, both Western and non-Western. I make no exclusive claim on behalf of my version of eudaimonism. However, I do think that good lives are possible for those who live according to it. If the same can be said for living according to other moral traditions, then human possibilities are correspondingly richer.

The connection between eudaimonism and contemporary Western moral practice is partly descriptive. For, if I am right, the types of conduct we find to have moral merit often reflect the prescriptions of eudaimonism. Yet we also act in violation of these prescriptions, and some of our practices follow the prescriptions of other moral traditions, so my description is bound to be partial. Another part of my account is intended to make explicit the discrepancy between eudaimonism and actual practice and to criticize some deviant conduct and conventions. But this criticism is not negative; it aims to guide conduct and conventions to conform more closely to the eudaimonistic recommendations; so my account is also prescriptive.

The justification of eudaimonism is that it produces a preponderance of good over evil and thus makes human lives better. Moral traditions differ, partly because they have different conceptions of good and evil. According to eudaimonism, good is what benefits human beings and evil is what harms them. *Moral* good and evil are benefit and harm brought about by human agency, while natural good and evil are benefit and harm occurring without human intervention. I shall be concerned with moral good and evil (good and evil, for short, from now on) and largely ignore natural good and evil, as well as possible benefit and harm to animals, plants, and inanimate things.

This conception of good and evil has important consequences. It follows from it that the question of what benefits and harms human beings at least sometimes has a factual answer. And if that is so, then good lives cannot be entirely dependent on what we want, believe, or feel, or what conventions we happened to have adopted. For the reasonability of our subjective responses partly depends on the objective fact that some things do, as a matter of empirical fact, benefit and harm us. Thus, insofar as morality is concerned with the achievement of good lives, it has some objective content. Of course, whether this is true cannot be settled merely by advancing a conception of good and evil. The conception needs to be justified, and I shall try to do so.

One possibility of good lives, according to eudaimonism, then, depends on maintaining a delicate balance between a particular moral tradition and the individuality of people trying to live according to it. It is delicate because the moral tradition is complex, its constituents are interdependent, and there are perfectly reasonable disagreements about the weight attributed to their often competing claims.

Among these constituents are the social and personal aspects of the moral tradition. The social aspect is concerned with people's responses to each other in the countless rather impersonal encounters of daily life. This is the sphere of social morality. In contrast, personal morality is concerned with people pursuing good lives by trying to realize private aspirations and establish enduring intimate relationships. We come to participate in social morality by being born into a society and by receiving moral education that initiates us into its ways. The development of personal morality, however, requires the complicated process of trying to find a fit between our characters, opportunities, and ideals and the forms and restrictions of good lives provided by the moral tradition. The conventions of social morality are generally simple; moderately intelligent people raised in a particular society usually know perfectly well what they are. Of course, this knowledge is not sufficient for appropriate actions, and complications can cause doubts about what actions are appropriate. But insufficient knowledge about the prevailing conventions is the exception, not the rule. Personal morality is a much less obvious matter, partly because our characters, opportunities, and ideals change, and the changes are sometimes due precisely to the growth personal morality makes possible. In personal morality we make moral requirements for ourselves, while in social morality we conform to the external requirements that prevail in our society. Thus, it is much more difficult to know the dictates of personal morality than those of social morality. On the other hand, the motivation to act on the knowledge is usually stronger in personal morality than in social morality. For the requirements of personal morality are dictated by our pursuit of what we think of as good lives, while the conventions of social morality often appear as restrictions on that pursuit.

Some of the conventions of social morality are deep, because conformity to them is thought to be essential to all good lives, and their violations are very serious offenses indeed. Other conventions are variable. They are more or less superficial customs whose observance or violation occasions only mild approval or disapproval. There is a continuum from deep to variable conventions, and the location of particular conventions on it keeps changing. For social morality is not static; it continually needs to resolve internal tensions and accommodate changing nonmoral circumstances. These changes are reflected by the relaxation of some deep conventions, by the increasing seriousness with which some previously variable conventions are regarded, by the desuetude of old conventions, and by the emergence of new ones.

In the first five chapters I concentrate on social morality. I begin with a rare but significant experience: moral horror directed at oneself. It occurs when moral agents realize that they, themselves, have unintentionally violated some deep convention they accept and, as a result, seriously harmed people whose welfare they were committed to protecting. If the agents conclude that the violations were not accidents but followed from their characters, they see themselves as defective human beings, and this is the root of their horror. Their horror is deepened because their own self-condemnation is matched by how others regard the violations of deep conventions. I argue that moral disapproval of these violations is appropriate, even if the agents had no choice in the matter. Thus, I reject the usual interpretation of the principle that "ought implies can." The significance of moral horror and of the reinterpretation of the principle is that the seriousness with which deep conventions are held is due to the fact that they are, in one sense, objective. For some of the ways in which people benefit or harm themselves and others depend on how the world is, and so it is not merely a matter of choice what conventions we adopt in trying to live good lives.

Next I discuss the desired moral attitude in social morality: decency. I argue that decency is highly important. Then, I go on to offer a general defense of social morality. My claim is that impersonal conventions are necessary for sustaining the framework in which individuals can make good lives for themselves. Yet social morality is not particularly demanding, nor is it difficult to maintain: usually, it makes its demands on us in simple moral situations. Well-trained moral agents are appropriately guided by their moral intuitions in such situations. Thus, the social aspect of eudaimonism does not usually confront us with important choices, and it does not require much thought. It consists, rather, in the routine customary transactions of daily life, which, nonetheless, constitute part of the background of the complex deliberations involved in personal morality.

As we approach the second half of the book, I begin to shift concentration to personal morality. This aspect of eudaimonism is characterized by complex moral situations in which conventions do not provide clear guidance, either because it is uncertain what they are, or because it is difficult to know what conventions are relevant. Thus, intuition must be replaced by judgment. The object of moral judgment in this context is the accurate interpretation of complex moral situations. The moral tradition of eudaimonism offers a wide range of moral possibilities. Making good lives requires a reciprocal adjustment between our characters and the possibilities we judge to suit us best. This process is self-direction, and since it involves the constant interpretation of complex moral situations, successful self-direction depends on good judgment.

One requirement of good judgment is objectivity, enabling us to see complex moral situations as they are, rather than as they appear through the distortions of our hopes and fears. Another requirement is breadth through which we become aware of other moral traditions and of the possibilities open to us within our own tradition. But the most difficult requirement of good judgment is depth, which depends on developing our own moral perspectives to evaluate the complex moral situations in which social morality gives no reliable guidance. Part of the reason for their complexity is that what these situations are depends on how we, the participants, interpret them. And we interpret them in the light of such moral perspectives as we have managed to develop. Adequate perspectives involve understanding the significance of the public moral vocabulary in the context of our private endeavors to create good lives, committing ourselves and consistently adhering to conceptions of good lives, while knowing and observing the limits imposed on us by social morality and circumstances. Thus, I argue, the development of adequate moral perspectives depends on the development of our characters in the direction of greater reflectiveness and integrity. How good our lives are depends on how good are our moral perspectives. Yet, this dependence is only partial. For the reason why we need moral perspectives is to realize the moral possibilities that, we think, would make our lives good. But our control over these possibilities is imperfect; whether we succeed in realizing them depends not only on our characters and judgment but also on circumstances we cannot decisively influence. Thus, not even the most excellent moral perspective guarantees a good life. Our situation is that if we are decent, as social morality prescribes, and if we direct ourselves reasonably, as personal morality requires, then we have done all we can toward making our lives good.

The view that emerges from my discussion straddles several dichotomies in terms of which moral outlooks are currently classified. If by conservatism we mean cherishing our tradition and being unwilling to tinker with it unless there are good reasons to do so, then my defense of social morality is conservative. If by liberalism we mean attributing central importance to individuals, to freedom to conduct experiments in living, and to pluralism, then my defense of personal morality is liberal. But since both of these are required for good lives, I am unwilling to accept either label.

Another distinction enjoying great currency is between moral naturalism and nonnaturalism. In one of its interpretations, naturalism is committed to rejecting a sharp distinction between facts and values. In this sense, my position is naturalistic, because I think that deep conventions are evaluative and yet they are derived from some facts about human nature and the world. Nonnaturalists, on the other hand, often defend the view that moral conventions are commitments to evaluating facts existing independently of these conventions. If this is what nonnaturalism is, then my position is also nonnaturalist because, if I am right, many variable conventions are like this. Thus, eudaimonism is both natural and conventional. Its concern is with good and evil, and some things are beneficial or harmful due to human nature. But the attainment of these benefits and the avoidance of harms guarantee only the minimum conditions of good lives. To go beyond them, we need to construct conventions, and these are underdetermined by the facts and vary from context to context.

One is also expected to take a stand on whether moral justification appeals to universal standards or to consequences. Once again, I am unable to do so because both kinds of justification are relevant in eudaimonism. Certainly, the justification of moral conventions is that conformity to them makes human lives better; this is an appeal to consequences. But many moral conventions are connected to good lives, not as means are to ends, but as parts are to the whole they form. And so good lives are not the consequences of conformity to these conventions; rather, they are partly constituted of such conformity, and so they are absolute requirements of good lives.

Nor can I wholeheartedly ally myself with those Kantians, utilitarians, and contractarians who see morality primarily as action-oriented and other-directed, or with those Platonists and Aristotelians who think of it mainly as virtue-centered and self-directed. For social morality is largely as the first claim the whole of morality is, while personal morality conforms to the second conception.

As I have already mentioned, the main historical figures who influenced my thinking are Aristotle, Hume, and Mill. The contemporaries who influenced me most are Isaiah Berlin, Stuart Hampshire, Iris Murdoch, and Michael Oakeshott. None of them has written only for professional philosophers, and in this at least I follow them. A rather different kind of influence on my thinking is exercised by literature. I have found that drama and novels combine just such general significance with palpable particularity as I have tried to express in a discursive manner. Many of my chapters are given focus by reflection on the lives and fortunes of fictional characters. However, the reflections are philosophical, and my treatment of the works I draw on is governed by what I have learned from them about good lives. Of course, this is a mixed provenance. I hope that what I have derived from it will prove illuminating.

CHAPTER ONE

Objectivity and Horror in Morality

> The pains we inflict upon ourselves hurt most of all.
> —Sophocles (1369–70)[1]

OBJECTIVITY AND ITS IMPLICATION

All moral traditions have some lightly regarded conventions whose violations incur only disapproving cluckings. But there are also others, and they go very deep indeed; they set limits not to be crossed, they are the moral equivalents of the sacred. Observing these limits may or may not be reasonable, depending on what makes conventions deep. I think that some conventions are deep because they protect factual, hard, and inexorable conditions of human welfare. They provide morality with some objective content, and that is why their violations are unreasonable. Our intellect and will are certainly involved in discovering these conditions and in formulating and conforming to the conventions that protect them, but the existence and identity of the conditions themselves are as objective as any other natural necessity.

If morality is concerned with good and evil—understood as human beings benefiting and harming each other and themselves—then the domain of morality is wider than the domain of human intellect and will. For what actually benefits and harms human beings need not coincide with what we can reasonably be said to know and intend. We may refer to the sphere within which our intellect and will operate as the domain of human autonomy. One consequence, then, of the objectivity of morality is that the domain of morality includes, but goes beyond, the domain of human autonomy. My aim in this chapter is to explore the significance of this consequence.

If the domain of morality is wider than the domain of human autonomy, then there must be possible cases in which moral agents violate the requirements of morality and, thus, act immorally, even

---

[1] Sophocles, *Oedipus the King*; numbers in parentheses throughout the text refer to the lines.

though they are ignorant of the relevant facts and have not intended to produce harm. Or, more strongly, in some cases agents are liable to adverse moral judgment on account of having caused harm, even though if they had known what they were doing and could have avoided it, they would have done so. Thus, the appropriateness of the charge of immorality in some cases depends on the harm produced and not on the beliefs and intentions of the agents.

This consequence of the objectivity of morality strikes our modern sensibility as positively barbarous. For it involves leveling the serious charge of immorality against agents of unchosen actions. Yet, it seems to me, if morality is objective, in the sense explained, then we must accept the appropriateness of this charge at least in some cases. Some people no doubt will find this an added reason for rejecting the objectivity of morality. But the possibility I shall argue for is that the fault lies with modern sensibility, which, I may as well confess, I share.

My argument requires a plausible case to support it. The most plausible case will not be one in which other people charge an agent with immorality for having caused harm without knowing or intending it. For the agent, or the agent's defenders, may indignantly reject the charge. The strongest case supporting my argument will be one where the charge of immorality for unknown and unintended harm is directed at oneself by oneself, where the agent is both the judge and the accused. Such a case is Sophocles' version of the tragedy of Oedipus.

Oedipus unknowingly and unintentionally violated two deep conventions he had accepted as fundamental to his moral outlook, and he caused serious harm. When he realized what he did, he was horrified. I shall refer to this experience as *self-inflicted moral horror*, or, for short, moral horror. Moral horror, in this sense, is a rare but significant experience. It is rare, because normally our actions are successfully guided by our intellect and will, and moral horror occurs only in some cases when their guidance fails. But it is significant that this may happen, because it shows that our intellect and will do not exercise a perfect control over the good and evil we do, and, hence, moral horror is highly suggestive evidence for my claim that morality extends beyond human autonomy. Even if modern sensibility rejects this and its consequences, the tragic figures, who experience moral horror on account of the evil they have unknowingly and unintentionally produced, do not. And so they are my allies in arguing for the objectivity of morality.

Sophocles' play, *Oedipus the King*, lends itself to many interpretations, and all of them are controversial. I have adopted one of the main contenders,[2] not because I deny the legitimacy of its competitors, but because it illustrates particularly well the significance and corrosive effects of moral horror. Oedipus experienced moral horror when he discovered that without knowledge and intention he committed parricide and incest. It happened that a man he killed—not unjustifiably, given the prevalent mores—was his father, Laius. And it also happened that he married a noble and desirable woman who was his mother, Jocasta. He did not know his parents, and they failed to recognize him since they were separated at birth. The separation was intended to circumvent the prophecy that Oedipus would kill his father and marry his mother. The prophecy was first made to Jocasta and Laius, and they had arranged to have their newly born son killed. But he survived and grew into adulthood, believing himself to be the son of the king and queen of Corinth. The prophecy was then repeated to Oedipus himself, who, upon hearing it, left Corinth to remove himself from the proximity of his supposed parents. Yet his prudent efforts to avoid the calamity actually hastened its occurrence, for it was to Thebes, to the city ruled by his true father, that his exile brought him. When the play opens, the prophecies and the parricide are many years in the past, and Oedipus is the respected king of Thebes. At the center of the play is Oedipus's discovery that he transgressed the limits of his moral tradition, a process that terminates in his moral horror.

Throughout the play, Oedipus is engaged in a quest whose objects are knowledge and the imposition of his will on his surroundings. Oedipus is a king, greater than his subjects, because his intellect is greater. It was his intellect that enabled him to solve the riddles of the Sphinx and thus liberate Thebes. It was in recognition of it that he, the stranger, was made king, in place of the dead Laius, and was given the hand of the queen, Jocasta. And it was his intellect that made him a good king, honored by his subjects:

> we do rate you first of men
> both in the common crises of our lives
> and face-to-face encounters with the gods.

(41–43)

So when plague descends on Thebes, people naturally look to him for help:

[2] This interpretation is in Lloyd-Jones, *The Justice of Zeus*, chapter 5, and in Knox, *Oedipus at Thebes*.

Oedipus, king, we bend to you, your power—
we implore you, all of us on our knees;
find us strength, rescue!

(50–53)

But, as usual, Oedipus is far ahead of them. He had already sent Creon to Delphi to ask what must be done so that the gods would lift the plague. The answer was that there was a stain on Thebes, that of harboring the murderer of Laius, and it must be removed. And so Oedipus resolved to find the murderer. But the murderer was himself: "he is both actor and patient, the seeker and the thing sought, the finder and the thing found, the revealer and the thing revealed."[3]

Once the resolve is made, nothing can stop Oedipus. Jocasta, whom he loved, begged him to stop; Tiresias, the prophet, warned him against proceeding; the chorus, speaking for common sense, urged caution; his own misgivings troubled him—but no matter, he went on:

I must know it all,
see the truth at last.

(1168–69)

That is my blood, my nature—I will never betray it,
never fail to search.

(1193–94)

In this quest, "Oedipus represents all that is intelligent, vigorous, courageous, and creative in man. In his relentless pursuit of the truth, he shows his true greatness: all the powers of intellect and energy which make him a hero are exhibited in his lonely, stubborn progress to knowledge."[4] He came to see that the key to discharging his responsibility as a king, to finding the murderer of Laius, to being true to his status, to deserving the respect of his subjects was to understand himself, his identity, his destiny. This is what makes him "a heroic example of man's dedication to the search for truth, the truth about himself."[5]

At the beginning of Oedipus's quest is the prophecy that reveals his fate. The status of this prophecy is crucial to understanding the play. On the one hand, the prophecy merely foretells that Oedipus will commit parricide and incest; the prophecy does not make Oedipus kill his father and marry his mother. But the prophecy could

---

[3] Knox, *Oedipus at Thebes*, 138.
[4] Ibid., 50–51.
[5] Knox's introduction to Sophocles, *Oedipus the King*, 135.

make the prediction because Oedipus has the character he has. The violations of deep conventions follow from Oedipus being the kind of person he is. On the other hand, Oedipus has the character he has because the gods made him that way. So, although Oedipus violates deep conventions, he does so because, in the last analysis, the gods made him do it. (If talk about gods grates on some ears, their owners should feel free to replace "gods" with "circumstances beyond Oedipus's control.")

In the play, Oedipus is shown as having choices and making them. But the alternatives among which he can choose and his character prompting the choices he makes are set by the gods. Thus, the temptation is to see Oedipus as a plaything of the gods, who manipulate him for their inscrutable purposes. But this is neither quite right, nor quite wrong. In a sense, Oedipus's character is set by the gods: they gave him the potentialities he can develop. Yet how he develops them is not set by the gods. Furthermore, the potentialities set by the gods are not merely for evil but also for good. Oedipus is prone not only to violate deep conventions but also to honor them. So the sense in which Oedipus is a plaything of the gods is not that the gods determine the particular actions Oedipus will perform. Rather, the gods determine that Oedipus's character will be a battlefield on which his good and evil potentialities fight for dominance.

Much of the great tension in the play comes from seeing the futility of Oedipus's reasonable and prudent attempts to avoid the prophesied horror. Oedipus left the people he believed to be his parents. He gave up his high status, exiled himself from Corinth, and became a stranger in a strange land. But the more he pitted himself against the potential evil in his character, the more he relied on his intellect and will to avoid the consequences of being the person he was, the closer he got to bringing them about. He was doomed, for he could not escape the fundamental conflict in his character. And when he finally discovered that this was so, a discovery that less intelligent and persevering people would not have made, he experienced the full force of moral horror.

As Aristotle observes, "A Discovery is . . . a change from ignorance to knowledge . . . in personages marked for good or ill fortune. The finest form of Discovery is one attended by Peripeties [reversals of fortune], like that which goes with the Discovery of Oedipus."[6] The play, then, is about Oedipus's discovery of his own character. He started out in ignorance of the significance of his past actions. He felt that he had achieved a lot, that he was "marked for good . . . for-

[6] Aristotle, *Poetics*, 1452a30–34.

tune," and he was satisfied with himself. The discovery that he had committed parricide and incest, acts that he regarded as most abhorrent, shattered his complacent view of himself and reversed his fortune. It was not just that he unwittingly sentenced himself to exile; that Jocasta, his wife and mother, hung herself; that he fell from the highest position to beggary; that he passed from the enjoyment of great respect to being an object of pity; and that he disgraced his children—Oedipus could have borne all that. The reversal of fortune that cut deepest of all involved Oedipus's view of himself. He discovered that he was not what he thought he was. He found what he regarded as the deepest form of immorality at the core of his own character. In his reaction lies his greatness. "Oedipus is great because he accepts responsibility for *all* his acts, including those which are objectively the most horrible, though subjectively innocent."[7]

THE HORROR OF OEDIPUS

The question I shall be struggling with is whether Oedipus was reasonable in accepting this responsibility. His actions violated deep conventions of his moral tradition—conventions he had made his own, and he caused great evil by seriously harming both those he loved and himself. Yet, Oedipus did not mean his actions as violations, and if he had had the knowledge and opportunity to avoid them, he would certainly have done so. The fact remains, however, that he did do them. He was stained by the evil he had caused, even though he was not a willing agent of it. Perhaps he should be excused, but it is crucial that excuse is needed. Morally speaking, Oedipus was not in the same position as other people, for he did and other people did not require excuses. Oedipus saw this, and he was rightly assailed by the horror of what he had done. He came face to face with having caused the evil deep conventions prohibit, and he saw himself connected with the dreadful details. And what made matters very bad indeed was that he harmed people he loved and whom he was specially obligated to protect. When Oedipus found that Jocasta, upon hearing the truth, hung herself, he was hit by the full force of moral horror:

> He rips off her brooches, the long gold pins
> holding her robes—and lifting them high,
> looking straight into the points,
> he digs them down the sockets of his eyes, crying, "You,
> you'll see no more the pain I suffered, all the pain I caused!

[7] Dodds, "On Misunderstanding *Oedipus Rex*," 48.

Too long you looked on the ones you never should have seen,
blind to the ones you longed to see, to know! Blind
from this hour! Blind in the darkness—blind!"
His voice like a dirge, rising, over and over,
raising the pins, raking them down his eyes.
And at each stroke blood spurts from the roots,
splashing his beard, a swirl of it, nerves and clots—
black hail of blood pulsing, gushing down.

(1402–14)

The key to what Sophocles is telling us is understanding why Oedipus blinded himself. It is true, we want to say, that Oedipus violated deep conventions and caused what he regarded as evil. But since he did it unintentionally and unknowingly, why should he punish himself in this horrible way? Why is the understandable moral horror he experienced such a corrosive experience? Why is he so hard on himself?

The answer is that he blinded himself because he realized that his violations of deep conventions were not tragic coincidences but direct consequences of the conflict in his character. What horrified Oedipus was his recognition that he is the sort of person who would violate deep conventions and cause evil. Moral horror was an appropriate reaction, for Oedipus came to regard himself as a fundamentally defective human being.

Oedipus's defect was that instead of trying to maintain the delicate balance between his moral tradition and individuality, he regarded them, as his life and conduct testify, as conflicting. And his way of dealing with the supposed conflict was, time and time again, to assert his individuality. But this self-assertion could not have helped Oedipus, because the deep conventions of his moral tradition had become part of his character. According to my interpretation, what Sophocles is showing us is that the ultimate conflict was in Oedipus himself. His allegiance to deep conventions and his characteristic confidence in his will and intellect were at odds with one another. Oedipus is emblematic of the human condition, and central to the theme of this book, because his conflict and his way of trying to deal with it exemplify one of the recurring mistakes that stands in the way of good lives. The play has permanent significance because the danger of treating as conflicting elements upon whose harmonious balance good lives depend is ever present.

Consider the pattern of Oedipus's life. He began by pitting himself against the pronouncements of the religious authority of his time: the Delphic Oracle. In doing so, he severed his ties with his supposed family, he left his city, he abandoned his great future as the next ruler of Corinth, and he gave up the rank, status, prestige, and wealth the conventions of Corinth vouchsafed him. Oedipus's decision to put all this behind him was a far more serious step in his times than it would be in ours. For in Greek city-states, character was partly defined by citizenship and family membership. This is why exile was such a severe punishment. But Oedipus was unlike others; he voluntarily exiled himself. He was able to do so, because he felt so secure about his character as to be able to dispense with what he regarded as the inessential accoutrements of it. And subsequent events only reinforced his self-confidence. On the road to Thebes, he proudly refused to behave like the beggar he was and give way to the conventional authority of Laius and his retinue; he got into a murderous fight with them and won it. When he arrived at Thebes, he fearlessly tackled the riddles of the Sphinx, which baffled the so-called wise men of Thebes, and by original, what we would call nonlinear, thinking, he succeeded in finding the answer. Then, Oedipus, "starting with nothing but his wits and energy," became "the despotic and beloved ruler of the city to which he came as a homeless exile."[8] The pattern of seeing events as conflicts between his character and the conventions that constrain him persisted when he faced the crisis produced by the plague in Thebes. He once again asserted himself and decided on a course of action. He was enraged by the warnings of Tiresias, who spoke for the conventional religious point of view; he ignored the pleas of Jocasta, whom he loved and whose misgivings expressed the claims of his family on him; he dismissed the respectful but brooding imprecations of the chorus, representing public opinion. Oedipus was compelled to go on, because his inquiry into the causes of the plague turned into an inquiry into his own character. To desist at this point would have meant to be untrue to himself. Given the pattern of Oedipus's life, the subordination of what he regarded as the claims of his individuality to the conventions with which he supposed them to conflict had become a psychological impossibility. And he acted in character to the last. For after his world collapsed, the futility of his self-assertions was fully revealed, the lives of those he loved were in ruin, he still performed the last gesture of self-assertion: blinding himself. And when the chorus asked,

> Dreadful, what you've done . . .
> how could you bear it, gouging out your eyes?
> What superhuman power drove you on?

> (1463–65)

---

[8] Knox's introduction to Sophocles, *Oedipus the King*, 14.

then Oedipus, true to himself, answered,

> Apollo, friends, Apollo—
> he ordained my agonies—these, my pains on pains!
> But the hand that struck my eyes was mine,
> mine alone—no one else—
> I did it all myself!

(1466–71)

What Sophocles tells us, I believe, is that if we conceive of good lives as the development of our individuality in conflict with conventions, then doom is unavoidable, as it was for Oedipus. For our individuality, apart from the conventions of our moral tradition, embodies precisely the danger of causing and suffering evil from which conventions are designed to protect us. The gods have understood Oedipus's character, and so they could predict that, since this conflict lay at its core, Oedipus will violate deep conventions. If we fail to find a way of avoiding this conflict, as Oedipus failed, we inflict great damage on ourselves and others.

Sophocles' point, of course, is not that this will lead us to kill our fathers and marry our mothers. For Oedipus, parricide and incest were among the most horrendous crimes, because one of the chief concerns of the deep conventions of his moral tradition was the protection of the fundamental social unit and the source of one's identity: the family. For us, in our changed circumstances, comparable crimes would probably be betraying those we love or torturing children.[9] If we had discovered that such betrayal or torture followed from our characters, and that we were guilty of them, then we would be as horrified as Oedipus was. Sophocles' point is that for all moral agents, in all moral traditions, there are some deep conventions whose violations cause crippling psychological damage. If the agents come to see that they have caused great evil by their violations, and that their violations were not accidental but flowed from their characters, then moral horror follows.

Oedipus is that quintessential Promethean figure many romantics, existentialists, and individualists insist we, too, are. They suppose that his predicament is also ours, and if he has a flaw, then so do we. Sophocles, according to my interpretation, rejects this view, not because he is opposed to individuality and reliance on our will and intellect, but because he is opposed to a mistaken understanding of

---

[9] A contemporary case is described by Murdoch at the beginning of *The Good Apprentice*.

what is involved in relying on them. I think that Sophocles saw deeply into this matter.

Sophocles shows us Oedipus as he intelligently, courageously, consistently, and heroically struggled with the conflict in himself and who experienced moral horror as a result of this struggle. He is tragic and he moves us because his mistake is one of the enduring human temptations, one that we all feel, at least on occasion. We bridle against conventions, we see them as impediments, and we suppose that freedom and goodness consist in regaining the innocence that living in the world with its conventions and compromises has corrupted. But this is an illusion, because uncivilized innocence is both good and evil, and the cost of good lives is the loss of this innocence. The remedy is not to struggle better than Oedipus did, for he did as well as anyone could. The remedy is to cope with the conflict in our characters that causes the struggle. How to do that is the subject of this book.

Conditions of Moral Horror

There are three conditions for the occurrence of self-inflicted moral horror. First, unknowingly and unintentionally, moral agents violate a deep convention of their moral tradition and cause, what they subsequently recognize as, great harm to themselves and others. Second, the victims stand in a close moral nexus to the agents who harmed them, and the agents, due to this nexus, are personally committed to the welfare of their victims. Third, the agents realize, after it is too late, what they have done, and this realization includes the absolutely crucial fact that the harm they have done followed from their characters. Thus, they find themselves horrified, not just by what they have done, but also by what they are.

The source of this horror is the agents' self-condemnation. They are committed to viewing themselves and others from the moral point of view, and they find themselves fundamentally flawed from that point of view. They want to be the kind of people who do not inflict undeserved harm on others, and they discover that they did just that, not only accidentally, on some rare occasions, but habitually. This is the salient fact that horrifies them. That the potentialities out of which they have formed their defective characters were not of their own making and that they had caused harm unknowingly and unintentionally are irrelevant to the unavoidable judgment that being the sort of people they were is a bad way of being. Their moral failure was not that they were deficient in knowledge or feeble in intention, but that they were people who habitually inflicted undeserved harm on others.

If deep conventions indeed protect objective conditions of human welfare, if, that is, morality is objective, at least insofar as it incorporates deep conventions, then the appropriateness of moral condemnation depends on the violation of deep conventions and not on the knowledge or intention of the agent. That moral horror is a possible experience, and that it is an appropriate response to the type of situations I have specified, is a consequence of the objectivity of morality.

Violations of deep conventions can be excused or extenuated. This may be the proper treatment of outsiders who are unacquainted with the moral tradition whose deep conventions they violate, or of the mentally defective and the insane who do belong but are unable to comprehend the significance of their actions. Further grounds for excuse are if the violations occurred when the agents were in unusual or extremely stressful situations and their actions were not in character, or if their violations were deliberate acts of protest against conventions that they rightly regarded as immoral. Consequently, the judgment that moral horror is an appropriate reaction is defeasible, and it can be defeated if excusing or extenuating conditions are present. But if they are not defeated in this manner, as they were not in Oedipus's case, then it is appropriate to be horrified by one's own characteristic violations of deep conventions, even if the violations were unknowing and unintentional.

Of course, this does not mean that the moral status of unknown and unintended violations of deep conventions is the same as that of fully conscious and deliberate violations. Oedipus has quite a different moral standing from Clytemnestra or Iago. Oedipus is like them in having caused evil when he acted in character; thus, he is like them in being liable to adverse moral judgment. But Oedipus is unlike them in having the character he had, as it were, under protest. Oedipus came to see that his way of being was a bad way, and he regretted and condemned it, but Clytemnestra and Iago did not. Consequently, while it follows from the objectivity of morality that adverse moral judgment is appropriate in all these cases, it does not follow, and it is not true, that the appropriate judgments should be equal in severity. I shall discuss in the next chapter how to draw a reasonable distinction between the appropriateness and the severity of adverse moral judgments.

Moral Horror and Self-Condemnation

Moral horror led Oedipus to blind himself. He judged himself and found himself guilty. Because he was committed to deep conventions, he was horrified by his own violations of them. Oedipus wanted to have a good life, but his way of trying to get it defeated his own efforts. He saw a conflict between moral tradition and individuality, instead of seeing the need for a carefully maintained balance between them, and he conceived of the good life as the resolution of the conflict by the assertion of his individuality. Thus he cultivated in himself dispositions whose natural expression was the violation of deep conventions he had accepted, and he ended by abominating the deeds that followed from his own deliberately cultivated character. He was divided at the deepest level of his character, and when he acted according to his divided character, he transgressed the boundary, marked by deep conventions, between barbarism in which anything goes and civilization, which morality makes possible. Because he was intelligent, strong, inquiring, and honest, he came to understand this about himself. And so he condemned himself.

I think that he was right, although I do not mean to suggest that similar self-condemnation now should take the same form. We need to abstract from the mores of ancient Greece and the thematic unity of the play that suggest that self-mutilation is an appropriate form of moral self-condemnation. The general claim that seems true to me is that self-condemnation is a justified moral attitude toward such violations of deep conventions as I have described, even if the agent did not know of or intend the violations.

To belong to a moral tradition is to see good and evil in its terms. For people in it, the violations of deep conventions must seem to be evil. They cannot make justifiable exceptions for themselves, because what counts as evil or good, in the context of deep conventions, is independent of who brings it about. Of course, it is an ingrained human tendency to judge one's own actions less harshly than those of others. But the people who experience moral horror are certainly free of this particular defect. They are horrified precisely because *they* violated deep conventions.

However, why should they not excuse themselves on the ground that they did not know of or intend the violations? The reason why this excuse is not available to them is that they realize that the actions that constitute the violations are, for them, characteristic ones. Oedipus's whole life was one conflict after another between his will and intellect, on the one hand, and conventional constraints, on the other. And in each conflict, he relied on his will and intellect, and so it is not surprising that he ran afoul of conventions. Even though he did not choose the specific violations of parricide and incest, it is readily understandable why he, of all people, would be guilty of them. And this, of course, is what I take Sophocles to imply when he has the oracle deliver the prophecy. Generally speaking, if weak, cruel, malicious, or dishonest people conduct themselves in characteristic ways, and, as a result, violate deep conventions and cause great harm, although without choosing to do so, they do not have available the excuse that they did not mean the violations. They are the sort of people who would do that sort of thing. They are right if they condemn themselves, because, through the experience of moral horror, they are brought to realize that, given their own conceptions of good and evil, they are, at least in part, evil.

If we reflect on this self-condemnation, we may be tempted to mitigate its harshness. It is understandable, we may want to say, that people in the throes of moral horror become overwrought and tend to make extreme judgments. But we, the witnesses, need not become their accomplices. We should remind them, when they have reached a cool moment, that it is, after all, only conventions they have violated, even if the conventions are deep and their own. The harshness of their judgments comes from being locked into their private world. They have lost, if indeed they ever had, a proper perspective. They should see that there are other moral traditions, and in their terms, what they have done would not be judged so severely. No present-day law court would convict Oedipus of incest or parricide; Kantians would give him much credit for the goodwill with which he acted throughout; and utilitarians would concentrate on the consequences produced by Oedipus's discovery but not, given the circumstances, on the violations this revealed. This is the voice of our modern sensibility, and I have two reasons for thinking that it is mistaken.

JUDGING ONE'S CHARACTER

The first is that at the root of moral horror there is self-condemnation. Moral agents condemn themselves in this way, because they find themselves seriously at fault in the light of their own view of good and evil. This view of theirs is not a working assumption, or a fickle attitude, but a settled disposition constitutive of their characters: it defines what they want out of life, it is the source of their hopes and fears, it informs their relationships with others, and it provides many of their norms for success and failure. If, accepting modern sensibility, we loosen the hold our moral tradition has on us, for that is what this settled disposition partly reflects, we undermine our own characters and thus deprive ourselves of the possibility of achieving good lives by destroying the capacity of knowing what they would be. But since the possibility of good lives is necessarily connected with the possibility of evil ones, we can mitigate the harsh self-condemnation involved in appropriate experiences of moral horror only if we weaken our desire for good lives.

The targets of this self-condemnation are the characters, not the choices and actions, of agents who experienced moral horror. Thus, it is pointless to try to acquit Oedipus on the grounds that he had done all he could to avoid the prophecy from coming true. Oedipus was doomed because of his character, not because of the choices and actions that followed from it. And it is for his character that he condemned himself. If his character had been different, the prophecy would not have been made. It was precisely the conflict at the core of his character between his moral tradition and his will and intellect that made it predictable that he would violate conventions and thus cause evil. If morality has to do with good and evil, understood as benefit and harm people produce for each other and themselves, then the characters from which beneficial and harmful dispositions follow are appropriate objects of moral judgment. And this is so quite independently of whether people choose their characters. The severity of moral judgments may vary with the extent to which agents struggle against their evil dispositions, but the appropriateness of moral judgments depends, primarily, on whether moral agents have produced evil when they acted according to their evil dispositions. The conclusion forces itself on us that some characters are morally bad even if the agents did not choose them.

Moral horror is the corrosive psychological experience we undergo when we realize that this is true of ourselves. We find ourselves fundamentally at odds with our moral tradition. Our deepest aspirations and fears are derived from it, yet our characters are condemned by the same moral tradition. Thus, an abyss opens up at the center of our being. If we are to recognize good and evil at all, we must judge ourselves adversely. And if we give our allegiance to a moral tradition, then this tragedy can happen to us. As moral agents, we run the risk of moral horror, but there is no alternative to taking it. For, if we resolve to stand outside and alone, we deprive ourselves of the possibility of self-definition and the mastery of the conventions by which we try to civilize our evil dispositions and develop good ones.

DEEP AND VARIABLE CONVENTIONS

The second reason for rejecting the voice of modern sensibility, speaking for the inappropriateness of Oedipus's self-condemnation, is that it involves a mistake regarding the place of nature, *physis*, and convention, *nomos*, in our lives. As I read him, Sophocles warns us, through the tragedy of Oedipus, of the serious consequences of ignoring the natural roots of deep conventions. His warning is still timely because we tend to think of all conventions as more or less arbitrary human inventions. Hence, we fail to see the serious evil their violations cause, and we are reluctant to grant the appropriateness of Oedipus's self-condemnation, especially since his violations were unintentional and unknowing. But if deep conventions articulate objective requirements of human welfare, then their violations are harmful quite independently of the knowledge and intention of trespassing agents, and, thus, Oedipus was quite right to be horrified by the harm he caused. If one central concern of morality is with good and evil—with the benefit and harm people cause each other and themselves—then the good and evil actually produced override secondary moral considerations having to do with what the agents knew or intended.

The thought underlying modern sensibility, however, is that good and evil are inseparable from our intellect and will, because, in the last analysis, we decide what counts as good and evil. Our moral conventions reflect decisions about how we should evaluate facts, including facts about ourselves, but they do not license objective moral evaluations that are independent of our decisions, since there are no such evaluations. Facts are one thing; evaluations are quite another. The first are found; the second, made. Facts are natural; evaluations are conventional.

One source of these doubts about the objectivity of morality is the belief in a sharp distinction between nature and convention. According to it, nature exists independently of human decision, while conventions are ultimately produced by it. The distinction is then applied to human lives. We are said to have innate or instinctive dispositions, independent of our social setting, such as many physiological and psychological drives, and they are supposed to be natural. We also have conventional dispositions that we have been conditioned or taught to have by being brought up in a society; they are shaped by etiquette, sports, rhetoric, styles of cooking, dressing, bargaining, courting, and the like.

But this sharp distinction is untenable, because natural and conventional elements are inseparably mixed in human lives. To begin with, it is natural for us to have conventional dispositions, for it is part of our nature to live by conventions. As spiders spin webs, so we construct conventions. It is a disposition to be found in all human beings everywhere. Furthermore, we are conscious of very many of our instinctive and acquired dispositions, and through consciousness we can, at least to some extent, control them, assign priorities to them, and, in normal circumstances, choose the manner in which we satisfy them. The first consideration shows that many conventions are natural; the second shows that much of our nature is inseparable from the conventions we have created. Consequently, while it is true that we have many dispositions that stem from our nature, and not from the conventions we have created, the fact remains that these dispositions are defined and identified in terms of the conventions provided by the moral tradition into which we are born and in which we are educated. Wanting food, for instance, is natural, but what counts as food and how it is prepared and consumed differs from context to context. Even the most natural of our dispositions appear in conventional forms. Hence, in such inevitable human practices as consumption and elimination, work and leisure, sex and marriage, the treatment of injury and illness, birth and death, maturing and aging, natural and conventional elements are inseparable. Thus, we cannot draw a sharp distinction between nature and convention.

The alternative I now want to argue for is that while conventions are human creations, there are some conventions that we could not have failed to create and live acceptable lives.[10] In other words, I claim that the existence of some conventions and general conformity to them are necessary conditions of human welfare. These are the deep conventions I have been referring to throughout the discussion. Of course, not all conventions are deep, because human welfare does not require conformity to all of them. I shall call these other conventions variable.

The distinction between deep and variable conventions straddles the distinction between nature and convention. Deep conventions are both natural and conventional. They are conventional, because they are human creations; but they are also natural, because they embody necessary conditions of human welfare that are independent of human creations. The natural roots of deep conventions should cause no surprise since human beings are, at least to some extent, part of nature, and so our welfare is bound to have some natural requirements.

The identification of the natural requirements of human welfare is at least partly an empirical question, and I do not have a full answer to it. But a partial answer, which takes us a long way, is available by reflecting on common human experience. The starting point such reflection provides is that there are some characteristics all human beings have, while others differ from context to context, person to person. The fundamental difference between deep and variable con-

---

[10] In formulating this alternative I have been influenced by Hampshire, *Morality and Conflict.*

ventions is that the former are derived from universal human characteristics, while the latter are not.

What, then, are these universal human characteristics? Many of them are physiological; they determine the structure and function of the human body; they include our shape, motor and sensory capacities, and organs; they regulate the rhythms of maturing and aging, motion and rest, sleep and wakefulness, consumption and elimination, pain and pleasure, conception, birth, and death, sickness and health. Since the brain is one of the organs, and since it is at least an empirically necessary condition of higher mental processes, I include among universal physiological characteristics the capacities to feel, think, will, imagine, use language, and so on. I shall refer to these characteristics as *the facts of the body*.

A second group of universally human characteristics is composed of *the facts of the self*. The facts of the body are truisms about our physiological apparatus; the facts of the self are truisms about human psychology. We all want our lives to conform to patterns that incorporate much of what we like and little of what we dislike. We all have capacities to learn from the past and plan for the future, and we all want to make use of these capacities in the course of our lives. We all have some view of our talents and weaknesses; we also have attitudes, which may not be conscious, toward our family, illness, death, toward the young and the old, success and failure, sexual relations, authority, and we want our lives to reflect these views and attitudes.

The facts of social life constitute a third group of universally human characteristics. Vulnerability, scarce resources, limited strength, intelligence, and energy, the facts of reproduction, child rearing, and division of labor force cooperation on us. This requires social organization that, in turn, depends on the adjudication of conflicts, handing down customs, respect for authority, the treatment of the ill, a system of reward and punishment, distinction between insiders and outsiders, and, generally speaking, the possession of a more or less clearly articulated set of rules regulating conduct.

The facts of the body, self, and social life constitute part of the foundation of human motivation. For we all want to protect the conditions in which we can obtain the benefits and avoid the harms these human characteristics define. Thus, the facts of the body, self, and social life establish what must be the minimum conditions for human welfare. To jeopardize these conditions is to harm us, and thus it is evil; to protect the conditions is to benefit us, and so it is good.

Just as the facts in question establish truisms about human beings, so the associated benefits and harms are truisms about the conditions in which we can have good lives. To guarantee the conditions in which physiological needs are satisfied, so that our lives are not in danger, is obviously good, and to undermine them is obviously evil. To cause death, dismemberment, lasting physical pain, prolonged hunger and thirst is normally evil. Similarly, it is good to make sure that we do not suffer these harms.

The same air of obviousness surrounds the satisfactions of psychological wants. It is obviously good for us to have the opportunity to exercise our faculties, direct our lives, assess what we regard as important, and equally obviously, it is evil to deprive us of them. The facts of social life provide the social conditions in which physiological and psychological wants can be satisfied. Thus, having a stable society, guaranteeing security and some freedom, providing an authority and known rules for settling disputes and adjudicating conflicts are good, and their opposites are evil.[11]

This account, however, calls for two qualifications. There may be situations in which individual welfare can be best served by violating some of the conditions just described. The satisfaction of some wants may conflict with the satisfaction of others; wants may be incompatible. Hence, none of the conditions is inviolable. The first qualification that needs to be made is that while there is a presumption in favor of guaranteeing the conditions and against their violations, the presumption can be overruled. Doing so requires reasons for depriving people of the benefit and for inflicting harm on them. These reasons can only be that the situation is special, so that what seems beneficial is not, or that small harm will avoid greater harm or it will bring great benefit. Thus we may say, for instance, that life is good and death evil. But helping the incurably ill, suffering from prolonged pain, to kill themselves may not be evil. The amended claim, then, is that these physiological, psychological, and social conditions hold normally, and, if they are supposed not to hold, then good reasons must be given for the claimed exception. Of course, what reasons are good is a very difficult question, but I shall ignore it at this stage.

The second qualification is a reminder that the relevant conditions are only necessary and not sufficient for human welfare. They are the minimum conditions required for human beings to live whatever they regard as good lives. For even mystics, devoting themselves to the contemplation of an extramundane world must, at least minimally, satisfy their physiological needs if they are to go on contemplating; they must be relatively free to exercise their faculties in the manner required by their esoteric discipline; and they must live in a relatively stable and secure environment so that their contemplation

---

[11] My argument is indebted to Gert, *The Moral Rules.*

is not disrupted by such mundane matters as torture, rape, and enslavement. Guaranteeing these conditions is good because it makes good lives possible. But the achievement of these goods does not assure that the people enjoying them will have good lives; the conditions specified provide only the soil in which good lives can flourish, but they do not, by themselves, make them flourish. And from this follows the obvious corollary that in addition to these universally human benefits and harms, there are also many others that vary from context to context, person to person.

Deep conventions are deep, then, because they protect the conditions defined by the facts of the body, self, and social life. They are universal and necessary, because the specific harms and benefits they are intended to avoid or protect would harm or benefit all human beings. They are also natural, because their universality and necessity are grounded on facts. Calling conventions natural seems like an oxymoron, because the error involved in the sharp distinction between nature and convention is reflected in language.[12] But it is an error nevertheless. The human situation, created by our nature and the world, requires the existence of some conventions, and although it is true that they are human products, it is also true that our welfare requires that we should make them and then conform to them.

Yet the universality, necessity, and naturalness of deep conventions do not consist in there being specific rules embodied in these conventions; rather, they consist in the existence of some specific rules or others. Moral traditions must have conventions protecting the physiological, psychological, and social conditions just described, but the specific contents of these conventions will depend on the context and circumstances. That these conventions are deep implies that all moral traditions must have them, but their depth does not rule out diversity.

By contrast, variable conventions are particular, social, and optional. They are particular in that they guide practices that may not exist in other contexts at all. Conventions regarding public confession, cohabiting extended families, the religious dimension of healing, prophesying the future, the arrangement of marriages, and the organization of pilgrimages are important practices in some moral traditions and absent in others. The particularity of these conventions results from their social origin. Their roots are in the contingent customs of the society rather than in the facts of human nature. Nothing in human nature would be damaged or frustrated if a moral

---

[12] For an anthropological documentation of this error and an extremely interesting attempt to avoid it, see Douglas, *Natural Symbols*.

tradition treated healing as a secular craft or if marriages were not arranged but were left to the inclination of would-be partners. And this means that the observance of these conventions is, in one sense, optional. These are the conventions against which nonconformists may rebel, the respects in which a moral tradition is most open to change, the arena in which conservatives and reformers wage their inevitable battles.

There is, however, another sense in which variable conventions are not optional at all. Human welfare does not require any particular variable convention, but it does require that there be some set of variable conventions. Thus, the existence of a system of variable conventions is not optional; what is optional is the identity of the particular variable conventions that compose the system. The reason for this is that conformity to deep conventions is not sufficient for good lives. Deep conventions merely secure the ground on which good lives can be built, but building them requires many of the variable conventions of a moral tradition.

Thus, both deep and variable conventions are required for human welfare, although they are required for different reasons. Deep conventions are needed to establish the conditions in which participants in a moral tradition can satisfy universal human wants created by the facts of the body, self, and social life. Variable conventions are needed to enable participants to make good lives for themselves, once these universal wants are satisfied. Yet the necessity of both kinds of conventions is compatible with their diversity. Once again, however, they are diverse in different ways. There is diversity in different moral traditions, both in the types of variable conventions they have and in the particular conventions within these types. By contrast, deep conventions are not diverse in respect to types but only in respect to the instantiations of the required types. All moral traditions must have deep conventions about sexual conduct, for instance, but they may and do differ in the specific deep conventions they have regarding it.

I want to guard against a possible misunderstanding of my account. What makes a convention deep is its connection with the facts of the body, self, and social life and not that it is strongly held. People in a moral tradition may jealously protect some conventions and regard them as deep in the absence of this connection. Nevertheless, a convention being strongly held is not sufficient to guarantee its depth. For this reason, a moral tradition may be criticized, and there may be perfectly reasonable disagreements in it about whether a convention ought to be strongly held. Furthermore, even if a convention is deep, because it has the required connection with the relevant facts, it may still be criticized on the grounds that the specific form it takes is less likely to protect the relevant conditions of human welfare than some other way of achieving the same end. So it is not a consequence of my account that the observance of deep conventions rules out the reform of moral traditions.

Nevertheless, a moral tradition must protect its deep and variable conventions, because if they survive critical scrutiny, it is reasonable to believe that conformity to them is necessary for human welfare. The assumption I have rejected, implicit in the sharp distinction between nature and convention, is that all conventions are products of human decision, and so the pursuit of good lives may well take the form of us making new decisions and create new conventions in the place of old ones. Against this view, I have argued that conformity to specific types of deep conventions is necessary for good lives, that the existence of some types of variable conventions is also necessary, and that good lives must include conformity to some specific variable conventions.[13]

We are now in the position to understand the far-reaching consequences of the second reason for rejecting the temptation to view Oedipus's self-condemnation as inappropriate. Modern sensibility is mistaken because Oedipus caused real evil: he seriously harmed others and himself. The deep conventions he violated protected universal requirements of human welfare; these requirements are objective conditions, not optional products of human decision. They mark the boundary between civilization and barbarism, and Oedipus transgressed it. He finally understood what he had done, and he condemned himself for it. His self-condemnation is not the symptom of an overzealous moral scrupulosity but evidence of the hard-earned moral insight that the source of the evil he caused was the conflict at the core of the character he so proudly cultivated. Thus, he came to see that the harm he had done was not accidental but a direct consequence of his being the kind of person he was.

It is true that Oedipus was not in complete control of the kind of person he was. The gods, or circumstances, provided him with the potentialities out of which he had to forge his character. It is also true that these potentialities were conflicting ones, moving him in different directions. And these truths hold not only of Oedipus but of all of us. Oedipus is a heroic figure, Everyman writ large, because his potentialities were exceptionally strong and so, therefore, was the conflict exceptionally sharp among them. The fact remains, however,

---

[13] Neu, "What is Wrong with Incest?" shows how this general point holds for incest in particular.

that, if the considerations I have adduced in favor of the objectivity of deep conventions are correct, then the primary concern of morality is with the evil caused by their violation and not with the amount of control violators have over their own motivation. If morality is concerned with the maximization of good and the minimization of evil, then Oedipus, having caused evil, must be adversely judged, even though he could not help doing what he did.

I think that skeptical readers, influenced by modern sensibility, may grant that deep conventions are objective, that Oedipus caused evil, that it followed from his character that he would do so, and perhaps even that *he* was right to condemn himself. But they may still balk at the appropriateness of *other* people's moral disapproval of Oedipus. I shall consider this in the next chapter.

CHAPTER TWO

Beyond Choice: The Grounds of Moral Disapproval

> Modern philosophers have often followed a course in their
> moral enquiries . . . different from that of the ancients. In
> later times . . . philosophers . . . were necessarily led to
> [regarding] . . . *voluntary* and *involuntary* the foundation of
> their whole theory. . . . [B]ut this, in the mean time, must be
> allowed, that *sentiments* are every day experienced of blame
> and praise, which have objects beyond the dominion of will
> or choice, and of which it behoves us . . . to give some
> satisfactory theory and explication.
>
> —David Hume[1]

THE PRINCIPLE: OUGHT IMPLIES CAN

Oedipus condemned himself, and, I have argued, he was right to do
so. But now let us change perspectives and consider *our* attitude toward him and others like him. In what light should we regard moral
agents in our moral tradition if, like Oedipus, their characteristic actions result in the violation of deep conventions, but they have not
chosen the violations and would have avoided them if they could?
The widely accepted answer is that we should distinguish between
actions and agents. The actions these agents perform are morally
wrong, but they do not reflect adversely on the agents, because they
did not choose to do them. This answer presupposes the principle
that "ought implies can." I shall refer to it as the *Principle*, and interpret it as follows: Moral disapproval of an agent for an action is appropriate only if it is in the agent's power both to do and not to do
the action.

What exactly is in our power is unclear. It is obvious that doing
what is logically and physically impossible is not in our power. But
there are other constraints as well. Physical and mental limitations
peculiar to individuals may also impose unavoidable limitations.
Unobservant people cannot respond to subtle clues, dilettantes can-

---

[1] Hume, *Enquiry*, 411.

not have depth, and the lethargic cannot be quick on the uptake. What individual limitations are unavoidable is controversial. I shall sidestep this issue and simply say that, in addition to logical and physical impossibility, there are also unavoidable personal limitations on our powers, but I shall leave it unspecified what personal limitations are unavoidable. The Principle is generally taken for granted, as the reluctance to disapprove of Oedipus shows, but I have considerable doubts about it. Let us start to question the Principle by considering two new cases.

The inspiration of the first is an episode in William Styron's novel, *Sophie's Choice*, but I have altered it a little. Sophie is a mother with two children, and they are about to be transported to a concentration camp. She rightly expects that they will suffer and die. However, she has a chance to save one of her children by giving it to an obliging stranger. Sophie has a few hours to decide which child she should save; she agonizes over the choice but cannot make it. By the time the decision must be made, she has collapsed: the psychological burden was too great for her, and she just could not bear it. Subsequently, all three of them suffer and die. There are strong reasons for saying that Sophie ought to have made a decision and thereby saved one of her children. We can understand how hard the decision was; nevertheless, it was her responsibility in that tragic situation to make it. Due to weakness, understandable as it is, she failed. She could not make the decision, yet, all the same, she ought to have made it.

The second case is like Stevenson's Mr. Hyde, "the evil that is present," but without Dr. Jekyll, who "would do good." Mr. Hyde cunningly entraps people and tortures them to death. His victims number dozens. He knows that others regard what he is doing as evil, but he does not care. He also knows that his victims suffer; indeed, he is torturing them precisely because their sufferings delight him. Let us assume that Mr. Hyde truly cannot help doing what he does; it is just not in his power to stop. Surely, we should say that he still ought not torture people to death. But if we accept the Principle, we cannot say this: if Mr. Hyde cannot help being cruel, we should not say that he ought not be cruel.

What can we say about the Principle in the light of these cases? To begin with, they show that it does not express a logical or a conceptual necessity. For if it did, then the conclusions that Sophie ought to have saved one of her children and Mr. Hyde ought not torture people to death would have to be logically or conceptually incoherent. It seems clear, however, that they are not incoherent. On the contrary, they express reasonable judgments about these situations.

But they are not the only reasonable judgments. For it can be argued that the tendency to disapprove of Sophie's weakness and Mr. Hyde's cruelty comes from thinking that it was at least to some extent in their powers to act otherwise. If they really could not help doing what they did, then we should not disapprove of them, for moral judgments are then inappropriate, and so, the Principle can be maintained after all. Assume, however, that it was totally beyond their powers to act otherwise, so whether the Principle is inconsistent with one judgment about these cases does not depend on further facts about them.

Now let us look more closely at the claim that lack of power makes moral judgments inappropriate. The implication is that it is inappropriate to disapprove of Mr. Hyde's cruelty and Sophie's weakness, because their vices were not of their own making. When we make moral judgments and disapprove of what people do, we should take into account how they came to do it. Mr. Hyde did not seek to be cruel, he had no choice about it; it just happened to him. Sophie did not choose to be weak, nor could she avoid being so. If people are driven to act cruelly or weakly by forces beyond their powers, they should not be subject to adverse moral judgment. But since, *ex hypothesi*, Sophie and Mr. Hyde could not avoid acting the way they did, their cases pose no real difficulty for the Principle.

However, we may be left unimpressed by this argument. We may say that kind and strong people are obviously better than cruel and weak ones, and this is true independently of how they came to acquire their virtues and vices. Part of the force of saying that one trait is morally better than the other is that we personally would rather have it than the other and that we would want our children, friends, teachers, and politicians to be similarly virtuous rather than vicious. What else do our approval of virtue and disapproval of vice betoken but a tacit moral judgment?

Of course, disapproval should be mitigated by extenuating circumstances. People who are vicious by choice should be judged much more severely than those who cannot help being vicious. But this is not to say that we should condone vice. We should always disapprove of cruelty and weakness, although we should also recognize that on occasion there may be extenuations. However, extenuation is needed only when wrongdoing is present. Cruelty and weakness are thus proper objects of moral disapproval. The Principle holds that such disapproval is always inappropriate in the absence of choice, and that shows that the Principle is faulty.

There is a possible way of reconciling these conflicting views, because there is a sense in which Sophie and Mr. Hyde could have acted differently: what they did followed from their characters, but they could have had different characters. Following this line of thought would permit a resolution of the dispute about choice being or not being necessary for the appropriateness of moral disapproval. However, I shall not take this way out because a more radical claim seems true to me: the moral disapproval of these people is appropriate regardless of how they came to have their characters. Whether and how people shape their characters is clearly relevant to the *strength* of the appropriate moral disapproval of them. But the very appropriateness of moral disapproval is independent of whether they could have different characters; moral disapproval attaches to what people are, to what characters they have, and not to how they came to have them.

VOLUNTARISM VS. EUDAIMONISM

In this dispute about the Principle, one side makes moral disapproval conditional on people's powers, while the other side includes their powers among the objects of approval and disapproval. What kind of dispute is this? We may say, initially, that it is a dispute about the limits of morality. One side holds that morality is coextensive with the domain of choice; the other side believes that morality embraces the evaluation of character and action even if they are not chosen.

Underlying this dispute are two conceptions of morality. According to one, morality depends on the human intellect and will; it is, thus, something we create. According to the other, morality is concerned with the benefit and harm people cause themselves and others. And since these benefits and harms are, at least sometimes, determined by the facts, such as the facts of the body, self, and social life, morality is, to the corresponding extent, something we discover or maintain but do not create. The first conception regards morality as a human artifact; the second regards morality as having a factual base that rules out it being entirely man-made. I shall call the first conception of morality *voluntarism*, to stress its connection with the human will. The second conception is the one I am engaged in developing and defending, *eudaimonism*.

According to voluntarists, the central moral question is what ought we to *do*. Since what we ought to do is one action rather than another, and since what we ought to do frequently conflicts with what we want to do, in voluntarism, the primary preoccupation is with choice and action, with the conflict between obligation and inclination, and with training the will to act on the choice guided by reason. Voluntarism is Kantian in spirit, if not in every detail.

According to eudaimonists, the central moral question is what sort of person ought we to *be*. The focus is not on action but on character.

The assumption is that what we ought to do follows from what we are, that actions follow from character. If our characters are good, our characteristic actions will be morally praiseworthy without us having to agonize over choice. The inspiration of eudaimonism is Aristotelian, although it is unclear how far Aristotle would agree with my present argument,[2] and I shall come to separate my version of eudaimonism from Aristotle's.

These two ways of thinking about morality are not logically inconsistent, for neither excludes any of the elements the other includes. Their dispute is one of emphasis. Voluntarists emphasize choice and action; eudaimonists emphasize character. According to voluntarists, what we are is formed by innumerable choices; according to eudaimonists, choice of action depends on character. Both hold that action and character are related. But the first think that action is primary and character, being formed by action, is secondary; the second think that character is primary and action, being a consequence of character, is secondary.

The Principle plays a role according to both, but, as it is to be expected, the roles are different. To distinguish between them, I shall say that the Principle has a *strong* version, favored by voluntarists, and a *weak* one, defended by eudaimonists. The strong version of the Principle expresses a necessary condition for the appropriateness of moral judgments. We should be disapproved of for what we do only if it is in our power to do it or not to do it. Thus, according to voluntarists, the strong version of the Principle has the crucial role of demarcating the domain of morality as that within which we can exercise our powers, that is, choose. According to eudaimonists, the weak version of the Principle plays a secondary role. They claim that disapproval depends on character. If our characters are vicious, we should be disapproved of even if it is not in our powers to be otherwise. But the disapproval should be mitigated by extenuating circumstances, and the weak version of the Principle expresses one possible ground for extenuation: it was not in our power to act otherwise.

I have observed that the dispute between voluntarists and eudaimonists is about the limits of morality. But it is more than that: it is a *moral* disagreement. For what is at stake is how we should judge people morally. Should we judge them on the basis of what they have

---

[2] Irwin, "Reason and Responsibility in Aristotle," is an excellent discussion of this difficult point. I stress more than Irwin does Aristotle's inclination to approve or disapprove of people's characters regardless of how they came to have them. Without this stress, it would be difficult to understand Aristotle's attitude to slaves and women, cf. *Politics*, book I, chapters 4–5.

become through their choices or on the basis of their characters independently of how they came to possess them?

If morality were a human artifact created by our will and intellect, then, of course, choice would have a decisive role in it, because it is through making choices that we express our intellect and will and thus create morality. But if morality is at least partly a matter of discovering what benefits and harms human beings and attempting to maintain a favorable balance between them, then what really matters is that people should have characters that prompt them to act beneficially and not to act harmfully. Whether they come to act in these ways through choice is of secondary importance. Hence voluntarists focus their moral evaluations on choices, while eudaimonists concentrate on characters.

Regardless of where we stand on this, it is clear that, since the dispute is moral, the Principle is a moral principle. Its strong version prescribes that we ought to judge people on the basis of choices they make, while its weak version prescribes that we ought not to judge those who lack the power to choose as severely as we judge those who have that power. I think that it is surprising that "ought implies can" turns out to be a moral principle.[3]

STRONG AND WEAK VERSIONS OF THE PRINCIPLE

The question I want to consider now is whether it is an *important* moral principle. The strong version is very important indeed, while the weak one plays only a subsidiary role. But whether the strong or the weak version is acceptable depends on what we say about the dispute between voluntarists and eudaimonists. As we have seen, the dispute between them is one of emphasis. I shall consider three contrasting pairs of notions; eudaimonists emphasize the first member of each pair at the expense of the second, while voluntarists reverse the emphasis. In each case, I think, eudaimonists have it far more nearly right. Consequently, I do not think that the Principle is important; its strong version is mistaken, while its weak version plays only a minor role.[4] It is helpful to have a concrete moral situation for discussing

[3] There is a logical and a moral question about "ought" implying "can." The logical question is discussed in Gowans, *Moral Dilemmas*, and in Rescher's *Ethical Idealism*. My interest here is in the moral question. To the best of my knowledge, only Brown, "Moral Theory and the Ought-Can Principle," shares this interest.

[4] There is a masterful discussion of how the emphasis has shifted to voluntarism in Greek ethics from Homer to Aristotle in Adkins, *Merit and Responsibility*. Adkins thinks that this shift represents moral improvement, while I, of course, doubt it.

these contrasting notions, and I shall use one strand in Mark Twain's *The Adventures of Huckleberry Finn* for this purpose.[5]

A dominant theme of the book is the relationship between Jim, the runaway slave, and Huck, the young white southern boy. At the beginning of their many adventures together, Huck's attitude to Jim is not much different from affectionate regard for a large friendly dog. When asked, for instance, whether anyone was hurt in an accident, he says, "No'm, killed a nigger," and finds the response, "Well, it's lucky because people sometimes do get hurt" (291), natural. On the other hand, when Huck hurts Jim's feelings, he apologizes, although "[i]t was fifteen minutes before I could work myself up to go and humble myself to a nigger" (143). Huck is confused. Friendship pulls him one way; his upbringing, of which slavery and contempt for blacks are an essential part, pulls him in the other. Most of the time he does not have to think about it, because he and Jim are alone and have great fun. But society intrudes, and finally a choice is forced on Huck: he can save Jim or inform on him. He says, "I was trembling, because I'd got to decide, forever, betwixt two things, and I knowed it. I studied a minute, sort of holding my breath and then says to myself: 'All right, then, I'll go to hell' " (283), and chooses Jim.

According to voluntarists, participation in morality consists in making such choices as Huck has done. He pitted himself against his religion and society, knowingly chose to be damned, and committed himself to Jim, whom he now sees as his friend. At the foundation of morality, as voluntarists have it, there lies radical choice concerning fundamental values, and we have to make a commitment one way or another. The assumption underlying voluntarism is that morality requires "one commitment whose ground is intimately personal and which comes before any other personal or social commitment whatsoever: the commitment to the principled mode of life as such. One is tempted to call this the supreme moral commitment."[6]

This way of looking at morality is obviously inadequate. For the mere fact that Huck finds himself in a moral dilemma about the conflict between friendship and social allegiance shows that he feels the moral pull of both. Huck's problem is not to choose a commitment but to weigh the hold on himself of his conflicting allegiances. Morality enters into such situations long before choice is made. So choice cannot be at its foundation.

A more realistic observation is that we are born into a moral tradition, and soon after birth our moral education begins. By adoles-

---

[5] Twain, *Huckleberry Finn*. References in the text are to the pages of this edition.
[6] Falk, "Morality, Self, and Others," 374–75.

cence, we are saturated with the moral views of our society. Of course, we can come to reject our morality, but no one starts with a decision to accept or to reject it, and if someone does come to reject it eventually, it is, short of suicide, to replace it by another morality.

In the normal course of events, "[m]oral change and achievement are slow, we [cannot] . . . suddenly alter what we see and ergo what we desire and are compelled by. In a way, explicit choice now seems less important: less decisive . . . and less obviously something to be 'cultivated.' If I attend properly I will have no choices left and this is the ultimate condition to aim at. . . . The ideal situation . . . is . . . a kind of necessity."[7]

The idea that choice lies at the foundation of morality is mistaken because it ignores the fundamental role conventions and education play. Conventions and education, however, require an object upon which they can exert their influence. This object is character. Moral education inculcates a morality. It takes young, unformed children and influences them to develop in a certain way, to cultivate habits, to strengthen or weaken dispositions, and to judge themselves and others in the light of prevailing conventions. This is the process by which character is beginning to be formed. And when we have well-formed characters, the actions we perform effortlessly follow from them. Normally, acting in many moral situations is not a matter of choosing but doing what comes naturally. People of good character spontaneously do what is right in the normal course of events.

This assumes that the credentials of the moral tradition are in order, but, of course, they may not be. Huck faced the choice he did partly because his moral tradition was faulty and partly because, being a young boy, his character was not well formed. Indeed, it was precisely his youth that made it possible for him to rise above his faulty morality and the upbringing that reflected it. If he had been fifteen years older, he, like the white adults surrounding him, would have learned to paper over the serious defect of their morality of treating some human beings in their society as if they were not human. Choice has to be faced in morality when the conventions are inconsistent, when our characters are formed by conflicting dispositions, or when unexpected and unusual situations occur for which moral education has not prepared us. But choice is the exception, not the rule. Most people, most of the time, act in accordance with their characters. And if their characteristic actions are good, we approve of them, while if they are bad, we disapprove of them. What people do is usually not the result of choice but the surface manifestation of

7 Murdoch, *The Sovereignty of Good*, 39–40.

the deeper structure of their characters. For these reasons, voluntarists are mistaken and eudaimonists are correct in the emphasis they
place on the contrasting notions of choice and character.

The second contrasting pair is agent and action. Voluntarists concentrate on action at the expense of agents, because they place choice
of action at the foundation of morality. Voluntarists allow, of course,
that actions require agents, but in the kind of situation Huck has
found himself, he was called upon to make a radical choice. The process of making it required, among other things, a decision about the
kind of agent he was going to be. The significance of his choice was
not just the act of friendship that saved Jim but also the long-term
influence it had on Huck's moral development. Huck, the moral
agent, according to voluntarists, is the result of the slow accretion of
many episodes of choices and actions that have gone into making
Huck. So Huck, the person, was there before he made any choices
and acted according to them. But Huck, the moral agent, came into
being as a result of choices and actions.

What is wrong with this way of looking at moral situations is the
resulting impossibility of explaining how identical choices and actions
can have vastly different moral significance. The bare bones of
Huck's situation were that he had to choose between loyalty to his
friend and loyalty to his social group. That the bare bones are inadequate for appreciating the moral significance of Huck's situation is
obvious if we transpose it to a postcolonial African state. We fail to
characterize the situation accurately if we leave out of account the
deep influence of Huck's moral tradition on his way of seeing Jim.
Huck began by not seeing Jim as a human being. He had to choose
and act because his moral perception of Jim has altered. But how
Huck saw Jim and how that way of seeing has changed left their mark
on Huck long before he had to choose and act. Huck, before the
choice and action, was not merely a nonmoral agent. He had the
views of his moral tradition, and in the light of his experience of Jim
as being as human as any white man, he began to free himself from
the hitherto unquestioned authority of his moral tradition. Choices
and actions do not make moral agents; moral agents make choices
and actions.

Eudaimonists reject the tacitly assumed distinction between persons and moral agents. People are moral agents, regardless of their
choices and actions, because they can benefit and harm themselves
and others. The inseparability of personhood and moral agency is
simply a fact of life. Everyone is born into a moral tradition, and
everyone undergoes moral training. Due to the nature of our species,
our characters begin to be formed before we have an opportunity to

make choices or perform actions that have moral significance. This could be otherwise: if we came into being fully mature, or if we could fend for ourselves immediately after birth, the relation between being human and being a moral agent might be otherwise. But as it is, the two go together, and voluntarists are mistaken in supposing that moral agency begins with moral choice-making.

Of course, it is true that choices and actions have a formative influence on the kind of moral agents we are. Eudaimonists recognize that this is so. What they reject is the supposition that choices and action create moral agents. Moral agents are born, and they are shaped by their moral tradition. Choices and actions alter moral agents, but they do not produce them. Thus, moral agency is a deeper, more fundamental notion than choice and action are.

The third contrasting pair is achievement and improvement. The emphasis voluntarists place on improvement goes hand in hand with their emphasis on choice and action. The underlying assumption is that human beings embark on a career of moral agency as they become choosers and actors. Before this happens, they are saddled with genetic and acquired dispositions, talents and weaknesses, capacities and incapacities. According to voluntarists, they are not subject to moral disapproval for any of these pre-moral characteristics, for they had no choice about possessing them. People should be subject to moral disapproval only for what they do with their pre-moral characteristics. Moral progress is moral improvement. But since people start with different pre-moral characteristics, moral improvement comes to quite different things in different cases. In moral progress, we measure the distance traveled from the starting point. And for some people, the starting point is way back, while others are more fortunately situated. The moral progress of Huck was greater than the moral progress of a contemporary boy would be in coming to the same conclusion. For Huck had to contend with his own racist upbringing, while a contemporary boy probably would not have to do that.

But this will not do. The clue to the inadequacy of this view is the question of how we gauge improvement. We are likely to agree that Huck has improved, because we agree in disapproving of racism. And we agree about that because we hold in common some ideal about human dignity and respect for others. Huck has improved because he got closer to that ideal. But now let us forget about Huck for a minute, so that his charm will not beguile us.

Consider two men, one of whom starts out as a dyed-in-the-wool racist, yet brings himself to the point where his racism dictates his choices and actions only in extreme situations. He has gone a long way toward ridding himself of it, but he has not quite succeeded. The other man has never encountered racism; the thought of discriminating against people because of their race has never entered his mind. If voluntarists were right, we should have to say that as far as racism is concerned, the first man, having improved so much, is more worthy of moral approval than the second man who has not improved at all. And this is extremely implausible. Surely, the man who is not a racist at all has better moral credentials on that score than the man who has not quite managed to shake off his vicious upbringing. One improved and the other did not. But the one who did not had no need to improve. As far as racism is concerned, he has no moral blemishes, so he deserves more moral credit than the reforming racist.

Voluntarism is encumbered with this implausibility because it underemphasizes the characters and tradition of moral agents in judging their choices and actions. The reason why improvement looms so important in choice-making is that that is what choice of action is supposed to bring about. And, of course, improvement matters, but it is wrong to regard it as the main determinant of moral standing. The considerable improvement of some people may just bring them to the lower rungs of decency, a position that others have achieved without effort. The truth is that some people are raised in moral traditions where vices flourish, and so they are beset by many vices. These are moral handicaps. And they are so even though people do not choose their tradition and characters, at least not during their formative years.

The strong version of the Principle is supported by the combined forces of choice, action, and improvement as the fundamental notions of morality. If morality is coextensive with the domain where actions are chosen, and the chosen actions are judged by evaluating the moral improvement they produce, then we should indeed determine the appropriateness of moral disapproval by asking whether the agent had the power to act otherwise. According to voluntarists, "ought implies can" expresses a fundamental principle of morality. As we have seen, however, they are mistaken in assigning fundamental importance to choice, action, and improvement.

The fundamental moral notions are character, moral agency, and moral achievement. Choice, action, and improvement matter, of course, but they matter as signs of something deeper, more fundamental. Eudaimonists give a more reasonable account of these basic considerations. But in eudaimonism, the strong version of the Principle has no place. Ought does not imply can, because we are perfectly justified in doing what we frequently do: morally disapprove of people for being in ways and doing things they have no power to change. This would lead to excessively severe moral judgments if the weak version of the Principle were not there to mitigate them. The proper function of the Principle is to remind us that people should not be judged harshly for the harm they could not avoid causing. The weak version is a civilizing force, because it restrains righteous moral indignation. However, let us be clear that "ought implies can" is a rather misleadingly expressed moral call for restraint and not the all-important criterion by which we can decide when moral disapproval is appropriate.

I conclude that, compared with voluntarists, eudaimonists give a more nearly accurate account of morality, and it is one in which the moral significance of choice and action can be readily accommodated. Thus, the voluntaristic account should be seen as a special case of the eudaimonistic one. For eudaimonists do not deny that in many, perhaps even in the majority, of the cases our will and intellect do, or should, inform our choices. What eudaimonists stress, in opposition to voluntarists, is, first, that the moral standing of choices depends primarily on the benefit and harm subsequent actions cause, and second, that benefit and harm may be caused by unchosen actions. Since morality is concerned with human welfare, and since both chosen and unchosen actions can contribute to or detract from it, the voluntaristic concentration on chosen actions does justice only to a part of morality. The voluntaristic account is a special case of the eudaimonistic one, because the latter includes the former and goes beyond it. The alternative to the eudaimonistic acceptance of the moral relevance of unchosen actions is to deny that the concern of morality is with the benefit and harm human beings cause themselves and others. But it does not seem to me that this denial can be reasonably defended.

THE APPROPRIATENESS OF MORAL DISAPPROVAL

It may be objected to my emphasis on the character-forming aspect of morality that it should lead us to disapprove the moral tradition rather than the agents whose characters were formed by it. The thought behind this objection is that if unchosen actions may reflect adversely on the characters from which they naturally follow, then unchosen characters may reflect adversely on the moral tradition whose products they are. If choice is not the ground of moral disapproval, then the causal chain whose effect is an action extends recursively into the remote past, and agents have no special standing as the locus of actions.

My reply to this objection is that being formed by a moral tradition is like mastering our mother tongue. Just as learning it leaves us much latitude both to say what we please and to violate its rules, so being brought up in a moral tradition leaves us similar latitude both to conduct ourselves in a richer variety of ways than anyone can possibly experiment with in a lifetime and to go, systematically or episodically, against the conventions. Morality does not exert its influence on us as billiard balls do on each other. Its control is a plastic one.[8] It is like the influence of the streets, cars, traffic regulations, the disposition of the drivers, and police patrol on the traffic patterns of a city. In language, traffic, and morality, there are conventions, both deep and variable, and there are individuals whose participation involves a constant and mutual adjustment of subjective purposes and objective possibilities. And just as we can distinguish between good and bad language-users and drivers, so we can distinguish between good and bad moral agents. Even if determinism gives the correct metaphysical account of how causes operate on us, it must still be recognized that the operation of all causes is not correctly represented by one billiard ball hitting another.

Another objection to the moral disapproval of agents whose characteristic actions violate deep conventions is to concede that people like Sophie and Mr. Hyde should be disapproved of but to deny that the appropriate disapproval is moral. The animating spirit behind this objection is the same as that which moves voluntarism. It is a reluctance to draw the distinction between morality and other realms in a way that permits moral judgments of people for doing what they could not help doing. We may say, in this spirit, that being cruel and weak are not good ways of being. But the goodness, or lack of it, has more to do with our overall attitude to the scheme of things than with morality. The world would be a better place, it may be felt, if it were more hospitable to humanity. It is an evil that some people are compelled by their nature to torture others and that extreme situations call for hard choices beyond the resources of some people. This evil, however, is not the fault of any human being; it comes from the world being what it is.

There are three reasons for rejecting this view. The first is that there is a confusion at its core. We need to remember the distinction between natural and moral evil. Natural evil is the harm that befalls people independently of human interference, while moral evil is harm done to people by people. On any view of morality, it is surely one of its major functions to minimize the occurrence of moral evil. And one way of doing so is to point out that some ways of being are

---

[8] The term is Popper's, see "Of Clouds and Clocks" in *Objective Knowledge*.

likely to result in harmful actions and then influence one's moral tradition and education in it so as to lessen the chances of people being in those ways. Moral disapproval is one of the ways in which this influence can be exerted. How could this activity fail to be part of morality?

But, it will be said, Sophie's weakness and Mr. Hyde's cruelty were more like natural than moral evil. They were the carriers of the harm they have done, not its agents. Being their sorts of carriers, however, are bad ways of being. Should we not teach people not to be like them? Should we not hold them up as examples to be avoided? Should we not say that one should not be like them? And what else would we be doing then but expressing moral disapproval?

However, critics may remain recalcitrant in the face of these considerations. They may continue to insist that the sphere of morality should be restricted to chosen actions. The force of this "should," however, is only that of an attempted linguistic legislation. It does not adequately reflect how we think or speak, so why should we accept it? And what would we or its champions gain if we did accept it? We would still want to say that it would be better if people did not have characteristics likely to issue in harmful actions; and this would still be an evaluative claim about human character and conduct that reflects adversely on those of whom it is justly made. We would merely have to invent another name for the evaluative category, if morality, its natural name, had been banned by this ill-advised legislation.

The second reason for not exempting people from moral disapproval, if their unchosen characters are likely to issue in harmful conduct, is that we do not hesitate in our moral approval of people whose unchosen characters lead them to benefit others. The inexact counterparts of Sophie and Mr. Hyde, approaching the other end of the moral scale, are the holy innocents: St. Francis, Melville's Billy Budd, Dostoyevsky's Prince Myshkin and Alyosha Karamazov. These are pure, simple, naturally good people. They act spontaneously, without moral struggle, without having to agonize over choice, so as to benefit others. As some people are born with moral handicaps, so some are born with moral advantages. We do not hesitate to give moral credit to the saintly, so we should not hesitate to express moral disapproval of their opposites. We may wish to reserve greater approval for those whose goodness is the hard-earned result of long struggle, but no one could reasonably balk at saying that the holy innocents live, morally speaking, in a good way. Why, then, should we hesitate to say that the ways of Sophie and Mr. Hyde are morally bad?

One source of hesitation may be that there is considerable unclarity about what follows from moral disapproval. Are we committed to blaming, condemning, or punishing people of whom we disapprove? This brings us to the third reason for rejecting the view that it is inappropriate to disapprove morally of agents of unchosen yet characteristic actions that result in the violation of deep conventions. Moral disapproval commits us to the appropriateness of adverse moral judgment, but it says nothing about the strength of the disapproval or the severity of the judgment. It would require great insensitivity to blame, condemn, let alone punish Sophie for her weakness. But this does not and should not stop us from saying that a similarly placed mother, who could make the dreadful choice Sophie could not, would have been a better person than Sophie. The point of saying this is to call attention to the fact that strength is better than weakness, because strength tends to reduce and weakness tends to increase the amount of harm people do to themselves and others. If we are morally committed, we must make judgments of this sort. In rejecting the strong version of the Principle, I have been arguing for the appropriateness of this kind of moral judgment. In accepting the weak version, I have accepted a guide to determining the strength of the appropriate moral disapproval: it should be proportionate to the extent to which it was in the agents' power not to do the action for which they are disapproved.

THE UNIMPORTANCE OF CHOICE

A moral tradition makes possible and defines for us various forms of good lives. Deep conventions mark the limits within which the pursuit of good lives can be conducted. To well-trained and reasonable moral agents, these deep conventions do not appear as more or less arbitrary constraints on what they feel like doing. What they feel like doing is seen as protected by these conventions. The fundamental reason why the appropriateness of moral disapproval of violations of these deep conventions is independent of the knowledge, intention, and choice of moral agents is that the potential harm thus caused is also independent of them. If the harmful conduct follows from the character of the agent, then we have no alternative but to disapprove of the character. Weak and cruel people are proper objects of moral disapproval if, through acting in their characteristic ways, they violate, as they are apt to do, deep conventions. Of course, those who violate them knowingly and by choice should be disapproved of much more strongly than unintentional violators. But I do not see how the conclusion can be avoided that some characters, some ways of being, are morally bad, regardless of how moral agents came to them.

When moral agents realize of themselves that their characters must be judged adversely, because they have led to violations of deep conventions they accept, the appropriate reaction is the self-inflicted moral horror I discussed in the previous chapter. When other people in the same moral tradition observe these agents, their appropriate reaction is the moral disapproval, mitigated by the weak version of the Principle, I discussed in this chapter. The conclusion supported by the argument in both chapters is that the limits of morality are set, not by the human capacity for choice, but by the capacity to suffer harms and enjoy the benefits, determined by the facts of the body, self, and social life. Therefore, morality cannot be entirely what we wish to make it. In this sense, the upshot of these chapters is that morality is partly objective.

CHAPTER THREE

The Great Guide of Human Life

Custom, then, is the great guide of human life.

—David Hume[1]

DECENCY: A FIRST SKETCH

The moral tradition of eudaimonism has two aspects: social and personal morality. But they are actually overlapping, interdependent, and, hence, not sharply distinguishable. Roughly speaking, social morality is the domain of impersonal conduct directed toward others, while personal morality is the sphere of the private and the individual. Honoring contracts, paying debts, helping strangers, doing one's job, obeying the law, being a good citizen are typical activities in social morality. Having love affairs, curbing one's temper, being loyal to a friend, trying to be honest, overcoming self-deception, being steadfast in adversity belong to personal morality. But since social conduct has a formative influence on agents, and since personal conduct invariably has some social significance, the two aspects are not sharply different.

In the first two chapters, I have discussed the conditions that any moral tradition must meet if it is to foster good lives. In this chapter and the next two, I shall concentrate on the social morality of eudaimonism. Following *The Oxford English Dictionary* (1961), I shall call conduct according to social morality *decent* and the attitude reflected by such conduct *decency*. The relevant definition of decency is as follows: "Propriety of behaviour or demeanour; due regard for what is becoming; conformity (in behaviour, speech, or action) to the standards of propriety or good taste." The definition permits both a moral and a nonmoral use of the term. The former stresses behavior and standards of propriety; the latter emphasizes demeanor and good taste. In its moral use, decency has both a wide and a narrow sense. The narrow one is sexual; it is in this sense that by indecency we mean offensive sexual behavior, the violation of standards of sexual propriety. The wide sense of decency connotes a much broader range of behavior; it includes civility, politeness, good will, helpful-

[1] Hume, *Enquiry*, 44.

ness, giving others the benefit of the doubt; this is what is often meant by common decency. I shall use decency exclusively in its wide moral sense. My aim in this chapter is to offer an analysis of decency thus understood.

Consider these glimpses of two societies: "I went a day or two later to see a friend who lives in a small town in Illinois. We went together to the corner drugstore to get ice cream for supper. It was a scene familiar enough to me . . . the Main Street of a small American town on Saturday night in late summer. . . . There was over the street and over the town that indefinable American air of happiness and ease. . . . There was that general friendliness and candor. . . . People called each other by their 'given names'; there were friendly inquiries and a few introductions of the visitor. It was a world in which the ominous word 'stranger' had been given a friendly flavor."[2] And now contrast it with this: "Wherever you looked, in all our institutions, in all our homes, *skloka* was brewing. *Skloka* is a phenomenon born of our social order, an entirely new term and concept, not to be translated into any language of the civilized world. It is hard to define. It stands for base, trivial hostility, unconscionable spite breeding petty intrigues, the vicious pitting of one clique against another. It thrives on calumny, informing, spying, scheming, slander, the igniting of base passions. Taut nerves and weakening morals allow one individual or group rabidly to hate another individual or group. *Skloka* is natural for people who have been incited to attack one another, who have been made bestial by desperation, who have been driven to the wall."[3]

In a society where *skloka* prevails, life cannot be good, for an essential ingredient of it is lacking. This ingredient is present in the society described in the first passage. It is decency: a mixture of spontaneous goodwill, casual friendliness, a spirit of mutual helpfulness. It is an attitude fellow participants have toward each other and friendly visitors. It assumes no intimacy; in fact, it holds between passing acquaintances and strangers who have nothing more in common than the mutual recognition that they share the same social morality. It does not involve deep feelings; it is not personal, for anyone may be its beneficiary; it is spontaneous, but hostility, rudeness, or abuse may destroy it. And if it is systematically destroyed, *skloka* will take its place.

Decency is generally admitted to be a good thing, but it is not generally supposed to be particularly important. I think that it is. De-

---

[2] Brogan, *The American Character*, xii.
[3] Mossman, *The Correspondence of Boris Pasternak and Olga Friedenberg*, 303–4.

cency is an essential ingredient of good lives, for it makes it possible to have more or less harmonious relationships with fellow members of one's society. I shall propose a way of understanding decency by considering three notions similar to it: Aristotle's *civic friendship* and Hume's *sympathy* and *custom*.

ARISTOTLE ON CIVIC FRIENDSHIP

Aristotle's central claim for my purposes is, "Community depends on friendship; and when there is enmity instead of friendship, men will not even share the same path" (*Politics*, 1295b23–25).[4] For us, friendship is an intimate personal relationship; Aristotle, however, uses the Greek *philia* (I transliterate it), which we translate as friendship, in a much wider sense.[5] It includes parental, filial, brotherly, sisterly, and marital relationships of a certain sort, as well as certain business relationships and relationships between members of religious, social, and political organizations. "The central idea contained in *philia* is that of doing well by someone for his own sake, out of concern for *him* (and not, or not merely, out of concern for oneself). If this is right, then the different forms of *philia* listed above could be viewed as just different contexts and circumstances in which this kind of mutual well-doing can arise. . . . *Philia*, taken most generally, is any relationship characterized by mutual liking . . . that is, by mutual well-wishing and well-doing out of concern for one another."[6]

This benevolence is altruistically motivated, but it is important to be clear that the altruism has its limits. The recognition that our friends want something is a sufficient reason for trying to satisfy that want. But their wants need not be our sole motive; we may also be moved by self-interest. Friendship involves caring about our friends for their sake; this is compatible, however, with caring for them for our own sakes as well.

Aristotle distinguishes between three kinds of friendship (*NE*, 1156a7–1157b1). The distinction is based on what brings the friends together. The highest form is *character-friendship*; the other two, in descending order, are *pleasure-friendship* and *advantage-friendship*.[7] Character-friendship is based on the mutual recognition of two

---

[4] Aristotle, *Politics*. My discussion is indebted to Cooper, "Aristotle on the Forms of Friendship" and "Aristotle on Friendship."

[5] Aristotle's account of friendship is in books VIII and IX of *Nicomachean Ethics* (*NE*); in *Eudemian Ethics*, book VII, chapter 12; in *Rhetoric*, book II, chapter 3; and in several scattered remarks in *Politics*.

[6] Cooper, "Aristotle on Friendship," 302.

[7] I follow Cooper, "Aristotle on Friendship," 305–8.

friends that the other possesses some particular excellence of character. The more excellences the friends' characters embody, the more perfect the friendship is. Pleasure- and advantage-friendship are less perfect, because the pleasure or advantage the friends derive from each other is not produced by qualities essential to their individuality but by incidental qualities, such as physical attractiveness, complementary skills, or mutually profitable commercial dealings.

Civic friendship is a form of advantage-friendship. There are different kinds of advantage-friendships depending on the advantage friends derive from their association. Civic friendship is the most general kind, for it is based on the advantage fellow members of a society derive from their association. As Aristotle says, "[I]t is for the sake of advantage that the political community too seems both to have come together originally and to endure, for this is what legislators aim at, and they call just that which is to the common advantage. Now the other communities aim at advantage bit by bit. . . . But . . . the political community aims not at present advantage but at what is advantageous for life as a whole . . . particular kinds of friendship will correspond to the particular type of community" (*NE*, 1160a11–30). Civic friendship, then, is the attitude members of a healthy society have toward each other.

It is an advantageous relationship, because it is essential to the existence of a society in terms of which individuals can live whatever they regard as good lives. The motivation for it is a mixture of altruism and self-interest. Altruism is present, because people are genuinely benevolent; they are habitually and spontaneously helpful. But self-interest also plays a role, because they expect others to treat them similarly. The fabric of society is permeated by the reliable satisfaction of this expectation. People feel well disposed toward each other and there is air of mutual well-wishing and well-doing. The health of the society prompts these attitudes, and the attitudes, in turn, reinforce the society. But nobody plans that this should be so. That it happens is a consequence of institutions that suit the people, because they articulate and satisfy their wants in the prevailing framework.

Like all forms of friendship, civic friendship is reciprocal, but the reciprocity is unlike what exists in character- and pleasure-friendship. It is not expected that the recipients of our benevolence will immediately or even ever return the favors done to them. Yet there is an expectation of return. Individual acts of civic friendship create a fund of goodwill from which the depositors can draw. Just as they are benevolent to strangers and passing acquaintances recognized to be fellow members, so they count on being benevolently treated by other members.

Aristotle expressed this by contrasting two types of advantage-friendships: "The *legal* type is on fixed terms; its purely commercial variety is on the basis of immediate payment, while the more liberal variety allows time but stipulates for a definite *quid pro quo*. In this variety the debt is clear and not ambiguous, but in the postponement it contains an element of friendliness. . . . The *moral* type is not on fixed terms; it makes a gift, or does whatever it does, as to a friend; but one expects to receive as much or more, as having not given but lent" (*NE*, 1162b25–33). Civic friendship is this latter, moral type.

One reason for the difference in reciprocity between civic friendship and character- and pleasure-friendship is that the former is considerably more impersonal than the latter two. Civic friendship holds between fellow members of a society, provided they have not disqualified themselves from it by hostility, rudeness, or inappropriate conduct. So the personal qualities of civic friends play almost no role in the reciprocally benevolent relationship. The relationship may not be lasting, for many instances of civic friendship occur in casual encounters; it does not require that the participants should know each other even superficially; nor is it necessary that if they get to know the recipients of their benevolence, they should like them. It is true that civic friendship is a relationship between two people, but this truth is superficial. Individual acts of civic friendship are acts of benevolence where the agent and the recipient are members of the same society. But since the identity of the recipient is almost totally irrelevant, any member would qualify. This is why it is impersonal and why it is unimportant that the advantage it yields should be conferred on one by the same person one happens to have benefited.

Aristotle's distinction between legal and moral advantage-friendship has the further significance of implying that civic friendship, being moral, goes beyond the claims of justice. In legal advantage-friendship, people come to trust each other because experience has convinced them of their mutual rectitude. Thus, they no longer exact from each other a punctilious discharge of contractual obligations. They still expect profit from their relationship, but the accounting is informal, the books need to be balanced only in the long run.

In civic friendship, however, a person "makes a gift, or does whatever [he] does, as to a friend." The conduct of civic friends is not governed by any rules but by mutual benevolence. As Aristotle puts it: "[F]riendship seems to hold states together, and lawgivers to care more for it than for justice; . . . when men are friends they have no need for justice, while when they are just they need friendship as well" (*NE*, 1155a23–28). The reasons behind this are the following.

To act justly is to give others their due. Since people tend to ignore what is due to others, especially when it conflicts with their own interests, it is necessary to have a legal system composed of explicit rules, judges who interpret the rules, and some authority to enforce the rules. But the legal system is needed only because people do not regard each other in the spirit of friendship. If they did, they would conduct themselves with mutual goodwill. So if people were friends, they would have no need of justice. The spirit that the laws attempt imperfectly to enforce would already permeate their dealings with each other.

This has the interesting consequence that civic friendship has no use for rights. For to conduct ourselves in the appropriate spirit is, not to honor the rights of our fellows, but to act toward them with benevolence that goes beyond what rights would vouchsafe them. Furthermore, in civic friendship we do not stand on our rights in dealing with others, for we find it unseemly, a violation of the spirit of friendship, to insist, in a mercenary way, on our slice of the pie. A society infused by civic friendship has little need of rights. And a society in which rights are jealously guarded provides incriminating evidence against itself. For in such a society, litigation attempts to exact what goodwill should freely give.

CIVIC FRIENDSHIP AND DECENCY

Civic friendship and decency share the following characteristics. Both involve an attitude that members of a society have toward each other: mutual benevolence, understood as wishing well and acting accordingly on appropriate occasions. The motivation for the attitude is a mixture of altruism and self-interest. We rely on social morality to establish some of the conditions enabling us to live whatever we regard as good lives. This is the advantage we hope to derive from conforming to it. But we recognize that our fellows are similarly engaged, that we mutually depend on each other, and that our interests coincide to a great extent. Hence we should do what we can to be helpful, both for the sake of our fellows and for society as a whole, since our welfare is part of the whole. This attitude is both reciprocal and impersonal. It is reciprocal, because we expect to be treated with the same benevolence with which we treat others. But it is impersonal, because the expectation is not directed at any particular individual; rather, its satisfaction is to be provided by whomever we encounter in our society. Thus, it does not require knowing, personally liking, or having a lasting relationship with other members. Yet the impersonality goes beyond mere rectitude. The attitude is one of goodwill, a willingness not to stand on our rights, to forgo immediate advantage, and to be friendly, helpful, and attentive to our fellows.

This, however, is an inadequate account of decency. One reason for it emerges if we notice the awkwardness of describing what Aristotle had in mind as a kind of friendship. Aristotle thinks of friendship on the model of a hierarchy. At its peak is character-friendship between virtuous men. Of course, few achieve this. The less perfect forms of friendship fall more or less short of the ideal. But what makes even the most imperfect kind of friendship an instance of friendship is the mutual liking, manifested as reciprocal benevolence, of the friends. We can see how this remains true of character-friendship, even if it is based on some particular excellence and not on overall moral goodness. Notably just, courageous, or wise people may recognize in each other these excellences, and they may like and admire each other for them, although they may admit failings in other respects. Stretching the notion a bit, pleasure-friendship can also be assimilated to this model. For lovers, for instance, can like and admire each other for the physical attributes that are the sources of their mutual erotic satisfactions. By the time we get to civic friendship, however, the notion of friendship requires such stretching as to challenge credulity.

We are invited to characterize people as friends who do not know each other and who have no lasting relationship; they may, in fact, be total strangers who happen to be thrown together in a casual encounter. The difficulty is not that the Greek *philia* is imperfectly translated as friendship. Rather, the mutual liking essentially involved in *philia* requires some ground, and Aristotle leaves us with an inadequate explanation of what it is in the case of civic friendship or decency. Why do fellow citizens in a good society treat each other with decency?

The Aristotelian answer is that civic friendship or decency is based on the recognition that by wishing and doing well to others the fabric of our society is maintained, and thus, one of the conditions of good lives is guaranteed. But this attributes far too much calculation and reflection to ordinary people. It is absurd to suppose that the spontaneous goodwill, casual helpfulness, ready friendliness of people is the result of a ratiocinative process, yielding the conclusion of a practical syllogism. We help each other, because one needs it and the other can provide it without too much trouble. We are not thinking of the fabric of society or of our own welfare; if we think at all, it is about how to help the other. Nor is it that lack of thinking at the time of the decent act betokens past thought. It requires greater theoretical preoccupation than most of us have to connect our conduct in our relatively narrow context with the implications of our conduct, and the conduct of others, for society as a whole. Moral education is presupposed by decency, but it consists of being told how we should act in particular situations. It teaches us how to behave, not the justification for behaving that way. Aristotle's answer is incomplete, because it does not tell us what makes us receptive to moral education and what predisposes us toward decency. One reason for turning from Aristotle to Hume is that he attempts to answer this question.

There is another difficulty in taking Aristotle's account of civic friendship as an account of decency. I have noticed that civic friendship may hold between strangers who encounter each other for a short time and never meet again. We need to consider how these strangers recognize each other as potential civic friends. Now, the society Aristotle had in mind was far more homogeneous and smaller than contemporary societies. In Greek city-states, citizens recognized each other on the basis of how they spoke, dressed, but, more importantly, they actually knew each other personally or by reputation. In current Western societies, neither personal appearance nor language is a reliable guide, and our societies are far too populous for their members to know or have heard of each other. Strangers truly are strangers; accents and dialects abound; styles of dressing no longer indicate nationality, social position, and occupation; yet decency is still possible and it often exists. How, then, do people establish their affinity? Once again, Hume suggests an answer.

HUME ON SYMPATHY

There are two reasons, then, for turning from Aristotle to Hume. The first is to give an account of what predisposes people to decency. Hume's answer is that *sympathy* does. Second, we look to Hume for an explanation of how people recognize each other as appropriate candidates for sympathy. And this explanation is based on *custom*. If we combine Aristotle's account of civic friendship with Hume's account of sympathy and custom, we shall obtain what I believe is an adequate understanding of decency.

Hume's general moral theory need not detain us. He believes that our moral judgments are based on the capacity to have feelings of approval and disapproval. If we approve of something, we call it good because it produces in us a kind of pleasure, and we disapprove of and call bad whatever produces in us a kind of pain. Moral qualities, thus, are not in objects; they are sentiments objects produce in us. These objects are human beings and the qualities that provoke the sentiments in us are their virtues and vices. Virtues and vices may be natural or artificial. Natural virtues are inborn; artificial virtues are habits cultivated to help society flourish. The paradigm of natural virtue is benevolence. It is natural because all human beings possess it and approve of possessing it. Benevolence and all the other natural virtues have a common ground in a basic inborn human tendency: sympathy. Thus, sympathy is the foundation of Hume's moral theory.[8]

Sympathy, according to Hume, involves the transference of an emotion from one person to another. We observe the behavior of others, infer their mental state, and come to have the mental state ourselves. In Hume's words, "When any affection is infus'd by sympathy, it is first known only by its effects, and by those external signs of countenance and conversation, which convey an idea of it. This idea is presently converted into an impression, and acquires such a degree of force and vivacity, as to become the very passion itself, and produce an equal emotion, as any original affection" (T, 317).[9] We see others crying, we infer that they are in distress, and we become distressed ourselves. The extent to which we come to sympathize with others is determined by imagination. Hume uses the word *imagination* in many confusing ways, but I shall use it to mean the faculty that combines ideas according to the principles of association: resemblance, contiguity, and causation. Thus, the more intimately we know others, the more we shall sympathize with them; the degree of intimacy is determined by the combined forces of the three principles of association.

Sympathy is involuntary, for it is determined by the natural workings of the mind. It is a feeling, for it necessarily involves having the same feeling as the object of our sympathy has. It is not restricted to feelings we morally approve of, for we may also sympathize with disagreeable feelings. Thus, sympathy, for Hume, is not a kind of pity, nor is it a kind of identification involving the attempt to put ourselves in the place of another. It is actually to have the feelings, good or bad, that the others have, and to have them not because morality prompts us so to choose but because the natural workings of our minds lead us, when connected by resemblance, contiguity, and causation, to sympathize with them. Yet sympathy has moral force. For we are not indifferent to the feelings, sympathetic or original, we have. Some are agreeable and give us pleasure, others are disagreeable and give pain.

[8] For a lucid and sympathetic account of Hume's moral views, see Mackie's *Hume's Moral Theory*. I am indebted for the discussion of sympathy to Mercer, *Sympathy and Ethics*.

[9] References in parentheses are to the pages of Hume's *Treatise* (T) and *Enquiry* (E).

Moral judgments derive from the pleasure and pain sympathy allows us to experience.

We are looking at Hume's account of sympathy to answer the question of what predisposes people to decency. Can we conclude that sympathy does? As the account stands, we cannot. Hume is right in observing that human beings tend to have fellow feelings for each other. Furthermore, although Hume's principles of association need much amendment, it is just plain common sense that the extent of fellow feeling depends on the combination of how far we find ourselves similar to others, on our proximity to them in time and space, and on the effect they have on us. No doubt, other factors also influence fellow feeling, but we can grant that, in insisting on the three principles of association, Hume was on the right track.

There are, however, two conspicuous inadequacies in Hume's account so far. First, sympathy lacks action-guiding force. Hume provides no reason why having fellow feeling would move us to do anything about it. Now, if sympathy were merely meant as an explanation of how we come to share some feelings with others, there would be no need to seek its action-guiding force. But Hume means sympathy to be the underlying motivation for the natural virtues, and the virtues necessarily issue in action. We have yet no explanation of how this happens. What makes this difficulty particularly acute is that in addition to benevolent feelings, we also have selfish, envious, jealous, and hostile feelings toward each other. Hume does not tell us how sympathy results in action, nor why agreeable rather than disagreeable feelings should be acted upon.

The second inadequacy in Hume's account is that it leaves unexplained the connection between sympathy and altruism. It is true that we have fellow feelings *with* other people, but why should we care *for* them? Others may occasion our agreeable and disagreeable feelings, and we do wish to have the former and not the latter. But this need not move us to help them; it may prompt us to withdraw from them if they produce disagreeable feelings in us. Decent people care for others, and since sympathy also gives rise to disagreeable feelings we wish to avoid, sympathy fails to explain yet another element of decency.

Both of these inadequacies are removed by supplementing Hume's treatment of sympathy as a feeling with an account of the role reason plays in sympathy.[10] The principal idea is this: "Human nature being compos'd of two principal parts, which are requisite in all its action, the affections and understanding; 'tis certain, that the blind motions

---

[10] I draw on Miller, *Philosophy and Ideology in Hume's Political Thought.*

of the former, without the direction of the latter, incapacitate man for society" (T, 493).

Crucial to understanding Hume's view of the relation between reason and passion is the recognition that his theory of moral judgment has a negative and a constructive side. The negative side de-emphasizes the role reason plays in moral judgments by stressing the role of feeling and the lack of the motivational force of reason: "[R]eason alone can never produce any action, or give rise to volition" (T, 413). The constructive side explains how reason can affect action by directing the passions.

By reason, I mean in this context the cognitive functioning of the mind. It results in judgments that can be true or false. Sense experience and memory are typical instances of it. Passion includes all the various forms of feelings, including moral sentiments, we may have. And by desire I understand the action-guiding component of our motivation. Hume's position is that reason, by itself, never results in action, because there is nothing in reason *per se* that could prompt desire; desire may follow only if reason is accompanied by passion. Passion may or may not result in desire. "Pride and humility are pure emotions in the soul, unattended with any desire, and not immediately exciting us to action. But love and hatred are not compleated within themselves . . . but carry the mind to something farther. Love is always followed by a desire . . . as hatred produces a desire" (T, 367). When a passion is accompanied by desire, we are moved to action. Reason can affect action by directing the passions. Reason can do this in three ways: by enabling us to recognize a particular object as satisfying our desire; by finding the appropriate means of obtaining it; and by acting as a corrective of the passions.

The first two do not require much explanation. If a passion is accompanied by desire, we are moved to action. The action is intended to satisfy the desire, and this requires accurate perception of the context in which we act. Reason directs the passion and guides action by providing the required information. But what about the third? How does reason correct the passions? One way is by determining whether a particular passion is appropriate. Passions have objects, and they are appropriate in the presence of their objects. Reason determines whether the object is present. The other way in which reason corrects passions provides the key to overcoming the inadequacies of Hume's account of sympathy.

Hume remarks, " '[T]is certain, that sympathy is not always limited to the present moment, but that we often feel by communication the pains and pleasures of others, which are not in being, and which we only anticipate by the force of imagination" (T, 385). That is, we sympathize with the past and future feelings of other people and also of people whom we have never met, such as, for instance, historical or literary characters. Our morality is not of the present moment. What makes it possible to extend sympathy from the immediate context to more distant occasions is imagination. Its basis must be in the present, but from that basis it can grow and embrace what is remote. "[H]owever we may look forward to the future in sympathizing with any person, the extending of our sympathy depends in a great measure upon our sense of his present condition" (T, 386).

But how does the imagination guide sympathy from the present to other occasions? Hume's answer is that "[g]eneral rules create a species of probability, which sometimes influences the judgment, and always the imagination" (T, 585). These general rules are indispensable to sound moral judgment, for without their guidance we are misled. For "sympathy with persons remote from us [is] much fainter than with persons near and continuous," and "were we to remain constantly in that position and point of view, which is peculiar to ourselves," we could not sympathize "with persons who are in a situation different from us." To correct these errors of judgment, we "form some general unalterable standard, by which we may approve or disapprove of character and manners" (E, 229).

The application of these "general rules" or "unalterable standards" may be more or less adequate. Judgment can be corrupted by superstition when we prefer some authority to the dictates of our critical faculties and, by enthusiasm, when we prefer violent passions to calm reflection. The result is that, thus misled, we may regard as virtuous what is not, such as "celibacy, fasting, mortification, self-denial, humility, silence, solitude, and the whole train of monkish virtues" (E, 270).

Another source of inadequacy is that "our natural uncultivated ideas of morality, instead of providing a remedy for the partiality of our affections do rather conform themselves to that partiality, and give it additional force and influence." As a result, "our strongest attention is confin'd to ourselves; our next is extended to our relations and acquaintances; and 'tis only the weakest which reaches to strangers and indifferent persons." But "nature provides a remedy in the judgment and understanding, for what is irregular and incommodious in the affections" (T, 488–89).

And with this we have finally arrived at the answer to what gives sympathy action-guiding force and why sympathy moves us to help people in our society. Reason corrects the partiality of our sympathy, because "men, from their early education in society, have become sensible of the infinite advantages that result from it." The protection of these advantages "can be done after no other manner, than by a convention enter'd into by all members of the society to bestow stability on the possession of . . . goods, and leave every one in the peaceable enjoyment of what he may acquire by his fortune and industry. By this means . . . the passions are restrained in their partial and contradictory motions. . . . Instead of departing from our interests, or from that of our nearest friends . . . we cannot better consult both these interests, than by such a convention; because it is by that means we maintain society, which is so necessary to their well-being and subsistence, as well as to our own" (*T*, 489).

To sum up, Aristotle's account of civic friendship does not explain what predisposes people to decency. According to Hume, sympathy does. But how does sympathy, regarded merely as fellow feeling, result in altruistic action? To explain it, we have to supplement Hume's account by showing how reason guides and corrects sympathy. Reason does so by postulating general rules that, if followed, save us from superstition, enthusiasm, and the partiality of our moral judgment. The reason for wanting to overcome these defects is that otherwise we undermine our society, which provides one of the conditions required for good lives for ourselves and for those we love. This is why we are predisposed to decency.

Two questions, however, remain. The first is left over from our discussion of Aristotle: How do we recognize others as appropriate recipients of decency? The second arises from the discussion of Hume: What are the general rules by which reason corrects and guides sympathy? Both will be answered by considering Hume's idea of *custom*.

HUME ON CUSTOM

Hume means by custom "a convention enter'd into by all members of the society" (*T*, 489). It takes the form of a generally approved and widely practiced pattern of action prevailing in a society. People regard custom as a norm of action. It determines what kind of conduct is appropriate. An important part of education is to teach children what custom demands. The customary is the traditional and old, and while it may be transgressed, it rarely is. Custom changes, but usually very slowly. Rapid change is dangerous, for custom includes all the uncodified ways in which people treat others and expect others to treat them. If these expectations are not met, because uncodified ways no longer prevail, two destructive options remain. One is that *skloka* will take their place. The other is that some authority will impose codified ways of conduct and thus make society more or less repressive. Thus, custom is both a civilizing and a liberating force.

According to Hume, customs are relative to societies. They are binding on their members but not on people living elsewhere. Visitors are expected to conform, but their transgressions are generally excusable due to their ignorance. Customs have an obvious connection with morality, but what that connection is, is controversial. The extreme skeptics Hume opposes, like Mandeville, who think of "all moral distinctions as the effects of artifice and education" (*T*, 578), identify custom and morality. The contemporary name for this position is moral relativism. On the other hand, moral absolutists, like Clarke and Wollaston, with whom Hume also disagrees, deny that custom has anything to do with morality, because moral principles are eternal and unchanging truths, while customs are variable. Hume's position, as mine, is between these two. Customs are variable, but not indefinitely so, because the facts of the body, self, and social life set limits to what can be established as customary. Within these limits, customs vary and change. But whether a society has customs is not optional, for none can endure without bonds of custom among its people.

What, then, is the relation between custom and human nature, according to Hume? The two parts of human nature are "the affections and understanding" (*T*, 493). Custom is related to them in different ways. As far as the understanding is concerned, "[c]ustom, then, is the great guide of human life. It is that principle which renders our experience useful to us, and makes us expect, for the future, a similar train of events with those which have appeared in the past. Without the influence of custom, we would be entirely ignorant of every matter of fact beyond what is immediately present to the memory and sense" (*E*, 44–5). How does custom guide us? By "principles which are permanent, irresistable, and universal; such as the customary transition from causes to effects. . . . [These principles] are the foundation of all thought and action, so that upon their removal human nature must perish and go to ruin" (*T*, 225). And the principles, of course, are the principles of association governing the natural workings of the mind. They organize and thus enable us to make sense out of the information provided by our memory and senses. Since it is on this basis that we must act, custom is, indeed, "the great guide of human life."

The relation between custom and the other part of human nature, affection, is as follows. "The minds of all men are similar in their feelings and operations, nor can anyone be actuated by any affection, of which others are not, in some degree susceptible" (*T*, 575–76). This similarity is due to the fact that "the chief actuating principle of the human mind is pleasure and pain; and when these are remov'd, both from our thought and feeling, we are in a great measure, incapable of passion or action, of desire or volition" (*T*, 574). Human nature is such that pleasure leads us to approve and pain to disapprove of qualities that provoke them. Some of these qualities are natural in that all human beings approve of them and "have no dependence on the artifice and contrivance of men" (*T*, 574). These are the natural virtues, and our approval of them is motivated either by sympathy or self-interest. In respect to these motivations, human nature is constant. We do naturally care for the welfare of others and ourselves. But human nature does not dictate how far we shall be motivated by one or the other of these desires.

Thus, Hume rejects both pure egoism and pure altruism: "I am of the opinion, that tho' it be rare to meet with one, who loves any single person better than himself; yet 'tis rare to meet with one, in whom all the kind affections, taken together, do not overbalance the selfish" (*T*, 487), but also that "we perceive, that the generosity of men is very limited, and that it seldom extends beyond their friends and family, or, at most, beyond their native country" (*T*, 602). The result is the distinctively Humean view of human nature as governed by limited sympathy: "It is wisely ordained by nature, that private connexions should commonly prevail over universal views and considerations; otherwise our affections and actions would be dissipated and lost, for want of a proper limited object" (*E*, 229). The role of custom is to guide our limited sympathies. It does so by taking the constant element of human nature, limited sympathy, and giving it direction through the social morality that a particular society has established.

We may say, then, that custom consists in limited sympathy and convention. Both elements are necessary, since without the natural disposition created by limited sympathy, benevolent conventions could not be maintained; while without conventions, our limited sympathies "would be dissipated and lost for want of a proper limited object." What is crucial for the welfare of society is that there be conventions that accord with human nature, but what these conventions specifically are depends on the historical influences upon different societies.

We are now in the position to answer one of the two outstanding questions: about the identity of the general rules by which reason guides and corrects sympathy. There are two kinds of such rules. The first are expressions of the constant elements of human nature, the principles of association, according to which the understanding functions, and the propensity to feel pleasure and pain in the presence of certain qualities, manifested by the affective side of our nature. These are among the deep conventions. The second are contributed by whatever happen to be the variable conventions prevailing in our society. Reason guides sympathy by giving it direction through both deep and variable conventions. And reason corrects sympathy by resisting its tendency toward superstition, enthusiasm, and partiality.

In my interpretation, then, the relation between custom, moral tradition, and social morality is as follows. Custom is the most inclusive of the three. It is the term for all the many different conventions prevailing in society. I have been using moral tradition to refer to the specifically moral conventions of a society. These conventions are moral, because they guide potentially beneficial and harmful conduct. But such conduct may be personal, having to do with realizing personal aspirations and with participating in intimate relationships. Or it may be social, concerning the more or less impersonal encounters of fellow members of a society. Social morality is the term I have reserved for the impersonal aspect of moral traditions. The peculiarly moral sense of decency, then, derives from conduct conforming to the social morality of one's society. This conduct conforms to deep conventions, some of which, following Hume, we can understand as expressions of the constant elements of our nature I have called the facts of the body, self, and social life, and it also conforms to historically and socially changing variable conventions.

DECENCY AND SOCIAL MORALITY

The other outstanding question has been waiting for an answer since we left Aristotle for Hume. It is about how we recognize each other as fellow members of a society, thus owing decency to each other, in such impersonal, populous, and heterogeneous contexts as ours. The answer is that mutual recognition is based on our conduct being governed by the same moral conventions. These conventions establish a language of conduct. They enable us, if we share them, to draw on common distinctions between what is good and evil, right and wrong, blameworthy and excusable, supererogatory and dutiful, pleasing and offensive. Thus, they give us a common way of assessing our perceptions of moral situations, beyond the ways dictated by the general rules that govern the operations of our thought and sensibility. The importance of this is that when we come to share a social morality, not because it is imposed on us, but because we find it suitable and pleasing, then we establish a common identity. We come to define ourselves in the same way, and so we feel allegiance to each other and to the society we constitute. This is what determines how far limited sympathy should go. And it explains why, if we are reasonable, in addition to caring about our own welfare and the welfare of those we love, we would wish to extend goodwill, friendliness, and helpfulness to some people and how we would select them.

The evaluative dimension of social morality is deep. It goes beyond knowing how to use such terms as good and evil, right and wrong. The depth comes from familiarity with the discriminations, nuances, judgments of importance and priority, and from an aliveness to sources of conflict and tension, all of which form the texture of the social life guided by social morality. What we, as participants, know is, not merely that this person is decent and that not, but also what makes them so and why one is better or worse, more or less culpable or admirable, weaker or stronger, more capable of improvement or hopelessly corrupt than other people in similar circumstances. It is to know what is outrageous, shocking, offensive, rather than a sophomoric attempt to provoke, an assertion of independence, or a cry for help.

As full-fledged participants in social morality, we know these and thousands of similar things in a particular manner. Not as a judge knows the law, for we do not reflect and then carefully select the appropriate convention that best fits the case at hand. Moral knowledge of the sort I have in mind has become our second nature. Making the distinctions, noticing the nuances, being alive to the conflicts, priorities, and temptations no longer requires reflection. Just as an accomplished violinist knows how to play adagio and a rock climber knows how to manage an overhang, so we, participating in a social morality, know about moral matters. Of course, we may have to stop and think, but that happens only in difficult cases. The daily flow of moral life can be handled spontaneously by well-trained participants in a social morality.

Nor is the knowledge like that of anthropologists observing a society. The crucial difference is that anthropologists stand outside of what they observe. They may approve or disapprove, feel sympathy, revulsion, or be indifferent, and compare the social morality favorably or unfavorably with what prevails in other societies. But as participants in a social morality, we are necessarily inside it. We may observe it perhaps as accurately as any anthropologist, but we cannot be indifferent. I do not mean that we are bound to judge our own conventions superior to others. What I mean is that whatever moral judgments we make, they are made in terms our conventions provide. Our participation in social morality means that we see the relevant moral aspect of the world in that way.

There is a sense in which this could not be otherwise. For we are given by our social morality a conception of what is a good society, what it is to be a decent member of it, what personal characteristics are virtuous and admirable, how we should treat each other, and what are the duties and privileges of the various stations in life our society affords. These constitute part, the social part, of the substance of our moral lives, and they inform our sensibility in terms of which we interpret and evaluate relevant events and situations. Indifference would mean the loss of much of our evaluative capacity.

Participation in social morality will, then, shape how we think and feel about our lives and how we judge the disclosures of our social experiences. But by being so shaped, we become part of a society whose members share the vision and sensibility of their common conventions. A social morality, then, not only defines part of the moral identity of its members, it also unites them in virtue of their common ways of judging and responding to the world. The visible marks of their identity and unity, in our times, are the behavioral clues, rituals, and ceremonies that play such a large, and largely unnoticed, part in our lives.

The behavioral clues are the gestures, frowns, smiles, nods, scowls, laughter and tears, sniffings and cluckings, winkings, head scratchings, yawns, clearings of throats, stares, gazes, looks and taking care not to look, gaze, or stare, the speed and emphasis with which something is said, the occasion and direction in which it is said, flushes, blushes, blanches, and the multitude of ways in which we emphasize, embellish, soften, indicate the seriousness or levity of what we say and do. But the clues are appropriate only if they communicate what was intended or meant by them, and this, of course, requires that the actor and the spectator, the agent and the recipient, should share an interpretation of the significance of what has passed between them. This, once again, is rarely a conscious reflective process. The clues are frequently given and understood without either party being aware of their passage. To a very considerable extent, participants in a social morality are united, feel comfortable and familiar with each other because they can depend on being thus understood.

This sense of belongingness is enhanced by the rituals that permeate everyday life: the how-are-yous, handshakes, openings of doors, taking off of hats, coats, jackets, the sharing of a meal, having a coffee or a drink together, the kisses and the embraces, the telling of secrets, sharing confidences, exchanging gossip, the uses of formulas for expressing regret, condolence, enmity, or sympathy, the occasions and manner of congratulations for success and commiseration for failure or misfortune. And the ceremonies marking significant occasions, like birth, marriage, death, graduation, birthdays, anniversaries, arrivals and departures, promotion and retirement, holidays and festivities, are similarly unifying forces. As fellow members of a society, we recognize our connectedness, because we share the knowledge of what is appropriate to the events of our lives and we share also the knowledge of the manner in which these events are to be marked. And this remains true even of those rebels, eccentrics, nonconformists, and iconoclasts who refuse to do what is appropriate. For the conventions against which they protest determine the occasions on which they express their disdain. Only genuine indifference, uninvolvement, and ignorance of what is appropriate place people outside of a social morality.[11]

Thus, the basis of social morality, the source that sustains it, is not that the participants know, love, or even like each other; there is no fundamental principle to which they have sworn allegiance; there is no overarching ideal whose inspirational force establishes their solidarity. There is largely spontaneous, unreflective, customary conduct, the unarticulated feeling of ease in each other's company, because there is much that need not be said, and there is the knowledge that when something needs to be done, they know how to do it. The signs of connectedness are the behavioral clues, rituals, and ceremonies, and their consequences are that people recognized as fellow members are given the benefit of the doubt, and they are treated in a friendly, polite way. The categorical imperative, liberty, equality, and fraternity, the happiness of mankind, or the imitation of Christ are intellectual abstractions that derive what force they may have from the concrete goodwill that participants of a social morality spontaneously have toward each other. Without this goodwill, the abstractions ring hollow. I have called the attitude that reflects this goodwill decency.

THE CONTENT OF DECENCY

By way of conclusion, I shall summarize the account of decency that has emerged from considering Aristotle and Hume. Aristotle provides the framework for the discussion. His civic friendship, and my decency, is a benevolent attitude, consisting of the well-wishing and well-doing of members of a society toward each other. It is motivated by both altruism and self-interest. Each derives from the realization that we can live what we regard as good lives only in a stable, cohesive society from which *skloka* is absent. The source of altruistic motivation is that, as fellow members, we view each other as partners in a joint

---

[11] Goffman describes these social transactions in many works. See, e.g., *The Presentation of Self in Everyday Life* and *Interaction Ritual*.

enterprise, we wish success to our fellows, and, if the opportunity arises, we spontaneously act on the wish. The source of the self-interested motivation is the desire to have others wish well and do well by us. Decency is thus reciprocal, yet impersonal. We do not treat others decently because we like them. Indeed, we could not like them, since the vast majority are strangers to us, and we meet such few as we do only in casual encounters. Decent people extend their goodwill to all their fellows without discrimination. They expect to be treated in as friendly and helpful a manner as they treat others. In good societies, this expectation is satisfied; in bad societies, it is not. What underlies this expectation is the tacit assumption that, not rights, but goodwill guides the conduct of fellow members. There is, of course, a codified system of law in the background. But it is there as a last resort to resolve serious conflicts. The more people are moved by decency, the fewer are such conflicts. For if people give each other the benefit of the doubt, if they are guided by goodwill, if they wish to be helpful and act on it, then most of the conflicts that do arise can be resolved privately without litigation. The more frequent is the appeal to the authority of the law, the less benevolent a society is. Thus, decency is the attitude that permits strangers, who are connected only by adherence to the same social morality, to live together harmoniously. By doing so, they meet one requirement of good lives.

But this Aristotelian account is too formal, too intellectualistic. It does not pay adequate attention to the emotive sources of decency and to the significance of the variable historically conditioned conventions that guide us. Hume's philosophical outlook, stressing sympathy and custom, is a corrective of the Aristotelian emphasis.

Decency is a spontaneous, nonreflective, habitual attitude. Its basis, according to Hume, is the inborn and involuntary feeling of sympathy, a fellow feeling people have for one another. It enables two people similar in some respects, not too distant in time and space, and affected by each other, to develop the feelings the other has. Some of these feelings will cause them pain and others pleasure. Subsequent moral approval and disapproval depend on these natural, universal, and instinctive feelings of pleasure and pain. This is the foundation of morality, but there is, of course, more to it; however, neither Hume nor I need to consider that for the present purposes.

Sympathy is the emotional source of decency, but it needs direction and correction. It must be based on accurate perception of the object of sympathy, it must move to action, its partiality must be overcome, and it must be strengthened against such competitors as superstition, enthusiasm, and selfishness. All this is the task of reason. And reason may accomplish it through the inborn principles that guide human judgment and through the general principles established by the customs prevailing in the society. So sympathy is guided by reason, and reason, in turn, operates in conformity with human nature and custom.

Social morality is the part of custom that guides people in particular societies in their impersonal contacts with each other. Its aim is to foster beneficial and avoid harmful conduct. And decency is the attitude that leads people to conduct themselves and treat others according to social morality. It is a mixture of feeling, reason, and custom. It is an indispensable condition of harmonious social living. Consequently, it is an essential ingredient of whatever anyone regards as a good life.

CHAPTER FOUR

Decency

> I see no harm in the bourgeois way of life, myself. I like
> regularity of behavior and courtesy of manner and due
> attention paid to the existence of other people. I like an
> ordered life and discretion and reliability. And honesty. And
> a sense of honour.
>
> —Anita Brookner[1]

WHARTON'S VISION

The importance of decency is that it protects a large area in which
people can seek what they regard as good lives. If we possess decency,
we tend to avoid harming fellow members of our social morality. But
decency is also a positive good, for it is an ingredient of good lives. I
shall discuss how decency is both by reflecting on Edith Wharton's
great novel, *The Age of Innocence*.[2]

   The setting of the novel is the social morality of upper-middle-class
society in New York during the last two or three decades of the nine-
teenth century. Against this background, we are given the love between Newland Archer and Countess Olenska. Archer is a highly respected member of this society. He is a lawyer engaged to May
Welland, a young woman who promises to be all New York would
wish. Countess Olenska was born in this setting, but her marriage to
a Polish count took her to Europe where she and her husband had
lived for several years. At the beginning of the novel, Countess Olenska returns to New York to seek the protection and comfort of her
family and society, for she left her corrupt husband and intends to
divorce him. She is received warmly and kindly. But it is made clear
to her that divorce is not countenanced by the prevailing social morality.

   The person who communicates this to her is Archer. He is dis-
patched, both as a lawyer acting for her family and as a representative of their society, to talk her out of it. And he does. He explains to

---

[1] Brookner, *Look at Me*, 59.

[2] Wharton, *The Age of Innocence*. References are to chapters. My discussion is indebted to Phillips, "Allegiance and Change in Morality."

her that the central values of their social morality are family, social allegiance, and unquestionable rectitude. Her intended divorce would violate these values, weaken their society, and hurt her family and friends. So she ought not to seek it. She listens to him, accepts the justification, and gives up the idea of divorce.

However, in the course of their several encounters, during which they are obliged to discuss deep and serious matters that are normally left well below the surface, they fall in love. She, having accepted the case against divorce, is, of course, not free to marry him. He, being first engaged and then married to May Welland, is similarly constrained. But this time it is Archer who would go against social morality and Countess Olenska is the one who explains to him that the case he previously made to her still holds.

In their different ways, Archer and Countess Olenska suffer, give each other up, opt for a life of decency, and accept that their love is impossible. Countess Olenska returns to Europe where she lives out her life in dignified separation from her corrupt husband. Newland Archer remains in New York and grows old as a good father, husband, lawyer, and citizen.

There are three levels of increasing depth below the surface of the simple story. On the first, decency forbids Countess Olenska's divorce; there appears to be a conflict between decency and happiness, and opting for decency, as she does, seems to call for a sacrifice. On the second level, we understand that both reason and sentiment favor decency; decency and happiness do seem to conflict, but their conflict has a ready solution, and opting for decency is not a sacrifice but doing what is reasonably and emotionally right. On the third level, we finally see that the conflict between decency and happiness is illusory, that neither Archer nor Countess Olenska has made a sacrifice.

Rule-Following and Identity-Conferring Decency

Let us begin with the conversation between Archer and Countess Olenska about her divorce. She says, "I want to cast off my old life, to become just like everybody else here." And again, "I want to be free, I want to wipe out all the past." She reminds Archer, "You know my husband—my life with him?" "In this country are such things tolerated? I'm a Protestant—our church does not forbid divorce in such cases." He replies, "New York society is a very small world . . . it's ruled by . . . rather old-fashioned ideas. . . . Our ideas about marriage and divorce are particularly old-fashioned. Our legislature favours divorce—our social customs don't." She asks, "But my freedom—is that nothing?" And he says, "The individual, in such cases, is nearly always sacrificed to what is supposed to be the collective interest: people cling to any convention that keeps the family together. . . . It is my business, you know . . . to help you see these things as people who are fondest of you see them . . . all your friends here and relations: if I didn't show you honestly how they judge such questions, it wouldn't be fair of me." She considers the case he put and acquiesces: "Very well; I will do what you wish" (chapter 12).

These words, Archer's case and Countess Olenska's submission, strike our modern sensibilities as outrageous. Here is an admittedly injured woman, wishing to free herself from an unmeritedly ugly past. And Archer, that plenipotentiary of decency, persuades her otherwise. We want to urge her to seize the day, be free, go after happiness, and sweep Archer's superficial conventions aside. Life is to be lived, not constrained by bloodless conventions. If we understand why this is a misguided view of their situation, we are ready to pass on to a deeper moral level.

Well, then, why are we misguided in seeing this as an obviously mistaken choice of decency, dictated by social morality, over freedom and the pursuit of happiness? A distinction between *rule-following* and *identity-conferring* decency will help with the answer. Rule-following decency is simply to conduct oneself according to social morality. It is to do or not to do what the conventions prescribe or prohibit; to behave appropriately, with propriety, respectably. Rule-following decency is akin to law-abidingness. Knowledge of the relevant prescriptions and conduct according to them are necessary and sufficient for judging whether the conduct conforms to the prescriptions. This knowledge is not hard to obtain for anyone familiar with the social context. Rule-following decency is all on the surface; in its case, things are as they seem. What matters is what is done, not why it is done.

Identity-conferring decency is essentially connected with motivation, with the reasons for doing what social morality prescribes. We are decent in this way if our moral outlook is informed by the one prevailing in our social context and if our motive for conducting ourselves in accordance with it is that we morally approve of it. We see the relevant aspect of good and bad lives, virtuous and vicious conduct, moral achievement and failure in terms provided by the social morality. We accept it, we are shaped by it, our moral vision is inseparable from it, we feel comfortable with it, we give our allegiance to it, and so it confers part of our identity on us. This kind of decency, therefore, is deep; it is connected with what we are and want to be.

Identity-conferring decency gives rise to rule-following decency. But we cannot infer from rule-following decency that it is motivated by identification with social morality. Rule-following decency may be hypocritical; identity-conferring decency cannot be. Furthermore, identity-conferring decency may actually motivate the violation of some conventions, if the agent is convinced that a particular convention is at odds with other conventions. Of course, such violations cannot be frequent. For if many conventions are supposed to be at odds with the prevailing social morality, then the social morality cannot command the allegiance of its participants.

Our modern sensibility regarding Countess Olenska's decision is misguided, because we tend to see the conflict between decency and happiness as juxtaposing superficial propriety to the deep and serious responsibility of directing our lives. We judge that Countess Olenska allowed herself to be persuaded to choose the superficial and she was wrong to give in, as Archer was wrong to lead her to it. The trouble with our sensibility is that it fails to recognize the significance of the distinction between rule-following and identity-conferring decency.

Countess Olenska's decision was an instance of identity-conferring decency. She decided not to seek divorce because it would have violated social morality. The reason why Archer could persuade her was partly that she was committed to social morality, but she did not realize that it prohibited divorce even in cases where the person seeking it was injured. Archer explained to her that this was so. Her conflict was not between superficial propriety and personal responsibility. It was between two directions in which personal responsibility simultaneously pushed her. She felt deep allegiance to the society whose social morality prohibited divorce, and she felt similarly deeply that she wanted to be free from her ugly past. Her conflict was between what she saw as social good and personal good, and she chose, with Archer's help, social good. If her choice is seen in this light, we may still think that it is mistaken, but it would be simpleminded to regard it as obviously mistaken. We do, after all, celebrate people as moral heroes who sacrifice their personal welfare for social welfare, as Countess Olenska appears on this level to have done. Modern sensibility, I am afraid, prompts us to be simpleminded, and that is why I think that it is misguided.

Of course, just because Countess Olenska and Archer are not obviously mistaken in favoring what seems to them social good over personal good does not mean that they are not mistaken. Their position calls for justification, and that is what we get on the second level.

IDENTITY-CONFERRING DECENCY AND HAPPINESS

We learn on this level that while there seems to be a conflict between decency and happiness, Countess Olenska, and a little later Archer, have a preponderance of reasons in favor of opting for decency. When this is understood, the conflict appears to be less important, the choice of decency over happiness is seen as involving much less sacrifice than before. What, then, are these reasons?

Countess Olenska and Archer discuss, on a later occasion, what made her accept his arguments. She says, "I felt there was no one . . . who gave me reasons that I understood for doing what at first seemed so hard and—unnecessary. The very good people didn't convince me; I felt they'd never been tempted. But you knew; you understood; you had felt the outside tugging at one with all its golden hands—and yet you hated the things it asks of one; you hated happiness bought by disloyalty and cruelty and indifference. That was what I'd never known before—and it is better than anything I've known" (chapter 18).

The essential point Archer put and Countess Olenska accepted was that since she finds the social morality of New York society better than anything she had known, it has a claim on her allegiance. The substance of that claim is that she ought to conduct herself, as identity-conferring decency requires, according to the conventions she judged to be superior to any others. Since the prohibition against divorce is part of social morality, she ought to observe it.

Both reason and sentiment force this conclusion on her. Sentiment claims her allegiance to social morality in two ways. First, she was born and raised in it, and she imbibed its conventions from cradle on. When she left it and marriage took her to another society, she judged her husband and his society corrupt by the standards of the social morality in which she was raised. As an observer says of her: "[I]f you are an American of *her* kind . . . things that are accepted in certain societies, or at least put up with as part of the general give-and-take—become unthinkable, simply unthinkable" (chapter 25). Social morality defines her limits; it does not do so consciously and certainly not argumentatively; she simply feels that certain things are unthinkable. She would not do them, and when she finds her husband accepting them as a matter of course, she feels abused and leaves him.

And what does she leave him for? For her own people, her family and society, for the social morality that formed her. "New York simply meant peace and freedom to me: it was coming home. And I was so happy at being among my own people that everyone I met seemed kind and good, and glad to see me" (chapter 18). This is the second way sentiment demands her allegiance. For how could she opt for divorce and show "disloyalty and cruelty and indifference" to her own people, whose social morality she shares, and who have been so "kind and good" to her?

But the force of sentiment is not strong enough to make her conform. For she also has sentiment pulling her in the opposite direction. As strongly as she feels allegiance to New York society, so she feels revolted by her husband's society. One prohibits, the other cries out for divorce. Furthermore, her state of mind is one of confusion and unclarity. It is an arena in which her feelings do daily battle for domination. And no battle is final; the victor of the day is the loser of the next. It is in just such situations that people feel the need for moral advice on which they can rely for clarification and judgment. Reason enters through the moral authority of Archer.

What makes Archer a moral authority, up to this point in the novel, before he falters, is that his conduct is exemplary and he is articulate and reflective about the social morality he accepts. His conduct is exemplary in that it is appropriate; he embodies identity-conferring decency. He is reflective about his social morality, because he has compared it with other social moralities and found it superior, and because he understands the hierarchy of values, the connection between deep and variable conventions, and he is able to judge their respective importance. Furthermore, he is articulate about the subject of his reflection. So he is not only able to judge reliably, but he can also explain to others in his context the reasons for his judgment. And this is what he does to Countess Olenska.

Seen in this light, the conflict between decency and happiness is modulated. It can no longer be seen as a special case of the conflict between duty and pleasure. And the social morality to which allegiance is the supposed duty can no longer be thought of as a collection of trivial and old-fashioned conventions imposed by the desiccated old to prevent the young from being happy. Well, why not? How does Archer's justification, properly appreciated, alter our perception of their situations?

Archer's justification shows that there is no sharp conflict between identity-conferring decency and happiness. For Countess Olenska's happiness is intimately connected with the same social morality that prompts identity-conferring decency. What would make her happy is identical with what decency demands of her, namely, conduct according to the social morality she accepts. She shares the moral vision of her society and this vision defines for her what a good life, a life she wishes to live, would be like. And divorce is not part of that vision. Yet she wants it. What Archer shows her is that the conflict she faces is not between decency and happiness but between a deeply and a superficially considered view of happiness. The superficial view is connected with her getting what she wants now; the shoe pinches, and she wants to take it off. Wanting that, viewed in isolation from her whole life, is reasonable and understandable. The deeper view, however, moves beyond immediate satisfaction and puts the conflict in the perspective of her whole life. Of course divorce would make her happier now. But divorce would also alienate her from the society in which she is happy; it would involve a signal act of disloyalty to those who were good to her when she turned to them for help; and it would tend to undermine the moral vision in terms of which she understands happiness. So her choice is not between decency and happiness but between the possibility of happiness in the immediate future and its possibility in the long run. This is what Archer shows her, and this is why she is led by both reason and sentiment to give up the idea of divorce.

However, we are in the hands of a master, and Edith Wharton's vision is too cool, too ironic, too understanding of human weakness to allow us to see Archer as the paragon he has so far appeared to be. In the course of all that advising and earnest talks and exercise of moral authority, he falls in love with Countess Olenska and she with him. And it is Archer now who is ready to go against social morality. He now wants her to divorce, and he is willing to break up his engagement to May Welland so that Countess Olenska and he can marry, and, presumably, live happily ever after. What has happened to our moral authority is that his feelings have grown too strong, and he has gotten carried away. The case he has made to Countess Olenska still holds, but he ignores it. If he were to reflect, he would realize that he is proposing to violate his own moral convictions; but in the throes of his passion, he does not reflect. This time, however, it is Countess Olenska who does for him what he previously did for her.

Archer tells her of his love, and she says, "Ah, my poor Newland— I suppose this had to be. But it doesn't in the least alter things." "It alters the whole world for me," says Archer. Countess Olenska replies, "No, no—it mustn't, it can't. You are engaged to May Welland; and I am married." But he does not accept it. "He reddened under the retort, but kept his eyes on her. 'May is ready to give me up.' " "What!" she says, "Three days after you've entreated her on your knees to hasten your marriage?" But, he says, the lawyer, the casuist coming to the fore, "She's refused; that gives me the right—." And to this, Countess Olenska has two highly significant rejoinders. The first is about Archer's appeal to his rights: "Ah, you've taught me what an ugly word that is." The second is about their love: "Ah, don't let us undo what you've done. . . . I can't go back to that other way of thinking. I can't love you unless I give you up" (chapter 18).

Why is *right* an ugly word? This brings us to the core of decency. Given their social morality, Countess Olenska has a right to divorce, and Archer explained to her why identity-conferring decency requires that she should not stand on it. Archer has a right to break up his engagement, and this time Countess Olenska explains to him why he should not take advantage of it. A right is a claim we have against others. This claim may or may not be cashed in. People may have a right to commit suicide, have an abortion, and see pornographic movies. But having such rights, of course, is not an invitation to engage in the activities. There is a question about when we should act on our rights. And what Countess Olenska is saying is that they ought not to act on theirs, that it would go against their social morality, and, thus, it would be indecent to do so. Why is this so?

Imagine a society whose members scrupulously observe the rules of their social morality, but their observance exhausts the extent of their moral involvement with each other. In such a society, people would punctiliously observe the rights of others and would expect others to do the same for them. Let us suppose that this mutual expectation is satisfied. Now, this society would be different from any existing society in several ways. But the difference that concerns us here is that normally societies depend on their members to act in a spirit of goodwill, with spontaneous helpfulness and friendly casual consideration toward each other. In a completely rule-governed society this spirit would, *ex hypothesi*, be lacking. There would be two alternatives: either rules would have to be designed for each of the many ways in which in other societies goodwill is the informal guide, or people would have to restrict drastically their moral expectations of each other and eliminate from their social morality all the informal nonrule-governed conduct that exists in other societies.

The first alternative could not work, because it is as impossible to devise rules for all the different moral situations that could occur as it is to have laws for all particular cases. The law requires precedents, judges, and the adversary system to determine what rule fits what case. A completely rule-governed morality would be like the law would be without the judicial apparatus. And that, of course, is unworkable. The letter of the law and the rules of social morality would have to be interpreted. An interpretation is successful, *inter alia*, if it represents the spirit of the interpreted rule. However, in social morality that spirit is just the mutual goodwill fellow members of a society have toward each other that the rules of a completely rule-governed society were trying to replace. So the replacement is bound to fail.

The second alternative would restrict social morality to situations for which rules can be devised. This would eliminate from social morality altruism, benevolence, generosity, charity, mercy, forgiveness, and all the other moral attitudes that call upon one to go beyond rules. It would make social morality into something like an extremely strict system of etiquette, although they would have different domains. I doubt that it needs to be argued further that neither alternative is desirable. And what follows from that is that social morality cannot do with rights only; it must also have the spirit of goodwill, spontaneous helpfulness, and friendly casual consideration I spoke of above.

When Countess Olenska says to Archer that *right* is an ugly word, she means that if she and he exacted their rights, they would violate the spirit, if not the letter, of their social morality. It would be indecent of her to divorce and of him to break up his engagement, because it would purchase their happiness at the cost of "disloyalty and cruelty and indifference." It is not that they would outrage the delicate sensibilities of "the very good people" who had "never been tempted." Rather, they would betray the social morality that is the fabric of their and their family's and friends' lives. By standing on their rights, they would be disloyal both to themselves and to others.

Archer, casuistically, says to her: we have the right; and he means: we would not violate rule-following decency if we did what was necessary to get married. Countess Olenska, having learned well the lesson Archer taught her, says in effect: exacting our rights would violate identity-conferring decency.

Identity-conferring decency is not merely customary conduct, it also, essentially, involves the spirit of goodwill toward fellow members of one's society. This goodwill is a sign of the frequently unarticulated belief that fellow members of a society share with one another a moral outlook, agree about good and evil, right and wrong, and about how they should treat each other. Identity-conferring decency is the translation of this deep allegiance into practical terms. It shows itself, on the surface, by rule-following decency and, more deeply, by not standing on one's rights if doing so is contrary to the spirit of goodwill.

The second of Countess Olenska's significant replies to Archer is, "I can't love you unless I give you up." By now it is obvious what she means: they love each other for what they are, and what they are is partly defined by their shared social morality. If they violated that, they would be destroying part of what they found worthy of love in each other. Their love, therefore, requires that they should give each other up. But Archer protests, "What a life for you!" and she replies, "Oh—as long as it's part of yours." "And mine," asks Archer, "part of yours?" She nodded. "And that's to be all—for either of us?" "Well; it *is* all isn't it?" (chapter 24). The last sentence is an affirmation, not a sign of resignation. The "all" their lives are is being part of the same social morality, sharing its deep and variable conventions, having a moral outlook in common, and seeing each other as companions in a common pursuit. That is why their lives will be part of each other's, even though they will be separated forever. She can truly say, "I shan't be lonely now. I *was* lonely; I *was* afraid. But the emptiness and darkness are gone; when I turn back into myself now I'm like a child going into a room where there's always light" (chapter 28). They gave each other up, and that is a sacrifice. But they gained in return the disappearance of loneliness and fear, and a sense of worth. And how many people have that?

DECENCY AND CHARACTER

This last remark of Countess Olenska leads us to the third and deepest level. On the first, their situation appeared to involve a conflict between decency and happiness; it seemed to be resolved by Countess Olenska making the great sacrifice of choosing identity-conferring decency over her happiness. On the second level, we saw the superficiality of the appearances on the first level. The conflict appeared to involve the choice between a naive and a reflective pursuit of happiness. Divorce and breaking the engagement have a place in the naive view but not in the reflective one. In opting for the latter, Archer and Countess Olenska do, to be sure, make a sacrifice. But if it is seen in the right proportion, the sacrifice is not great. Betraying their social morality, society, friends, family, and their love would be much worse. On the third level, we realize that, properly understood, their situation does not involve a conflict at all. We shall come to see this if we reflect on a question that comes naturally to contemporary readers of the novel: Why do they not leave? They are independent unencumbered adults. They have money. Why do they not move to France or Italy and enjoy each other and life?

The answer is suggested by a pair of lovers who did just that: Vronsky and Anna Karenina did pack up and go to Italy. And, of course, what happened to them was that their love faltered. The anticipated joyful abandon, made possible by having left behind the intrusive presence of their society, did not occur. They became listless, distracted, irritable, bored, although they continued to love each other.

However, their love was at least as troubled in Italy as it had been at home in Russia. I think the same would have happened to Countess Olenska and Archer, although perhaps not so soon, for they had greater resources than Tolstoy's pair.

But the question should be pressed: Why need anything bad happen? If the love between two people is true, they want each other's company and the world is irrelevant. Undoubtedly, flawed love will be quickly revealed as such, if the lovers are left to their own resources. However, presumably the love between Countess Olenska and Archer was not flawed, and if it had been, they would still be better off having found that out. If it is fear of the truth that stops them from leaving New York, they are weak, and they bring their separation upon themselves. If they are strong and really love each other, they have nothing to fear. So a contemporary reader may impatiently respond to all the nuances, fine discriminations, and interior struggle that Edith Wharton presents. This, however, is another simpleminded response.

The mistaken supposition underlying it is that our relation to our social morality is contingent, changeable, and has little importance. It is supposed that we can change our social morality with as little loss as we can change our clothes when the fashion changes. But this is not so. Both Countess Olenska and Archer have defined themselves partly in terms of their social morality. It is from it that they have derived some of their deepest convictions about good and evil, the meaning of life, and their happiness. To discard them would be to damage themselves psychologically and morally. And that is not all: their love for each other also depends on it. For part of the reason they love each other is that they admire and respect each other's character and sensibility, and these, of course, have also been shaped and formed by their social morality.

All this may be acknowledged by skeptical readers, but they could still ask why it is supposed that if they were to leave their society, they would be obliged to leave their character and sensibility behind. Presumably, they would carry with them their deep convictions and values, and they would continue to love each other partly because of them.

This is partly true and partly false. Character and sensibility are not possessions we can be deprived of by customs officials as we are leaving the country. But they do depend on the social background that is left behind. Our characters are constituted of dispositions to conduct ourselves in certain ways in certain situations. Changing societies, leaving our social morality for another, involves a basic change in the situations to which we have to respond. The standards of appropriateness shift, our judgment and perception are no longer reliable, what was natural and matter of course in the old setting is no longer fitting, or fitting in the same way, in the new setting. The conventions are different. And it is not just that new ones are added and old ones are omitted but also that the ones occurring in both contexts have different significance and importance. If we find ourselves in a new society, with its own social morality, we have to learn what counts as politeness or insult, forthrightness or forwardness, mockery or compliment, supererogation or duty, a strong or a weak commitment; we do not know the signs of guilt, shame, modesty, flirtatiousness, or irony; we do not know how to express gratitude, appreciation, annoyance, friendliness, resentment, or generosity. We lack the vocabulary of the language of conduct; we know what we want to say, but we do not know how to say it.

Now, of course, we can learn it. But the more we learn, the more our characters and sensibility alter. The better we fit into our new context, the less remains of our previous identity. And if we decide to stay aloof, to maintain our old selves, we shall fail. For the circumstances in which our old selves could express themselves will be lacking. So, while it is true that we can carry our characters and sensibility into new contexts, it is false that these contexts will not change us in fundamental ways over time. And if Archer and Countess Olenska love each other partly for their character and sensibility, they are wise and show good judgment in rejecting the option of leaving behind the social morality that nourishes their love. She is right in saying to Archer that "I can't love you unless I give you up." She cannot love him and have him in New York because their allegiance to social morality makes it impossible; and she cannot love and have him elsewhere because she and he would soon cease to be the people who fell in love with each other.

Skeptical readers may still think of all this as making too much of the importance of changing societies. They may point at immigrants, exiles, and refugees who have changed societies and many of whom adjusted perfectly well to ancillary moral changes. But Countess Olenska and Archer are in a different situation. For immigrants, exiles, and refugees left behind a bad way of life, and they exchanged it for something they believed to be better; and they frequently left because they were driven to it. Nobody drives Countess Olenska and Archer, and they both believe that New York society is "better than anything I've known." Their judgment is not based on ignorance of other possibilities. Archer "had felt the outside tugging . . . with all its golden hands" and rejected it. And Countess Olenska fled in horror from the corruption "accepted in certain societies, or at least put up with as part of the general give-and-take." They are the kind of Americans for whom certain things "become unthinkable, simply unthinkable." And what is unthinkable is what their social morality regards as such. So they cannot just pack up and go; it is psychologically and morally impossible.

One significant fact about Archer and Countess Olenska is that they see this clearly. They realize that they are what they are partly because of the social morality of their society; their continued life together in a manner they regard as worthwhile is inseparably connected with it. Their identity and self-respect depend on living according to their social morality, on conducting themselves with identity-conferring decency. This sort of decency is a condition of their well-being. So when they fall in love, and circumstances render their love indecent, the emotional dislocation is only temporary. Their reason and calmer passions are powerfully there in the background awaiting the violent emotion of their love to subside a little, and then they reassert themselves. They both understand and feel that their love is impossible. It is not social pressure, a sense of sin, or strong conscience that stands in the way. If it were any of these, there would be a conflict between decency and happiness. What stands in the way is their realization that such happiness as they are capable of depends on identity-conferring decency. So they recognize as illusory the prospect of happiness involving its violation. For the reflective moral agents they are, there can be only a flicker of a doubt before they understand that there is no conflict facing them: as soon as they realize what is at stake, the supposed conflict disappears. It is only the achievement of clarity that involves struggle.

We should not, therefore, think of Archer and Countess Olenska as making a big sacrifice to resolve a dramatic conflict, as we are misguided enough to do on the first level. Nor should we think that they have made a small sacrifice in a less dramatic conflict, as they are erroneously thought to do on the second level. They have sacrificed nothing and faced no conflict. They have been momentarily tempted to betray all that mattered to them, including themselves and their love, but due to identity-conferring decency, aided by their reflectiveness and sensitivity, the temptation was resisted. Of course, the degree of happiness they desired eluded them. They have resigned themselves to a self-respecting life in which their deepest feelings lay fallow. But the alternative for them was not to cultivate them; given their characters and circumstances, they could not have done that. That alternative would have deprived them of both happiness and self-respect.

The Value of Decency

What general conclusion follows from this discussion of decency? Decency is conduct according to social morality. Social morality is essential to the welfare of a society, for it prescribes the ways in which fellow members of a society should treat each other. Thus, decency is an important moral attitude. It appears to be superficial, on the surface of morality, and failing to reveal its depth, because the difference between rule-following and identity-conferring decency is overlooked. Rule-following decency is to do what social morality prescribes. Identity-conferring decency is to do so because the agent feels a deep allegiance to social morality. Rule-following decency can be taught, learned by imitation, and acted on hypocritically. It is the superficial aspect of decency. Identity-conferring decency is not only the disinclination to violate conventions; it is also the reluctance to exact our rights, if doing so is contrary to the spirit of social morality. Through identity-conferring decency, moral agents show that their allegiance to social morality is more than scrupulous adherence to rules; it involves goodwill toward fellow members of the society, a reluctance to injure others in pursuit of our own ends, even if we have a right to pursue our ends.

The motivation for identity-conferring decency is neither altruistic nor self-serving. These are crude notions for understanding allegiance to social morality. If decency prevails, everyone, including the agent, benefits. But the motivation for decent conduct is not to benefit ourselves or others. Its motivation is general approval of the social morality we share with others. And we approve of it because it provides part of the substance of the evaluative dimension of our lives. Nor is approval a matter of weighing the facts and then judging. For we weigh the relevant facts and situations in terms of our social morality. And judgment is the application of the conventions of our social morality to particular cases. The motivation for decency, the reason why reasonable people would want to be decent, is to strengthen the ground on which they stand and from which they evaluate themselves and others.

Nothing I have said should be taken to imply that we could not be justified in rejecting the social morality of our society. If we are justified in doing that, then the case for decency is correspondingly weakened. So my defense of decency is not unconditional. But the conditions in which the case for decency does not hold are bound to be rare and tragic. Rare, because the rejection of the social morality of our society requires exceptional circumstances. What usually happens is that people criticize part of their social morality by appealing to other parts. Thus, we may criticize our social morality on the grounds that it is unjust to women and homosexuals. But we do so in the name of equality and human dignity, which are deeper aspects of the same social morality. The wholesale rejection of social morality, not reform, but revolution, can be justified, I think, only in two cases.

One is that systematically and over a period of time it produces a preponderance of evil over good. But it is difficult to see how social morality could do that, since its continuity depends on the allegiance of its members. If the moral experience of its members is mainly or largely of evil, their allegiance will not last, and the social morality would crumble by itself. The situation of decent people in a disintegrating society is tragic. For whatever they do, evil follows. This seems to me to strengthen the case for decency, since what it requires of us in a faulty social morality is to work for its reform and thus prevent disintegration. We can do this by criticizing evil practices in the name of conventions with which these practices conflict. The second possible justification for the wholesale rejection of social morality is that we come to appreciate and to adopt a social morality superior to it. But in transferring our allegiance in this way, we do not reject decency. We arrive at a deeper appreciation of what decency is.

Rule-following decency goes a long way toward satisfying the requirements of social morality. Identity-conferring decency goes beyond it and constitutes a beginning of personal morality. For identity-conferring decency becomes, as its name suggests, part of the identity of moral agents who possess it. They define themselves and construe their conceptions of good lives partly in terms of their social morality. Through the development of identity-conferring decency, moral agents internalize their social morality. In this process, they transform the largely impersonal social aspect of their moral tradition into the primarily intimate personal aspect. This is precisely what Archer and Countess Olenska have done. But this internalization of social morality, the transformation of the requirements of harmonious social life into a conception of good life for oneself, is a matter of degree. I have argued that some degree of it is a moral necessity, for rule-following decency is hollow unless it derives from identity-conferring decency. Archer and Countess Olenska, however, carried the process of internalizing their social morality far beyond the required minimum. They internalized social morality to such an extent as to allow it to swallow up the space occupied in other lives by personal morality. Their conception of a good life became largely identical with living according to social morality. They resolved the brief conflict they experienced between social and personal morality by making social morality their personal morality. I have tried to present their moral stance with as much understanding and sympathy as I could muster. But we must notice that their way of dealing with the conflict between social and personal morality is only one option, and there are others. The dissatisfaction we continue to feel with what Archer and Countess Olenska did with their lives is due, I think, to our disinclination to give as great a scope to social morality in our personal morality as they did.

But if we do not do as they did, we must face the kinds of conflicts they avoided. One such conflict is between social and personal morality. Its resolution would require us to set limits to the extent to which social morality is allowed to influence our personal morality; the extent, that is, to which our conceptions of good lives and intimate personal relationships conform to the prevailing conceptions. The other type of conflict is between the various conceptions of good lives and forms of intimacy that present themselves as options for us. To settle on one option in a reasonable manner, we need to balance our understanding of ourselves, our strengths and weaknesses, hopes and fears, against the promise held out by these various options. The private aspect of eudaimonistic moral tradition, personal morality, is concerned with the resolution of these conflicts.

CHAPTER FIVE

A Defense of Social Morality: Intuition of Simple Moral Situations

> The moral life . . . does not spring from the consciousness of
> possible alternative ways of behaving. . . . [M]ost of the
> current situations of life do not appear as occasions calling
> for judgment, or as problems requiring solutions; there is no
> weighing up of alternatives or reflection on consequences,
> no uncertainty, no battle of scruples. There is, on the
> occasion, nothing more than the unreflective following of a
> tradition of conduct in which we have been brought up.
> —Michael Oakeshott[1]

THE *PRIMA FACIE* CASE

The social morality of eudaimonism has the primary role of guiding
impersonal interactions in contemporary Western societies. But its
guidance is imperfect, because there is a discrepancy between the
prescriptions it endorses and actual conduct. This adds urgency to
the defense of social morality, but it also presents a difficulty. For if a
social morality is indeed customary and widespread, then the discrepancy between its prescriptions and prevalent behavior cannot be too
great. Thus, the defense of social morality must involve both a realistic description of relevant conduct and a justification of the claim
that people ought to conduct themselves like that. The description
should be of the sort of conduct that is the norm, while the justification of the prescriptions should show why such conduct is reasonable.
If the descriptions were often false, then the defense would fail on
account of social morality not being customary and widespread. And
if conduct conforming to social morality actually failed to make lives
better, then the defense would be vitiated by faulty prescriptions.

An additional complication is that there are tensions and inconsis-
tencies among the prescriptions endorsed by social morality, due to
the fact that several moral traditions have influenced it. In defending
our social morality, I shall argue from the point of view of the eudai-

---

[1] Oakeshott, *Rationalism in Politics*, 61.

monistic moral tradition. The result is that the defense is doubly pre-scriptive: in intending to guide conduct and in intending to guide it in a particular direction. The success of the defense depends on the justification of both sorts of prescriptions.

Up to now, we have been considering the attitudes of moral agents who have accepted social morality. In the first two chapters, we looked at attitudes occasioned by the violations of accepted conven-tions; in the next two, we examined attitudes behind conformity to accepted conventions. The question here is whether either type of attitude is reasonable. I shall give an affirmative answer, involving the combination of three theses: the existence of our social morality is necessary for the welfare of contemporary Western society; everyone in this society has a *prima facie* obligation to conform to its social mo-rality; and this society is *prima facie* justified in upholding its social morality.[2]

Describing an individual's obligation and a society's justification as *prima facie* is intended to indicate an initial presumption in favor of them; unless there are overriding reasons, the obligation and the jus-tification hold. This implies both that there could be such reasons and that the responsibility for providing them lies with those who claim exception.

The upholding of social morality includes measures ranging from moral education to parental praise and blame, to the approval and disapproval of friends, acquaintances, teachers, and strangers, to cen-sure and ostracism, to legislation, and to various degrees of legal en-forcement. From our society being *prima facie* justified to uphold its social morality, nothing follows about how it should be done. I shall argue that the severity of justifiable measures depends on the con-text.[3]

Social morality in general may be understood in a sociological or in a normative sense. In both senses, its concern is with good and evil. In the sociological sense, a society can be said to have a social morality even if it produces vastly more harm than benefit; in this sense, we can speak about Nazi morality, for instance. In the normative sense, social morality must be more beneficial than harmful; hence Nazi mo-rality, given this usage, is a contradiction. How one interprets social morality is not very important, provided the sense is made clear. I

---

[2] My thinking is deeply influenced by the controversy between Lord Devlin and Pro-fessor Hart. The chief texts are Devlin, *The Enforcement of Morals*, and Hart, *Law, Lib-erty, and Morality*. An excellent summary of the controversy, including a bibliography, is Mitchell, *Law, Morality, Religion in a Secular Society*.

[3] Devlin and Hart concentrate on the *legal* enforcement of morality. This is one of the ways in which my treatment differs from theirs.

shall interpret it in the normative sense. Accordingly, our society can be said to have a social morality only if our conduct produces a preponderance of benefit over harm. This, of course, does not settle the issue by definition, since moral reformers may reject social morality for something they regard as better. The normative interpretation merely establishes that not just anything deserves the name of social morality. Thus, in defending social morality, one is not committed to defending whatever happens to be the moral *status quo*. Yet the *status quo* has a presumption in its favor, if it has a social morality, normatively interpreted.

Our social morality contains deep and variable conventions. Conformity to deep conventions is necessary for the welfare of society, for it protects the conditions of well-being set by the facts of the body, self, and social life. Thus, widespread adherence to deep conventions is a minimum requirement for counting the system of conventions as a social morality. Tyrannical and disintegrating societies do not have a social morality. They may endure, for tyranny can be perpetuated by repression, and disintegration may take a long time. But in such societies people cannot have good lives, for the minimum conditions are lacking.[4]

Deep conventions, however, give only a meager content to social morality; there must also be variable conventions. But what particular variable conventions a social morality endorses differs from society to society. To further the clarification of our social morality, here are some examples of variable conventions embodied in it: politicians speaking in their public capacity should not lie; winners must not gloat over losers; people ought not to brag about their talents; a life of idleness is wrong; following one's conscience is right; eating people is wrong; one must not torture animals; disagreements should not be settled by physical violence; people should be allowed to express unpopular views; it is wrong to spread malicious lies about one's rival; one must ask for permission before borrowing anything; handicapped people should not be laughed at; white lies are permissible; people should not rejoice publicly at the misfortune of their enemies; one should be loyal to friends; confidential information should not be made public; being cheerful, considerate, and unassuming are good, and their opposites are bad.

These and other variable conventions of our society form an intri-

---

[4] Hart distinguishes between the disintegration thesis and the conservative thesis. The former is that without social morality, society disintegrates, and that is why the enforcement of morality is justified. The latter is that society is justified in enforcing its social morality, even if it would not disintegrate without it. See "Social Solidarity and the Enforcement of Morals." I am defending a version of the conservative thesis.

cate interdependent system. Much of it is uncodified, unconscious, and conformity to it is habitual. Of course, people often go against it, but when this happens, they accept moral blame or can be shown its appropriateness. If people habitually violate it, then, according to eudaimonism, they are either immoral or abnormal.

Social morality is the normative background of social conduct. It is what many moral lapses are deviations from, the standard by which much of what we do is judged, the criterion often appealed to in establishing what requires excuse and what sort of excuse is acceptable. Yet, social morality is only part of the eudaimonistic tradition. Personal morality, supererogatory conduct, and relationships with people outside the context of society are other parts. Nor is social morality meant to be a guide in moral crises or in extreme situations. It guides only social conduct in everyday life: a large, although not all-embracing, task.

MORAL INTUITIONS

The typical concern of social morality is with simple moral situations where there is a clear unambiguous answer to the question of what constitutes decent conduct. On the other hand, personal morality tends to involve more complex situations. Conscientious moral agents are more likely to experience conflicts among various personal aspirations and forms of intimacy than among the conventional requirements of keeping promises, paying debts, doing their jobs, and helping others. I shall concentrate here on simple moral situations. In the next chapter the transition to personal morality and to complex situations will begin.

Simple moral situations can be characterized in terms of the Aristotelian scheme of practical reasoning, consisting of two premises and a conclusion. In simple moral situations, the major premise is a convention of the social morality, expressed as a principle, and known to all normal adults living in the society. We learn these principles in the course of our moral education. The minor premise involves the recognition that a particular situation instantiates the principle stated by the major premise. In simple cases, this recognition is immediate, and it requires no reflection. Normal adults just know that what they may do constitutes making a promise, incurring a debt, giving help, or telling a lie. Recognizing that a certain principle governs a particular situation, they draw the conclusion of the practical syllogism and perform the action the principle requires.

This scheme is an intellectual reconstruction of what is involved in countless transactions of social morality. Most of the time, people are unaware of these steps, precisely because they are well-trained moral agents. Thus, they do not hesitate, there is nothing to ponder, doubt has no foothold. Of course, not even in simple situations does it always go as smoothly as this. People are often tempted not to do what they know they should, and they often give in to this temptation. Things can and do go wrong.

For the moment, however, let us concentrate on cases in which moral agents possess identity-conferring decency and acting according to social morality is natural for them. The conventions, expressed as principles, their bearing on the cases at hand, and the implied actions form a seamless web. These agents choose their actions only in the most attenuated sense: as they understand a situation, so they automatically know what it calls for. It does not occur to them to do anything else. When people act in this manner, they are guided by moral intuition. In simple moral situations, intuition is an appropriate and reliable guide.

Reliance on moral intuition was traditionally thought to involve unquestioning obedience to an authoritative inner voice, requiring no justification. This is a dogmatic and obscurantist view, and it has done much to discredit old-style appeals to moral intuition. But the new-style appeal I propose to make here proceeds differently.

At the dividing line between old and new styles stands W. D. Ross.[5] Before him, moral intuitions were generally regarded as involving self-evidence, unconditionality, and as being the product of a moral sense. Self-evidence was supposed to yield infallible and incorrigible knowledge, guaranteeing that intuitions could not be mistaken. Unconditionality led to categorical moral judgments expressing the fruits of intuitive knowledge. And the psychological apparatus making intuition possible was assumed to be an inborn human faculty whose proper functioning required only maturity and normality. This view was rightly criticized on the grounds that intuitions were often incompatible with each other, what a person or a society regarded as an intuition others rejected as dubious, and that there was to be no trace found of a faculty of moral sense.

Ross jettisoned the idea that intuitions were produced by a moral sense, and he replaced unconditional intuitions with *prima facie* ones. He gave a list of *prima facie* duties and claimed that all mature and normal human beings intuitively recognize their obligatoriness, provided they did not conflict with each other. In cases of conflict, we must put ourselves, actually or vicariously, in the concrete situations and try to intuit which *prima facie* duty has the stronger claim. We

---

[5] Ross, *The Right and the Good* and *Foundations of Ethics*.

could err in such conflicts, but morality involves risks. Conflicts do not show that intuitions are unreliable, only that, in some cases, they are difficult.

The new-style defense of moral intuitions follows Ross in rejecting their certainty and unconditionality and likening moral sense to a sense of humor or a sense of honor in not requiring a sense organ. Yet, as they do in other spheres, intuitions are assumed to play an important role in social morality. "There are vast areas of belief necessary for survival within which intuition is not discreditable, and in which the mind operates by a mechanism of causes and effects normally unknown to the thinking subject. . . . If it were possible to count beliefs, one could say that most of one's beliefs about the environment are of this character."[6] The recognition of pattern, color, size, persons, sounds, tastes, smells, texture are some examples of intuitions involved in perception. But intuitions also play a role in logic, when we see, for instance, that a conclusion follows from the premises; in mathematics, when, if we understand a proof, we see that it is proof; in judging people; estimating distance; getting the point of a joke; and so on. It seems indisputable that we rely on intuitions in many areas of life, and, I shall argue in the new-style, we also do so in social morality.

Intuitions are *moral* if they centrally involve seeing situations in terms of good and evil: human beings benefiting or harming themselves and others. Seeing in this way is *immediate*; there is no conscious inference, reflection, or thought involved in it. Our reaction is spontaneous, instant, automatic. As soon as the facts present themselves, they fall into a pattern for us. This is not to deny that there had been inferences in the past. The fact that our reaction is immediate now is no doubt explained by our having learned in the past to see similar situations in that way. But the lessons have been so thoroughly absorbed that we no more have to rely on them consciously now than we have to remember how to walk or talk. The need to think occurs only in complex situations. Thus, we are led to recognize that intuitions occur *routinely*. They are not sudden revelations or striking discoveries but rather pedestrian, matter-of-course apprehensions of something being so. Therefore, the contexts of intuitions are, not moral dilemmas and conflicts, but the innumerable spontaneous occasions on which we do our jobs, keep appointments, help others if we can without too much trouble, and pay our bills.

Moral intuitions come to us as *imperatives*: they move us toward action. The motion may be arrested for many reasons, but unless some-

---

[6] Hampshire, *Two Theories of Morality*, 7.

thing intervenes, we feel called upon to do something about the intuited situation. In this respect, moral intuitions differ from sensory intuitions. For we can intuit some empirical aspect of the world and be quite indifferent to it. Nor is it a sufficient explanation of the action-guiding force of moral intuitions to say that, unlike sensory intuitions, they are evaluative. For aesthetic intuitions are also evaluative, but they need not move us to action. Aesthetic intuitions are often passive, moral intuitions are typically active. We may be uplifted by beautiful objects and repelled by ugly ones without wanting or needing to do anything public about them. But moral situations call for a different response: we feel obliged to do something, at least to register public approval or disapproval. We typically want others to know where we stand, even if we do not participate in the situation.

Following Ross, we should recognize that intuitions are *presumptive*. Their occurrence establishes a *prima facie* case for the situation being as intuited. If there is no good reason to disbelieve them, it is reasonable to accept our intuitions. This initial presumption in favor of intuitions should be contrasted with the unconditionality old-style intuitionists attributed to them. The difference is that according to the old view, provided something really were an intuition, nothing could overrule it. By contrast, the new view allows for this possibility.

Moral intuitions are *interpretative*, rather than merely descriptive. They involve seeing *as*, not just seeing. They are perceptions of patterns formed by the relevant facts. But what we intuit is not a moral fact over and above nonmoral facts but an interpretation of nonmoral facts. In moral intuitions, we see nonmoral facts in a certain light. This involves the formation of a pattern of the nonmoral facts in which some facts are regarded as significant, while others are assigned no decisive influence. So there are two components of an act of intuition, although they are separable only in thought. One is identifying the facts, and the other is recognizing their significance. Reasonable people identify the same facts comprising a situation. And if they share a social morality, then there will also be many situations in which they will attribute the same significance to the facts.

A further characteristic of moral intuitions is the agents' *unquestioning acceptance* of them. In old-style intuitionism, this was identified as self-evidence. There is something right and something wrong with this idea. It is clearly true that if we have no doubts about the nonmoral facts of some situations, then their moral patterns may present themselves to us immediately and authoritatively, much as objects appear red, rectangular, or heavy. We are not aware of having made an inference, we are not entertaining a hypothesis, so we are not in need of evidence beyond what we already have. It is not unreasonable, therefore, to talk about self-evidence. But self-evidence carries with it a connotation of the impossibility of error, and this is not true of moral intuitions. Although we unquestioningly accept our intuitions, they may be mistaken, we may come to see that they are, and we may correct them.

Consequently, we should recognize that intuitions are *fallible*, and as we recognize it, so the appearance of self-evidence weakens. Old-style intuitionists thought that intuitions were infallible, thus strengthening their supposed self-evidence. For, according to them, if we get the facts of the case right, then, intuitions being the apprehensions of facts, we *ipso facto* get the intuition right, and so there is no room for error. Since I hold that intuitions are not merely of facts but also of the interpretations of facts, fallibility enters through possibly mistaken interpretations. We could get all the facts of the case right and still be mistaken, because in our interpretations of them we may have misjudged their significance.

Since the source of fallibility is misplaced significance and faulty interpretation, it is possible to knock out yet another pillar supporting self-evidence. Intuitions were supposed to be incorrigible because, if the facts were rightly apprehended, then the sources of error were eliminated, and so correction was neither needed nor could it be provided. But if mistakes could happen in the way I have just described, then it becomes possible to correct them by putting right the misplaced emphasis. An essential step toward correcting intuitions is understanding what could produce faulty interpretations.

One source of misinterpretation may be that the social morality in the background is disintegrating or undergoing far-reaching changes. In such cases, moral situations cease to be simple and intuitions no longer give reliable guidance, because the conventions fail to protect the conditions of individual welfare set by the facts of the body, self, and social life. In a disintegrating society, such as France during the Terror, Russia shortly after the fall of the tzar, Germany under Hitler, not even the most decent people could trust their intuitions, for the conventions were breaking down. In societies whose social morality is fundamentally changing, the situation is less dangerous, for intuitions may still be reliable in areas free of changes. For instance, just because in our present circumstances we cannot trust our intuitions about sexual conduct does not mean that we cannot trust them about cruelty, exploitation, or fraud.

Another way intuitions can become unreliable, even if social morality is at its healthiest, is if the balance between tradition and individuality is upset. This can occur by the personal usurping the social or by the social intruding into the personal. The classic example of the former is Oedipus. As we have seen, his error was to suppose that his personal morality required him to develop his character in conflict with the conventions of his social morality. He did not see that social and personal morality need not be in competition, that the moral conventions of a society provide a hospitable setting in which moral agents can develop their characters and thus create good lives for themselves.

The opposite error is illustrated by Archer and Countess Olenska, who made themselves into entirely conventional people. They had simplified the complex moral situations they encountered by viewing them entirely from the vantage point of social morality. They allowed their individuality to be engulfed by their social morality. Thus, decency swallowed up their love. They failed to see that, just as social morality must be protected against violations, so also must personal morality. For unless there is a domain left for personal morality, in which people can try to realize personal aspirations and enjoy intimacy with others, the protection vouchsafed by social morality loses its point.

Thus, the proper balance between social and personal morality requires setting limits beyond which the social should not intrude into the personal; or, to express it from the other direction, limits that personal morality should not lead people to transgress. These limits are set by the strongly held deep and variable conventions of a social morality. It is reasonable for moral agents to conform to them, provided the conventions protect the participants; the social morality is not changing radically in areas guided by the relevant conventions; and the *prima facie* case for conformity has not been defeated. The eudaimonistic claim is that there will be very many simple moral situations in which these conditions are met. These are the situations correctly represented by the Aristotelian scheme. And it is in them that well-trained moral agents can justifiably rely on their moral intuitions.

JUSTIFICATION OF MORAL INTUITIONS

In support of this claim about justification, consider people who have moral intuitions. They interpret the facts of the situation immediately, noninferentially as involving benefit and harm, and they spontaneously, matter-of-factly respond; they have beliefs, feelings, and intentions about the situation, but they need not be formulated in conscious explicit judgments to be translated into action; they unquestioningly accept their intuitions, yet the interpretations involved in them are both fallible and corrigible, and they may come to regard the interpretations as mistaken and attempt to correct them. As we have seen, such conduct is ubiquitous and essential to social morality.

Suppose that when intelligent and normal people behave in this manner, we ask them to justify their intuitions. Their perfectly proper reaction would be incomprehension. For why should they need justification for the obvious? They bought the goods, and that is why they pay the bill; a friend asked, and that is why they help. What more needs to be said?

Now, of course, situations are not always as simple as these; there may be hidden facts, unrecognized complexities, deeper conflicts. If so, the conditions for intuition are absent. When complications occur, reasonable people no longer respond immediately and spontaneously; intuition is appropriate only in routine simple moral situations. But the routine is what occurs most of the time, so in social morality, intuition is, most of the time, a reliable guide. If someone regards a situation as simple, and yet it is complex, then reliance on intuition is mistaken. If the demand for justification is based on some evidence that this has happened, then it has a serious point and deserves an answer. But if there is no reason to doubt the obvious, then there is no need to advance additional arguments for it either.

Furthermore, moral intuitions do not occur in a vacuum; people act on them, compare them, and they figure in each others' intuitions. Thus, there is a ready public test for them. If our intuitions are not shared by others in our social morality, then, once again, there is ground for doubting them. But if what seems to us to be unquestionably so is reinforced by the concurrence of others, then there is no room for reasonable doubt of our intuitions in simple moral situations.

This justification for relying on moral intuitions and acting according to them appeals to our social morality from which the intuitions follow. Thus, the justification is internal. Of course, there remains the question of whether conformity to our social morality is itself justified. The answer is that since social morality is an essential ingredient of everyone's welfare in our society, because it protects the conditions in which we can make good lives for ourselves, conformity to it is justified.

One sign of conformity is that deep and some variable conventions are strongly held. If these strongly held attitudes are widespread, then they define simple moral situations and the proper sphere for moral intuitions. The relevant conventions are then expressible as the major premise of the Aristotelian scheme. Ideally, it is in terms of these that well-trained moral agents spontaneously, unreflectively, immediately react to the appropriate moral situations.

In this happy state, society is cohesive and enduring partly because its members largely agree about how they should treat each other, what sort of lives are good, and what constitutes benefit and harm. Their agreement rests on attachment to shared and strongly held deep and variable conventions, and social morality embodies them. Many of the conventions have endured for generations, so they have been tested in practice and survived. Members of a society express in terms of these conventions what they want, and the conventions also prescribe the permissible ways of trying to get it. Their lives make sense in the moral tradition of which the social morality is an essential part. So they value and they are rightly protective of social morality.

One of the benefits of this happy state is order, making it possible for people to have reasonable expectations about each others' conduct. These expectations rest on the justified assumption that members of a society are guided by many of the same conventions. Thus, they know what is appropriate and inappropriate, expected and unusual, backsliding and supererogation in many different contexts. This knowledge comes from their shared moral education. Their individual identities are partly defined in terms of the general context established by their society, and so they recognize others as having the same allegiances and count on others having them as well.

Thus, it is not merely that the welfare of our society requires the existence of some social morality or another. There is good reason for holding that the welfare of our society requires the particular social morality we have. For our social morality protects the fundamental requirements of the welfare of its members, it guarantees the cohesion of the society by supporting order and the fulfillment of people's reasonable expectations about each others' conduct, and it establishes a framework in which decency rather than *skloka* prevails.

If we, as moral agents, reflect on our own and other people's conduct within social morality, then the first things that strike us are the conflicts, the turmoil, the violations, and the changes. This is the natural consequence of the disposition to notice the unusual and the unexpected, rather than conformity to the conventional pattern that most of us take for granted. In the vast majority of our impersonal interactions with other people, we simply—and correctly—assume that they, like ourselves, will do their jobs, keep their appointments, be routinely helpful; that, generally speaking, they will conduct themselves decently. It is only because this assumption normally holds that we become indignant at its violations or that we agonize over the exceptional situations in which the assumption, for some reason, breaks down. Why else would be so noticeable the rudeness of a clerk, the nonappearance of the person with whom we had an appointment, the overbearingness of a public official, the indifference of a physician, or the incompetence of a supposed expert if not because our justified expectations are disappointed? So deeper reflection on our social conduct will lead to the recognition that behind the deviations we remark on there is the order and predictability we, as a matter of course, assume. And it is only because we are justified in assuming their existence that we can go on to live the lives we want to live. Social morality is the guarantor of this possibility, and that is why it is reasonable to uphold it.

Of course, this is not to say that our social morality is not in need of much improvement. My claim is only that the general framework is in order, and this is compatible with the obvious truth that many parts of the framework are faulty. It is not as if the boat were sinking; rather, it requires constant repair to remain afloat. Hence, social morality must be capable of repair, and the repair must always go on.

This raises the question of how the *prima facie* case for upholding it can be consistent with the need for these changes. The answer depends on understanding how the need for changes comes about. One source of it is the alteration of nonmoral conditions. For instance, secularization and the discovery of the birth-control pill produced a change in our social morality. A generation ago, our social morality was opposed to heterosexual affairs among young unmarried adults; nowadays, such affairs are generally accepted. Does this show that the *prima facie* justification for upholding social morality is mistaken?

On the contrary: it shows that the *prima facie* case holds, unless good reasons can be given against it. There were two kinds of objections to such affairs before the pill: practical and religious. The practical objection concerned the dangers of unwanted pregnancy, and the pill has removed that. The religious objection was based on the biblical notion of sin, and secularization has cast widespread doubt on that. The *prima facie* case has been defeated. However, it was reasonable before defeat, for neither unwanted pregnancy nor damnation was a desirable prospect. The conventional moral attitude was reasonable in the face of these supposed dangers.

But now consider would-be reformers of social morality, before the pill. Their opposition to the conventional prohibition of heterosexual affairs was based on objections to the notion of sin. Suppose that they were right in this. Their opposition was still weak, because the practical objection, on account of the dangers of unwanted pregnancy, still held. So defenders of social morality had a strong *prima facie* case. That the reformers' position came to be adopted later is not due to the merits of their case as they then were but to the subsequent availability of the pill, which removed the practical objection.

Another source of change is the discovery that social morality is inconsistent. There could be conflicts between deep and variable conventions and also between variable conventions. In America, an example of the former was slavery. Deep conventions were said to protect everyone, yet the lives, security, and property of slaves were customarily in jeopardy. Change came about because abolitionists aroused public indignation about this inconsistency. Political prejudice against Catholics was an example of the inconsistency between two variable conventions: the one guaranteeing religious freedom and the other conceiving of statesmen on a limited number of WASP models. But this, too, came to an end when John F. Kennedy enlarged the existing vision of the possibilities of being statesmanlike.

Therefore, changes in social morality do not show that the *prima facie* case for upholding it is mistaken. They show that social morality is capable of improvement. For the existence of a *prima facie* case establishes a guideline about when change is desirable and how to bring it about. Change is desirable if some parts of social morality are affected by changing nonmoral conditions or if they are inconsistent. And the way to bring change about is to defeat the *prima facie* case against it.

Many of the current changes in our social morality affect conventions guiding sexual conduct. The *prima facie* cases against homosexuality, various forms of sexual experimentation, the equality of women, abortion, and so on, are being defeated. Defenders of social morality ought to be in favor of changes coming about as a result of reasoned objections against the *prima facie* case. But in the heat of the moment, sexual reformers often imagine themselves to be opposed to the whole of our social morality. This is a mistake. Sexual conduct is only a small part of social morality. Our social morality also guides conduct in commerce, war, sports, education, in the relationships between competitors, colleagues, neighbors, and in such human affairs as winning, losing, working, borrowing, joking, promising, and arguing. Some defenders of social morality mistakenly think that they are defending it when they oppose reasonable changes in sexual conventions. The defense of social morality should be more attractively and plausibly put in terms of opposition to hypocrisy, overbearingness, cruelty to people and animals, exploitation, fraud, nepotism, bribery, and similar indecent practices; the *prima facie* case against them holds as firmly as ever.

There are two general reasons why changes in social morality strengthen rather than weaken the *prima facie* case for upholding it. One is that the defeat of the *prima facie* case by overriding reasons in one area suggests the absence of such reasons in other areas. We know what sort of argument would show that the *prima facie* cases for telling the truth, paying debts, honoring contracts, being polite to each other, doing our jobs, and respecting privacy are in the same area of doubt as the conventional case for sexual conduct. But we also know that there is no ground for such doubts. Hence, these areas of our social morality are strengthened by the favorable contrast between them and the changing area.

The other reason why change strengthens social morality is that arguments about the nature and direction of changes are resolved by appealing to the deeper conventions of social morality. Conflicts about the relations between the sexes are debated in terms of the deeply rooted convention of treating like cases alike; the controversy about abortion takes for granted the deep convention protecting human life; and the issue about homosexuality is partly how far the freedom guaranteed by our social morality extends. In all these cases, the changes in social morality actually involve the reaffirmation of the more fundamental aspects of social morality. Reasonable change, therefore, is not only consistent with social morality, but it is strongly endorsed by it.

Thus, the *prima facie* case for social morality allows for both continuity and change; continuity, because the case for change must be made, justified, and accepted, and this is going to occur in terms of the temporarily stable aspects of the social morality; change, because the case for it can be put, it is known how to put it, and what a good case is. Both continuity and change presuppose social morality, for that is what is being continued and changed. And the justification of change also presupposes it, because the recognition that social morality needs changing in some respects must depend on it being adversely evaluated in terms of other parts of the same social morality.

ENFORCEMENT OF SOCIAL MORALITY

Even if social morality is in good order over all, its conventions are still going to be violated. This is the context of immorality, in which social morality must be upheld by encouraging conformity to it and discouraging its violation. Encouragement and its opposite begin with moral education and end with legal enforcement. How severe should society be in discouraging violations depends on how harmful they are to society. Since this can be determined only by understanding the significance of the violations in their contexts, and since contexts change, there is no principle we can appeal to in answering the question. However, there are some guidelines.

The justification for encouraging conformity and discouraging violations is that the first strengthens and the second weakens social morality. Since the welfare of our society partly depends on social morality, upholding social morality is justified, because it establishes one necessary condition of individuals having lives in which there is a preponderance of benefit over harm.

It follows that the more important something is to the survival of social morality, the more important it is to discourage its violation. Now, the most important parts of social morality are the deep conventions. No social morality, and, *a fortiori*, no good society can do without protecting the conditions established by the facts of the body, self, and social life. Therefore, the most severe form of discouragement, legal prohibition and its enforcement, is justified in the case of violations of deep conventions.

Strongly held variable conventions need not require severe measures for upholding them. The reason for this is that each violation of social morality produces two kinds of harm: one is to the people directly affected; the other is to society as a whole. The former harms people directly; the latter, indirectly by weakening social morality upon which everyone's welfare depends. All violations of social morality produce direct harm, although it may be slight. The violations of strongly held variable conventions, however, produce only negligible indirect harm, since, being strongly held, social morality is not likely to be appreciably weakened. So, the severity of the measures for upholding strongly held variable conventions should depend on the seriousness of the direct harm produced by their violation. The violations of deep conventions always cause serious harm; hence, legal enforcement is always justified. The harm produced by the violation of variable conventions, however, may range from the very mild one of being made indignant, say, by malicious gossip, to the serious one, for instance, of being blackmailed.

The severity of the measures for upholding weakly held variable conventions depends on the motivation for violating them. For if a variable convention is weakly held, its violation is unlikely to produce serious harm. Furthermore, a variable convention is likely to be weakly held, because it is peripheral to social morality, or because social morality is changing in that respect. Motivation becomes important when social morality is changing. If violation is motivated by moral reform, it is one thing. If it is motivated by trying to take advantage of the existing moral confusion, it is another. If decent people publicly declare that they are homosexuals, they may aim to aid the reform of social morality by showing that homosexuality is compatible with decency. If, however, people finance the production of pornographic films, they intend to profit from the unclarity of social morality, and, although they are unlikely to cause serious harm, their conduct is still deplorable. Both violate weakly held variable conventions, but the homosexuals may be justified moral reformers, while the pornographers are likely to be seamy profiteers.

The upholding of social morality should be combined with as much tolerance as is consistent with the welfare of society. This follows from it being part of the purpose of social morality to prevent harm to members of the society. Upholding social morality is justified partly because its violation causes harm. But the upholding of it harms violators. This is inevitable and justified, but the harm should be as little as possible. Minimizing the harm depends on the willingness of society to allow the case being put for moral reform. Reasonable defenders of social morality realize that conventions are always changing in some ways and that they are frequently inconsistent. The *prima facie* case for upholding them may be defeated, and if it is, society benefits from the salutory change. What appears to be violation may be a case of justified moral reform. It is often difficult to decide how to judge conduct, because motives are mixed, the arguments inconclusive, and the context unclear. Tolerance involves giving the benefit of the doubt in ambiguous cases and making the severity of measures for upholding social morality proportionate to the harm produced.

The most severe measure for upholding social morality is legal enforcement. Defenders of social morality ought to be willing to take that measure if the harm is great or the threat to society is serious or deep conventions are being violated. In this respect, there is no disagreement between eudaimonism and prevailing political practice. For the causes favored by a wide consensus in contemporary America frequently involve legal enforcement, such as desegregation, graduated taxation, and welfare legislation. So the legal enforcement of both deep and some variable conventions is a measure favored by the vast majority of the American public. And if the most severe measure for upholding social morality is justified, there can be no objection to my case for the justifiability of milder measures. I find it surprising, therefore, that critics often respond to arguments for the enforcement of morality as if they advocated barbarism. Such arguments merely articulate the reasons for a practice supported by most thinking people.

PLURALISM AND SOCIAL MORALITY

In closing, I note that a society that encourages pluralism, freedom, and the development of individuality actually presupposes the eudaimonistic view of social morality. For social morality, thus conceived, is intended to guarantee freedom and provide the plural forms of individuality. Just as language supplies the forms in which whatever we want to say can be said, so social morality provides the forms among which members of a society can freely choose and, thus, develop their individuality. The great defenders of such a society have not supposed that the free development of individuality requires people to create their own forms of life in opposition to their society. What they have insisted on is that people should be able to choose freely the forms they want their lives to take. I have been arguing that our social morality aims to protect the conditions in which choices can be free and to maintain the kind of society in which freely chosen lives can be lived.

Consider, for example, Mill's principle that "the only purpose for which power can be rightfully exercised over any member of a civilized community, against his will, is to prevent harm to others."[7] The eudaimonistic argument is that our society is justified in upholding its social morality, because doing so prevents harm to others. Nor is there a disagreement between *On Liberty* and eudaimonism about the range of permissible cases of exercising power. Mill thought, and I agree, that some "conditions society is justified in enforcing at all costs to those who endeavor to withhold fulfillment" and also that "the acts of an individual may be hurtful of others or wanting due consideration for their welfare, without . . . violating any of their constituted rights. The offender may then be justly punished by opinion, though not by law."[8]

Social morality is a necessary condition of a society in which pluralism can prevail, because it establishes the conditions in which a plurality of forms of lives can exist. That this is so has often been missed, because the prohibition of conduct violating social morality has been mistakenly supposed to be the prohibition of experiments in living. The violation of social morality is objectionable because it causes harm. The experiments in living Mill advocated can go on unimpeded by social morality, provided they do not involve harm to others. Moreover, they can go on only because social morality guarantees the conditions of their possibility.

It is central to my case that social morality is only part of the eudaimonistic tradition. Social morality offers no guidance about personal morality, saintly or heroic conduct, and it applies only to relationships within the context of our society. It is silent on the subject

[7] Mill, *On Liberty*.
[8] Ibid., 91–92.

of choosing among the manifold ways in which we can earn our living, form friendships, enjoy ourselves, find relaxation, be creative, appreciate the riches of our culture, given that the minimum conditions set by the relevant conventions are observed. Social morality aims to guide impersonal, routine social conduct. But since there is also personal conduct, and since social conduct is vast in number and various in kind, social morality leaves ample room for individuality.

It would be remiss to end this chapter without taking account of one emotional source that sustains poor arguments against social morality: revulsion toward moralizing. Defenders of social morality are often taken to be defending the conventions of the last generation, as, I fear, some of my readers will suppose me to be defending a repressive attitude toward sex, despite my repeated claims to the contrary. And in defending the *status quo ante*, one is supposed to foist on people the attitudes from which it was their achievement to have freed themselves. But what eudaimonistic defenders of social morality are in favor of is the moral *status quo*, provided the *prima facie* case for it has not been defeated. As to moralizing, only the convictions of a previous generation can seem to be overstated in the opinion of its children. The relentlessly labored contemporary opinions about ecology, equality, racism, and commercialism cannot, apparently, be moralizing. Our parents mutter *tu quoque* as they turn in their graves. And if we shall complain likewise about our children, then all is well, for the moral life of our society is going as it should.

CHAPTER SIX

Self-Direction in Complex Moral Situations

> I wish my life and decisions to depend on myself, not on
> external forces of whatever kind. I wish to be the instrument
> of my own, not of other men's acts of will. I wish to be . . .
> moved by reasons, by conscious purposes, which are my
> own, not by causes which affect me, as it were, from outside.
> I wish to be a doer . . . deciding, not being decided for, self-
> directed, and not acted upon by external nature.
> —Isaiah Berlin[1]

FROM SOCIAL TO PERSONAL MORALITY

Let us begin the transition from social to personal morality by noticing that simple and complex situations may occur in both, but while
the typical situations in social morality are simple, those in personal
morality are complex. In complex situations, conscientious moral
agents may want to act as they should, but the complexity often
makes it difficult to know what that is. If we recall the Aristotelian
scheme, we can locate the source of this difficulty either on the general level, pertaining to the conventions expressed as principles in the
major premise, or on the concrete level, where a particular situation
is subsumed under a principle, as represented by the minor premise.
The difficulty on the general level may be due to the unavailability of
principles. Witness, for instance, their lack in marriage, raising children, opposing authority, learning self-discipline, acquiring self-
knowledge, or distinguishing between loving and indulgent responses to another person. The principle that married partners
should love each other says very little about how to resolve fights,
distribute chores, or allocate responsibility; that unjust authority
should be opposed leaves it open how much injustice is tolerable or
how far we should endanger our well-being by offering resistance;
that we should know ourselves does not tell us when introspection
turns into narcissistic self-obsession or when analysis kills spontaneity.

The difficulty on the concrete level stems from not knowing which
principle has jurisdiction in a particular situation. In these cases, con-

[1] Berlin, *Four Essays on Liberty*, 131.

scientious moral agents aim to do the right thing; they are familiar with the relevant principles, but they do not know whether the situation in which they find themselves comes under a particular principle. For instance, they know that they ought not to be cruel, and they do not want to be, but they do not know whether telling a hurtful truth or punishing a child would be cruel.

Complex moral situations are characterized by these kinds of difficulties. Consequently, intuitive responses become unreliable. No matter how much we may want to act as we should, we cannot, because we are not sure what specifically it would be. If we are to do the right thing, we must first discover what it is. But this discovery is not a matter of learning some principles that we happened to have missed in the course of our moral education. It is more a matter of trying to understand how general claims apply to us in particular, given our characters and circumstances, and how to balance the competing demands they make on the way we try to live our lives. Of course, what we are trying to do, others have done before us. But the marriage we want to go well, the temper we want to control, the friend to whom we want to be loyal are ours, and success depends on finding a way in situations rendered unique by the conjunction of our special contribution to them and by the mutual influence we and other participants have on each other. The requirements of simple situations impose themselves on conscientious moral agents, and they apply impersonally. What we are called upon to do is the same as other people would have to do were they in our position. But complex situations are created by our participation. We do not just find ourselves in them: we make them what they are.

Personal morality involves complex situations, because personal aspirations and intimate relationships, the chief concerns of personal morality, typically go beyond the simple requirements of social morality. We have many more wants than we can satisfy, and social morality provides no clear guidance about satisfying them. Thus, in personal morality conflicts loom large. We must evaluate and choose between our conflicting wants and their possible satisfactions. We do so by developing our conceptions of good lives, and we choose and evaluate from the perspective that conception provides. This process of developing, choosing, and evaluating is self-direction. My aim in this chapter is to take the first steps toward understanding it, but a full account will emerge only at the end of the book.

Self-direction, of course, does not occur in a vacuum. The lives we wish to direct are lived in the framework of our moral tradition. Reason and decency dictate that we should conform to its deep conventions and also to many of its variable conventions. But it is difficult to know how far our attempts at self-direction should be curtailed by decency. We have seen how Sophocles and Edith Wharton struggled with this problem. Another instructive approach is D. H. Lawrence's. He fulminates against Benjamin Franklin's prudent creed that would "satisfy the professors of every religion, but shock none."[2] "Who knows what will come out of the soul of man?" asks Lawrence. "The soul of man is a dark forest, with wild life in it. Think of Benjamin fencing it off! Oh, but Benjamin fenced a little tract he called the soul of man, and proceeded to get it into cultivation." This Lawrence will not have. "I defy you. I defy you, oh society, to educate me or to suppress me, according to your dummy standards." No civilizing conventions for him. Instead, "[r]esolve to abide by your own deepest promptings, and to sacrifice the smaller thing to the greater. Kill when you must, and be killed the same: the *must* coming from the gods inside you." In place of Franklin's decency, we have Lawrence's savage creed celebrating the primitive urges in the dark forests of our souls. There is something at once very right and very wrong here.

Suppose we follow Lawrence and resolve to abide by our deepest promptings. Provided we are not prevented by ignorance, nor by the promptings being vicious and life-diminishing, the question of how we are going to abide by them still remains. The gods in the dark forests of our souls are urging us to say Yes! or No! to conforming to the conventions of our moral tradition. They are the options open to us; they are the possible ways of life afforded by our society. Our private urges are given shape by these public conventions. And if the private urges prompt the rejection of possibilities provided by our society, then there are two alternatives: either a life doomed to frustration within our society or a life requiring conformity to the conventions of some other society. Lawrence's idea that we should free ourselves from "dummy standards," because "they take away my wholeness and my dark forest, my freedom," is romantic nonsense. The aspiration is impossible, for our deepest promptings are inevitably modulated by conventional forms. The language we learn; the information we have; the goods we seek; the education we receive; the objects of our thoughts, feelings, and efforts; the good lives we want to have are all necessarily conditioned by the conventions of our society. To reject them is to reject part of ourselves. Lawrence is banging his head against human limitations, and that is why his agonized rage is quixotic.

All the same, Lawrence has a point, for it is hard not to read Franklin's pious homilies without suspicion. He positively relishes confor-

[2] Lawrence, *Selected Essays*, 231–42.

mity to convention. We suspect the absence of rough edges, the lack of rebelliousness, the great ease with which he fits into his surroundings. Where, we want to know, is the wild life of Franklin's soul? The life of decency he recommends is so prudent, insipid, expedient; it is so very useful and practical that we cannot help suspecting that the dark forest of his soul has been turned into a vegetable garden. So Lawrence is right about Franklin, although he goes too far and spoils his case. In self-direction, deep private promptings and conventional forms need to be balanced. Too much of the former, and barbarism and frustration loom. Too much of the latter, and decency destroys its own source by stifling the impulses it aims to civilize. The great question about self-direction is how to achieve and maintain the necessary balance between them. I shall approach it by considering a tragic case of self-direction: Sophocles' Antigone.

A CASE OF SELF-DIRECTION: ANTIGONE

The facts of the play are that Creon, king of Thebes, Oedipus's successor, has forbidden the burial of his nephew, Antigone's brother, Polynices, because he betrayed Thebes. Religious tradition dictated the burial of the dead, and doing so was the responsibility of the women of the family. The responsibility fell to Antigone, and she accepted it. She disobeyed Creon and buried her brother. And so occurred the confrontation between Creon and Antigone.

CREON: You, tell me briefly, no long speeches—
           were you aware a decree has forbidden this?

ANTIGONE: Well aware. How could I avoid it? It was public.

CREON: And you had the gall to break this law?

ANTIGONE: Of course I did it. It wasn't Zeus, not in the least
           who made this proclamation—not to me.
           Nor did Justice, dwelling with the gods
           beneath the earth, ordain such laws for men.
           Nor did I think your edict had such force
           that you, a mere mortal, could override the gods,
           the great unwritten, unshakable tradition.

                                                    (495–506)[3]

Antigone had to choose between human and divine law; she chose divine law; and Creon, representative of human law, exacted the penalty she knew she would have to pay: her death.

---

[3] Sophocles, *Antigone*; parenthetical references are to the lines.

Antigone was forced to choose. What forced it, however, were not conventions but her strong self-direction. Ismene, Antigone's sister, was in exactly the same situation without being forced. To Antigone's question whether she, Ismene, would help to bury Polynices, Ismene replies:

> we must be sensible. Remember we are women
> we're not born to contend with men. Then too,
> we're underlings, ruled by much stronger hands,
> so we must submit in this, and things still worse.
>
> (74–78)

So Ismene opted out, and Antigone could have, too, if she had not been compelled to take a stand. The compulsion, however, came from within. Like Luther, on another occasion, she said, Here I stand, I can do no other. But why could she not? Because she had committed herself to live in a certain way, and her commitment was so strong that she judged life not worth living at the cost of betraying it. Ismene could disengage herself because she was not thus committed.

There is a longstanding suspicion that self-direction, at bottom, is self-interested. Let us consider, therefore, whether Antigone acted self-interestedly. If by self-interest we mean doing what we want, then Antigone was self-interested. But if it is understood that self-interest may involve sacrificing our lives to serve others, as Antigone did, then very little is left of the confused notion that self-interest is necessarily selfish; whether it is, depends on what that interest is taken to be. A deeper notion of self-interest requires us to be clear about what we want and be firm in our commitment to what we believe would make our lives good. To act self-interestedly, then, is to try to achieve a good life. Antigone acted self-interestedly, because she decided that ending her young life was preferable to having a long dishonored life. As she put it to Creon:

> So for me, at least, to meet this doom of yours
> is precious little pain. But if I had allowed
> my own mother's son to rot, an unburied corpse—
> that would have been agony! This is nothing.
> And if my present actions strike you as foolish,
> let's just say that I have been accused of folly by
> a fool.
>
> (519–24)

The folly of Creon was not to see that self-direction is essential to good lives and that what moved Antigone was not an urge to rebel against Creon's authority but her own strong sense of what she had to be and do to remain true to her moral vision. Lawrence would have been proud of her.

Yet, Antigone's self-direction, flowing from her conception of good life, was deeply informed by the past. The promptings she obeyed did not spring from the dark forest of her soul unmediated by the tragic history of her family, a history that is inseparable from the violation of deep conventions that rendered it tragic. Self-direction is informed both by the past that formed the self being directed and by the future toward which the self aspires. Antigone was impressed by deep conventions, because their violation caused her father, Oedipus, to be

> hated,
> his reputation in ruins, driven on
> by crimes he brought to light himself
> to gouge out his eyes with his own hands.
>
> (61–64)

And the same cause acted on Jocasta,

> his mother and wife, both in one,
> mutilating her life in the twisted noose.
>
> (65–66)

Antigone's self-direction reflected her tragic past. She had been taught the hard way to respect the law Creon ordered her to break. But Creon was just a king and not even a very good one; her father, Oedipus, had been a much greater king and a better man, yet even he had been brought low. What Antigone learned is expressed by the chorus:

> yours is the power, Zeus, what man on earth
> can override it, who can hold it back?
>
> (678–80)

> And throughout the future, late and soon,
> as through the past, your law prevails.
>
> (685–86)

Oedipus broke the divine law against incest and parricide, and, although he did so unknowingly and unintentionally, he suffered for it. Antigone did not even have the excuse of ignorance; she knew that she must bury Polynices; the gods ordered it.

It would be a misunderstanding to represent Antigone as having faced a conflict between her individuality and moral tradition. It is not that her personal religious convictions dictated burying her brother, while traditional responsibility called for obeying the king and leaving the corpse to rot. Antigone's religious convictions were just as traditional as her responsibility was to obey the king. Both her religion and the law to which she was subject were the products of her moral tradition. She had to choose between two elements of her tradition: human and divine law.

The personal aspect of Antigone's situation may be understood if we reflect on the fierceness of her commitment to the religious tradition she accepted. This becomes especially obvious when we contrast her attitude with the prudence with which Ismene tried to avoid the tragic confrontation and with the faltering of Creon in the face of Antigone's relentlessly uncompromising stand. Nobody had as much at stake as Antigone. At first, Creon acted in an official capacity and Ismene was distressed by all the intransigence surrounding her. But Antigone was guided throughout by what was most important to her. If she had lost that, nothing else would have come even close to compensating for it. She could not afford to lose this battle, for she was making her last stand. The barbarians were at the gate. Antigone's commitment to her conception of a good life was the personal aspect of her situation. Antigone is tragic because she sacrificed all for self-direction, but instead of gaining the good life she had hoped to have, she had to give it up altogether to avoid having to endure the opposite.

The lives of all of us, just as Antigone's, are formed of both individual and traditional elements. The traditional elements include the demands of nature and society, and we are compelled to cope with them by the inevitable circumstances of human existence. But we want more than merely coping: we want to do so in accordance with our conceptions of good lives. And these conceptions are also informed by the traditional elements of our situation. Our lives must be lived within the limitations imposed by nature and society and reflected by deep and variable conventions. This, however, is only one aspect of our situation. The other is that within these limits lies a personal sphere where we can direct our lives. Our nature and society provide many of our wants and the conventions that guide their satisfaction. Yet, how we regard our wants, which ones we aim to satisfy, and how we rank their respective importance is within our personal control. And so are our conceptions of good lives. For what we take over from our moral tradition and adapt to our characters and circumstances are matters for individual decision. The aim of self-direction is to exercise that control and make reasonable decisions of this sort. Properly understood, therefore, self-direction is not a Promethean enterprise pitting the individual against the tradition, as Lawrence supposed, nor is it an exercise in social conformity, forcing the individual into social molds, as Lawrence opposed. Rather, it is an attempt to reach a reasonable balance between individuals and their moral tradition.

SELF-DIRECTION VS. PERFECTION

The balance between individual aspirations and traditional constraints upon which reasonable self-direction depends can be upset by allowing one to dominate the other. As we shall see, the two forms of this mistake have a common root in an overly optimistic view of human nature. Perfectionism is one way of upsetting the desired balance.[4] Its fundamental idea is that it is possible to formulate a conception of the good life, a *summum bonum*, for all human beings. The goodness of a life, then, depends on how closely it approximates this conception, and the task of self-direction is to aim at it. Although such perfectionists as many Platonists, Aristotelians, Thomists, and Marxists differ among themselves about what the *summum bonum* is, they agree about its existence.

There is an inevitable metaphysical dimension to perfectionism. For underlying the belief that there is only one good life for human beings is the supposition that the scheme of things is good, human nature is part of it, and the good life consists in living in harmony with the scheme of things. Thus, the explanation and justification of there being a *summum bonum* is that it alone rests on the correct view of the nature of reality and our place in it. It is an embarrassment to perfectionists that they disagree in their metaphysics, but I shall ignore this problem, for my objections to perfectionism are independent of the particular metaphysics its defenders favor and also of the particular interpretation of the *summum bonum* that goes with it. It is the very idea of there being a *summum bonum* that is at fault.

One early formulation of perfectionism is in Aristotle's *Nicomachean Ethics*: "For man . . . the life according to reason is the best and pleasantest, since reason more than anything else *is* man. This life therefore is also the happiest" (1178a). A standard interpretation of this passage is that the *summum bonum* is life according to reason, progress consists in approximating it, and perfection is its attainment. Given the nature of reality, rational life is the only beneficial form of life for us.[5]

---

[4] For an account of the many versions of this idea, see Passmore, *The Perfectibility of Man*.

[5] That Aristotle need not be interpreted in this way is convincingly argued by Har-

The claim that we are perfectible assumes that human nature dictates a way of life toward which we naturally strive, if we are uncorrupted. But this way of life can be interpreted positively, to involve the pursuit of the *summum bonum,* or negatively, to prompt the avoidance of what is harmful for us. I think that the negative interpretation is correct. There are certain things that all normal human beings do naturally want to avoid, because they are harmful. These are the violations of the minimum conditions for living good lives, derived from the facts of the body, self, and social life. Of course, we may be prepared to accept their violation in exceptional circumstances, as Antigone was prepared to accept death. But such acceptance is highly unusual and calls for special explanation. Normally, we do strive to avoid being harmed in these ways, and doing so is dictated by human nature.

However, the avoidance of harm cannot be interpreted as perfecting ourselves. Harm avoided can only guarantee that the pursuit of good lives can proceed unimpeded, but it still leaves the all-important question of what we are going to do with ourselves. So the thesis of human perfectibility is necessarily connected with the positive interpretation, with there being a *summum bonum* to give aim to our harm-free lives. And the assumption on which perfectionism rests is that just as there are evils we naturally want to avoid, so also there are goods we naturally seek. The issue, then, is this: Are there goods all normal human beings seek, and is this search essential to good lives?

An affirmative answer requires showing what these goods are. The most frequently offered candidate is happiness. Is it true, then, that all human beings pursue happiness, that doing so is essential to good lives, and that the rare exceptions can be explained in terms of unusual circumstances or abnormal agents?

Happiness may be understood in a general or in a specific sense. In the general sense, it means roughly a contented state of mind, with the nature and causes of the contentment left unspecified. If so understood, the claim that we all and always pursue happiness becomes an old and mistaken thesis. It fails because human conduct routinely contradicts it. There are many people who consciously give up contentment: for social justice, like Orwell; to explore the world, like Marco Polo; to pursue intellectual passion, like Nietzsche; because they regard themselves as unworthy, like Simone Weil; for a cause they believe in, like Christian martyrs; or to carry on with their art, like Van Gogh. Surely, many people seek lives whose achieve-

---

die, *Aristotle's Ethical Theory,* chapter 3, and by Cooper, *Reason and the Human Good in Aristotle.*

ment has very little to do with contentment. So, if happiness is interpreted generally, it is a mistake to suppose that all human beings always pursue it; and the instances where we do seek this contented state of mind do not support the perfectionist claim that if we are normal and uncorrupted, then we are compelled by our nature to pursue it.

The specific claim about the pursuit of happiness is that there are some particular goods whose attainment would ensure good lives. If happiness is interpreted in this way, then it must be explained what the particular goods are. The difficulty here is that we cannot reasonably suppose, as this interpretation of the perfectionist thesis obliges us, that a life is less than good simply because it lacks an appropriate supply of some particular good. Saints, martyrs, and puritans repudiate pleasure; power is renounced by many artists and scholars; romantics and fundamentalists of various sorts scorn reason. Many think that beauty is a dispensable frivolity; wealth, the root of all evil; the esteem of others, worthless; and truth, an illusion. We must conclude, I think, that while people do seek these and other goods, not all goods are sought for the sake of happiness, and the goods that are supposed to bring happiness are so numerous and varied that none of them can be said to be a universal requirement for all good lives.

This version of the claim that humanity is perfectible would be true only if there were a fixed and specified number of goods whose achievement would satisfy all of us. In contrast, we can be self-directed even if the number of goods is indefinite. Self-direction is open-ended; the pursuit of perfection is not. Self-direction presupposes that while part of human nature, set by the facts of the body, self, and social life, is constant and universal, other parts can be and are being transformed. Thus, self-direction commits one, negatively, to the rejection of the kind of perfectionism I have been criticizing and, positively, to a pluralistic view of good lives.

Of course, this is not to deny that there is a connection between happiness and good lives. It is to deny only that their connection is necessary: good lives need not be happy and happy lives need not be good. One traditional interpretation of eudaimonism is that good lives are happy lives. But this is not the interpretation I am defending. According to my view, lives can be good only if the people living them find them satisfying. However, while happiness, in the specific sense, may be the source of such satisfaction, it is not the only source. People may find their lives satisfying, because they involve achievement, adventure, love, struggle against evil, quiet contemplation, creativity, service, or honorably doing their duty. These kinds of satisfying lives may occasion happiness, but they may not.

The pluralistic thesis is that diversity is a condition of eudaimonistically conceived good lives. Accordingly, the claim is that a moral tradition should embody a multiplicity of equally important and yet irreducibly different conceptions of good lives; consequently, it must exclude the idea that there is a best, highest, or ideal way of life. Pluralists do not merely accept diversity within this moral tradition as necessary evil, produced perhaps by human blindness; they regard diversity as a requirement of human welfare, understood eudaimonistically.

The fundamental reason for this is that if there were a *summum bonum*, human life would be instrumental to a predetermined end. The goodness of a life, then, would be proportionate to the degree this end has been approximated, and evil would be deviation from it. But 2,500 years of search has not revealed a generally, or even widely, accepted *summum bonum*. The moral life of humanity is characterized by diverse conceptions of good lives, as historians, anthropologists, dramatists, and novelists, agreeing on little else, never tire telling us. No good reason exists for rejecting their evidence. Those who nevertheless claim the supreme status for the way of life they favor have failed to convince the rest of us that theirs is a best life, rather than just one possibility among others.

Underlying pluralist morality is the view of self-direction I am developing. The facts of the body, self, and social life provide the starting point for all of us. The first steps we take beyond them are guided by the various social moralities into which we are born. But good lives involve more than the satisfaction of common wants and decency. They involve a creative forging of an amalgam of our wants and capacities and of the conventions of our society. Thus, good lives are similar in some respects and different in others. My version of eudaimonism is in agreement with perfectionism about there being some requirements all good lives must meet no matter what forms they take. The two views diverge, however, because perfectionists assert and I deny the possibility that the full content of good lives can be specified in advance. Good lives differ, because they essentially depend on going beyond their natural and conventional aspects that we share with others. This transcendence is an affirmation of individuality, an effort in self-creation.

None of this would be desirable if there were a *summum bonum*. For, then, trying to live good lives would require forcing ourselves to conform to the predetermined pattern that is the blueprint for all good lives. This would require the repression of individuality and the deliberate cultivation of just those aspects of our nature that we share with others and that conform to the blueprint. Furthermore, social and political arrangements ought, then, to reflect the moral assumptions of society. If there were a *summum bonum*, establishing wherein the good life consisted, it would be the responsibility of a society to promote it with such legal, political, and educational measures as would best facilitate its achievement. Whereas if the assumptions of pluralists prevailed, society would aim at an organization that would encourage the cultivation of individuality. Given the historical record of the two kinds of society, there can be no serious doubt about which is likely to foster good lives.

SELF-DIRECTION VS. SELF-REALIZATION

The second way of upsetting the balance between individuality and moral tradition is to emphasize individual aspirations at the expense of the moral tradition. This tendency is shown by the self-realizationist approach to morality and good lives.[6]

In the *Symposium*,[7] Plato has Alcibiades compare Socrates to a sculpture by Silenus. Inside the sculpture, hidden from view, there is encased a golden figure. The point of Alcibiades' comparison is that beneath the unprepossessing exterior of Socrates there is an infinitely more precious interior, the true Socrates. The self-realizationist view is that what Alcibiades says of Socrates is true of everyone. The gold figure in each of us represents our potentialities. Self-realization is to discover our potentialities and to live according to them. Associated with self-realization is the "ethical doctrine (which achieved its first systematic formulation in the words of Socrates and the writings of Plato and Aristotle) that each man is obliged to know and live in truth to his . . . [potentialities] . . . thereby progressively actualizing the excellence that is his innately and potentially."[8] The two fundamental requirements of self-realization were inscribed on the temple of Apollo at Delphi: "Know thyself" and "Accept your destiny." To know oneself is to know one's potentialities, and to accept one's destiny is to live so as to realize them. This is the view implicit in Lawrence's remarks I quoted at the beginning.

Our potentialities, then, are what we should aim to realize. They provide the internal conditions for our conceptions of good lives, and they act also as criteria for distinguishing good and evil. Good is what

---

[6] The best contemporary account of self-realization is Norton's *Personal Destinies*. Norton calls his view eudaimonism. To avoid confusion between his view and mine, I am referring to his as self-realizationism, a term Norton also uses, and reserving eudaimonism for my own view.

[7] Plato, *Symposium*, 216e.

[8] Norton, *Personal Destinies*, ix.

accords with our potentialities; evil is what conflicts with them. So the supreme moral injunction self-realizationists direct toward each human being is as follows: "to become the person he potentially is and . . . cultivate the conditions by which others can do likewise."[9]

There are two serious difficulties with this view. One is that our potentialities may be vicious, and the other is that self-realization tends to endanger the social context necessary for good lives. I shall discuss these in turn.

The terrible hero of self-realization, or of authenticity, as we now tend to refer to it,[10] is Kurtz in Conrad's *Heart of Darkness*.[11] Kurtz was a civilized man who undertook the journey to darkness, to barbarism. As the layers of civilization that stood between him and his ominous destination were peeled away, the closer he got to the heart of darkness. And the terrible realization that awaited him when he finally reached his goal was that the true center of barbarism was in himself. His authentic self beneath the protecting covering of culture, education, and civilized comforts, his true nature hidden by the easy hypocrisy of his European *persona* was evil. It is this discovery that explains his last words: "The horror! The horror!"

Conrad's narrator, Marlow, speaks with the voice of civilization. What adds to my mind a truly frightening dimension to Kurtz's journey and its end is Marlow's comment on it. He says, "Kurtz was a remarkable man. He had something to say. He said it. . . . He summed up—he judged. 'The horror!' . . . Better his cry, much better. It was an affirmation, a moral victory paid for by innumerable defeats, by abominable terrors, by abominable satisfactions. But it was a victory!" Why does Marlow think that it was a victory? Because Kurtz came to know himself, accepted his destiny, realized his potentialities. The horror was that his potentialities directed him to do abominable deeds. Nevertheless, Marlow admires Kurtz because he was true to himself.

Kurtz's life and Marlow's judgment of it point to the great danger of self-realization or authenticity: the potentialities we are exhorted to realize may be evil. Living according to them may destroy and degrade both ourselves and others. If good and evil indeed depend on whether or not we are true to our potentialities, then self-realization may lead to the destruction of everything good in life. In that case, Sade's depraved characters in *120 Days of Sodom*, Huysmans's protagonists engaged in systematic self-destruction in *Against the Grain*, and

[9] Ibid., 358.

[10] For a discussion of authenticity in contemporary Western culture, see Trilling, *Sincerity and Authenticity*.

[11] An excellent discussion of this is Kolenda, *Philosophy in Literature*, chapter 5.

the Nazi epigones of Wagnerian heroes would all be admirable moral characters. Of course, defenders of self-realization are opposed to viciousness. We must ask, therefore, why they do not find this consequence of their position frightening.

The answer, I think, is that they suppose that our potentialities are talents, virtues, and excellences. If this were true, I would have no objection to self-realizationism, and I would not want to dissociate my version of eudaimonism from it. But sadly, it is not true. Our potentialities are also weaknesses, vices, and destructive life-diminishing dispositions. As I shall shortly argue, the picture of human nature self-realizationists accept is too simple.

The second difficulty with self-realization emerges if we reflect on a passage from Thomas Mann: "The finest characteristic of the typical German . . . is his inwardness. . . . The inwardness, the culture of a German implies introspectiveness; an individualistic cultural conscience; consideration for the careful tending, the shaping, deepening and perfecting one's personality or, in religious terms, for the salvation and justification of one's own life; subjectivism in the things of the mind, therefore, a type of culture that might be called pietistic, given to autobiographical confession and deeply personal, one in which the world of the objective, the political world, is felt to be profane and it is thrust aside with indifference."[12]

As Mann implies, self-realization has strong affinities with the Protestant tendency to search our conscience and allow nothing, no institution, tradition, convention, or authority, to come between it and God. Its hero is Kierkegaard's Abraham, the man with pure heart, who wills only one thing: to follow his conscience. If it prompts going against social morality, then so be it. This may come to being prepared to do what the world regards as evil, as Abraham was prepared to kill Isaac, or to recoil from involvement with politics, reform, or improvement because they are seen as impure.

Self-realization tends to yield extremes: heroes of conscience who stake their lives on what they think is right, like Luther, and irresponsible weaklings who are so preoccupied with their inner lives that they fail to notice the world around them, like Werther. One great danger of self-realization is that it easily leads to political irresponsibility, to a detachment that *is* indifference, to a repulsive fastidiousness about the fine-tuning of one's soul. It may produce admirable people of great integrity, but it may also produce self-indulgent ones.

Eudaimonistic self-direction shares with self-realization the empha-

---

[12] From a lecture Mann gave in 1923; see Bruford, *The German Tradition of Self-Cultivation*, 2.

sis on living according to one's vision of good life. But self-direction does not easily succumb to the kind of extremes that plague self-realization, for it has a moderating element essentially connected with it. This is the recognition that the personal and the social aspects of self-direction are inseparable. Self-direction is prompted by our wants, and we aim to satisfy them in accordance with conventions. But these conventions embody the accumulated experiences and reflections of people in our moral tradition who, like us, have struggled to live good lives. If we are immersed in our tradition, we have a repertoire of options from which we can choose to be guided. Self-direction requires us to direct our attention inward, to understand ourselves, and outward, to imaginatively appreciate and learn from the lessons other real and imagined lives can teach.

Self-realization, however, tends to breed extremes, because it recommends that attention be directed largely inward. It rightly emphasizes personal judgment over conformity to convention, but it wrongly supposes that personal judgment is abdicated if we conform to conventions. This is an error, because personal judgment can and ought to be involved in deciding whether to conform to conventions in choosing the ones appropriate to our cases and in weighing the importance of the guidance thus received. Self-direction calls for this; self-realization resists it.

Self-direction involves the contemplation of the riches of our tradition and a willingness to make use of them within our lives. There goes with it a liberality of spirit, a toleration born of understanding that others, no less reflective and virtuous than ourselves, may choose to be guided by conventions whose historical roots we may recognize but do not choose. Self-directed lives are experiments in living, and it is good that these experiments should go on. For, although we can live only one life, self-directed experiments in living enlarge our moral possibilities by widening the scope within which the lives we choose will fall.

By contrast, self-realization tends to pit us against society. The social reality surrounding us is seen as an obstacle to our becoming what we should. "The political world," as Mann says, "is felt to be profane and it is thrust aside with indifference." There is always a battle going on between the personal and the social. The fortress of conscience is always besieged. To protect it, self-realizing people must rely on their own resources, and the social world is seen as soiling; to participate in it is to compromise "the careful tending, the shaping, deepening and perfecting of one's personality."[13] Thus, the second

---

[13] Bruford, *The German Tradition of Self-Cultivation*, 2.

difficulty with self-realization is due to the mistaken attempt to separate sharply the social and the personal and to suppose that the first necessarily encroaches on the second.

Eudaimonistic self-direction avoids these difficulties by urging participation in moral tradition. Self-directing people, therefore, have the resources of their tradition at their disposal, and they are correspondingly strengthened by them. "There are some minds which give us a sense that they have passed through an elaborate education which was designed to initiate them into the tradition and achievements of their civilization: the impression we have of them is . . . of the enjoyment of an inheritance."[14]

GOOD AND EVIL IN HUMAN NATURE

Underlying the pursuit of self-realization, and also of perfection, there is a view of human nature from which the neglect of evil potentialities directly follows. This view is that the scheme of things is good, there is a rational order in reality, and we, human beings, in our natural state, are part of this rational order. Evil comes from the failure to conform to it. The source of this failure may be external or internal to human beings.

That the failure is predominantly internal is one standard interpretation of the perfectionism implicit in the thought of Socrates, Plato, Aristotle, the Stoics, many Christian thinkers, and Spinoza. It is our weakness or ignorance that is responsible for the evil we do. Christians tend to stress weakness as the chief cause. Indeed, this is the significance of the Fall and Original Sin. The Fall is the separation from the benign and rational order created by God, and it is brought about by giving in to the weakness in our nature, a propensity referred to as Original Sin. Spinoza, being more intellectually inclined, attributes evil to lack of understanding, to allowing our unruly emotions to cloud our intellectual grasp of the scheme of things, including ourselves, and, thus, futilely and frustratingly pitting ourselves against rational necessity. Socrates, Plato, and Aristotle occupy a middle ground between Spinoza's intellectualism and the Christian stress on human frailty and the consequent need for salvation. Aristotle, for instance, recognizes two sources of evil: wickedness and moral weakness. He attributes wickedness to acting on the wrong principles, because the agent is ignorant of the right ones, while morally weak agents know the right principles but fail to act on them, due to some defect in their characters. The implication is that if moral agents are

14 Oakeshott, *Rationalism in Politics*, 2.

not ignorant and if their characters have not been ill-formed, then their actions will reflect the dictates of rationality and morality. Consequently, moral goodness is seen as health, and evil as disease. The natural physical state of an organism is healthy, just as its natural psychological state is morally good. Evil is a psychological sickness, an interference with the natural course of events.

If this is a straight empirical thesis, then it is plainly false. For there are countless evil actions performed by agents who are not ignorant of the moral principles their actions violate, who mean their actions as violations, because they are indifferent to the principles, or because they care about satisfying their own wants much more than about not harming others. Such actions are not attributable to moral weakness, for their agents often show great strength of character in performing them (think of Clytemnestra, Iago, or Stalin) and they feel no subsequent remorse or regret.

But defenders of this view would not accept these cases as counterexamples, and this shows that they are not making a simple empirical claim. Their rejoinder would be that the ignorance or weakness responsible for these evil actions may not be obvious, nevertheless one or the other must be there. For if it were not, the performance of evil actions would be incomprehensible. If evildoers understood the rational order of reality, and if they were not deterred by some sickness in their souls from acting accordingly, then they would not do evil; they would understand that evil agents are more fundamentally harmed than their victims. For evil actions tend to increase the agents' separation from the rational order, while living according to it is essential for the agents' welfare. The good life is the rational life, because the moral principles to which good lives conform are the applications of the laws implicit in the rational order to human affairs.

When we encounter this full-fledged metaphysical theory, we must conclude, I think, that no evidence supports it and that there are plausible alternatives to it. Why should we think that, contrary to common human experience, which provides innumerable counterexamples, it is always ignorance or weakness, and never selfishness or malice, that lurks behind evil actions? The only answer defenders of this view give is that it must be so, because there are no other explanations available. But there are. One is that the order of nature implies no moral conclusions, so knowledge of the scheme of things, or actions conforming to it, cannot lead to moral improvement. Another is that while reality does imply moral conclusions, the scheme of things is evil, or a mixture of good and evil, so living according to it will actually increase the amount of evil in the world. The explanation of common facts must be one of the touchstones by which metaphysical theories are judged, because if even facts incompatible with such theories are said to confirm them, then any pretension to offering a reasonable explanation has been abandoned.

There is yet another difficulty with the view that the scheme of things is rational and benign and that evil is internally caused by human ignorance or weakness. Human beings are either part of the natural order or they are not. If they are, then the evil they do, and the propensities that lead them to do it, are also part of the natural order. But if evil is irrational, then the natural order of which it is part, must also be partly irrational and evil. And this, of course, is precisely what the underlying metaphysics denies.

Christian thinkers have struggled with this difficulty, in vain, it seems to me, under the name of the problem of evil. It is worth noticing that the problem is not uniquely theirs but that it must be faced by everyone who thinks both that human beings are part of a natural benign order and that they do evil. If, however, it is denied that human beings are part of the natural order, because, for instance, free will enables us to transcend it, then there is no longer any reason for supposing that conceptions of good and evil, inferred from the natural order, could or should guide the conduct of our lives in their transcendent aspects.

In contrast with this, the self-realizationist view tends to look to external causes for the explanation of evil. The usual explanation is to blame civilization, or some aspect of it, for corrupting our essentially good nature. Just what aspect of civilization is the culprit is a matter of disagreement. It may be the division of labor and exploitation, poor education, competition for scarce resources, growth in population and the consequent increase in impersonal relationships, repression by rulers, and so on. In its more sophisticated versions, it is inevitable structural features of social life that are held to be corrupting, rather than such specific and local causes as, for instance, industrialization, capitalism, or the dissolution of extended families. The common metaphor representing the different versions of this view is that there was a Garden of Eden and the snake was responsible for our expulsion. This is the view of those countless millenarian movements that aim to make us good and pure and simple again by returning to a legendary haven supposed to have existed in the misty past, but this time, they say, we shall know better than to listen to the snake.

The first thing to notice is how very tenuous must be the connection between this view and any evidence that could be adduced for or against it. The state of nature in which the savage was noble is necessarily elusive. We have two kinds of evidence about preliterate forms of life: the extant bones of the beings and the artifacts they produced. The bones are uninformative about the moral dispositions of the agents who were once wrapped around them. The testimony of the artifacts, on the other hand, is bound to be suspect because they are products of civilization. Since it is to civilization that corruption is supposed to be due, we must look for a state prior to it. But in that state artifacts will not have been produced. If, forced by necessity, we look at the earliest artifacts, then testimony adverse to the present theory can always be attributed to the corruption that has already set in, while favorable evidence can always be dismissed by critics on account of its anachronism.

However, self-realizationists are not given to historical or archeological argumentation. Rather, they tend to appeal to observation of human beings, supported by sociological and anthropological evidence. They call attention to isolated primitive tribes who live peaceful lives until the corrosive effects of contact with the outside world corrupt them, and they reflect on the causes of evil in our context. They show how poverty, boredom, soul-destroying work, war, exploitation, injustice, and other social ills breed crime, vices, brutality, cynicism, and despair. What are we to say in response to this?

I think that it is obvious that external influences may corrupt people. The question is whether all corruption is due to external influences. To this question the above argument does not address itself. If it did, it would have to notice that identical external causes have different effects on people living in the same context (not all Italian immigrants joined the Mafia); that evil actions are often done by people who enjoy the benefits that are the other side of social ills (think of white collar crime); that patterns of evil recur in vastly different social contexts (aggression, greed, selfishness, malice, and hostility are ubiquitous); and that for each idyllic primitive tribe, countless others cultivate indigenous brutality. What observation of our fellows in our own and other contexts tends to suggest is that corrupting external influences are neither necessary nor sufficient for very many evil actions. For, since people sometimes do evil in the absence of specific external influences, and they sometimes do not do evil in their presence, it is reasonable to look for an internal propensity that makes us receptive or resistant to specific external influences.

The defect vitiating both external and internal explanations of how our essentially good nature is corrupted is that they are nourished by a one-sided diet of facts. Surely, the reasonable procedure in embarking on generalizations about human nature is to begin by observing human conduct in a variety of settings. What such observation reveals is that human beings perform a multiplicity of good and evil actions.

And if we want to explain why they perform them, then it is surely reasonable to look at the patterns these actions form. We find, then, that there are patterns of both beneficial and harmful conduct. Malice and philanthropy, greed and generosity, selfishness and altruism, hostility and friendliness, aggression and gentleness exist in juxtaposition to each other. They are not idiosyncratic products of specific cultures but the commonplaces of human life. The reasonable question to ask about them is why it is that they are so entrenched in such a variety of historically, climatically, religiously, economically, and socially different contexts. And the answer that suggests itself is that the patterns are ubiquitous and enduring, because they derive from culturally invariant human propensities. This evidence suggests that human nature contains both good and evil potentialities, and they exist and exert their influence side by side.

The Mixed View of Human Nature

In place of the view that human nature is essentially good, I offer the suggestion that human nature contains a mixture of good and evil dispositions. We have them innately, and neither has essential priority over the other. Some of our dispositions readily fit into morality; others conflict with it. Some are difficult to develop, so others have to be frustrated if we decide to foster them. Some present themselves clearly, with urgency; others are muted, and it is unclear what they call for. Dispositions also have to be harmonized with each other and with the conventions surrounding us. Some need to be encouraged; others, curtailed; choices have to be made about areas in ourselves where discipline is called for and where indulgence is permissible. All this calls for reflection, understanding, calm judgment, and a willingness to change our minds if, as it is too likely, we have made a mistake. Eudaimonistic self-direction is this complex, difficult, fallible process.

Self-direction differs from both the pursuit of perfection and self-realization, because it involves the rejection of the mistaken idea that the attempt to realize our potentialities, with or without the guidance of a *summum bonum*, is bound to be good. Unlike what self-realization and perfection are supposed to be, self-direction is not a guarantee of good lives, merely a necessary condition of them. If we are self-directed, we choose the wants we aim to satisfy, the dispositions we encourage, and the conceptions of good lives toward which we aim, but we may be mistaken in our choices. And if we are, we shall have caused harm to ourselves and to others.

One obvious advantage of the view I am offering is that it can readily accept as true both that our animalistic, barbaric selves often break out of the channels of civilization by which we aim to control them and that we have a natural tendency to goodness. It also escapes the embarrassment of having to explain away the obvious fact that there are culturally invariant patterns of both beneficial and harmful conduct. It sees human beings as possessing a limited amount of energy. Much of it is spent on perpetuating ourselves and on generating more energy. Our nature is animalistic, but there are two reasons for thinking that it is not only so. The first is that self-perpetuation involves cooperation with others. Reproduction, raising children, a measure of security, the achievement of some comfort would be impossible without mutual reliance. So our barbaric selves cannot be entirely evil and evolutionarily successful. There are evolutionary pressures on us to develop and cultivate beneficial dispositions. The second reason is that one implication of our evolutionary success is that our stock of energy is not exhausted by the requirements of self-perpetuation. No doubt, we do want that, but we have enough energy left over, at least in civilized contexts, to choose between alternative courses of action, to reflect on how we should make these choices, and, thus, to take a hand in determining the manner in which we perpetuate ourselves. We are not wholly driven by relentless necessity: there is a gap between what we must and what we can do. Our recognition that this gap exists makes it possible to encourage or discourage the natural tendencies we find in ourselves.

These two views of human nature have conflicting implications affecting the way we think about morality. If human nature is essentially good, as perfectionists and self-realizationists believe, then morality is seen as a way of developing our native goodness, as a liberating force. Its task is to remove impediments from the way of good lives. I have been arguing that the great problem for this conception of morality is the existence and frequency of evil. The ubiquity of evil shows that alongside our potential benevolence exists potential viciousness. Thus, a morality that removes impediments from the way of developing our potentialities actually encourages evil. We cannot afford the kind of liberation perfectionists and self-realizationists hope for and advocate, because we need the civilizing restraints of moral conventions to curb and channel our native aggressive, hostile, greedy, selfish, and malicious propensities. If perfectionists and self-realizationists accept that this is so, then they can no longer hold that human nature is primarily good and that evil is a corruption of it. They must recognize that morality is, not only a liberating, but also a constraining force.

The view of morality implied by my view of human nature is centered on this realization. Morality is concerned with good lives, but it has two equally necessary aspects: the evil-avoiding and the good-approximating. These aspects are asymmetrical. In trying to avoid evil, we aim largely to refrain from harming ourselves and others; we try not to act on our potentially evil dispositions; the moral effort required of us is not to do what we often feel like doing; we cultivate passivity in the face of contrary urges. In pursuing good, we are active; we try to foster our beneficial dispositions; the moral effort we need to make is to try to develop our characters so as to transform ourselves in accordance with our conceptions of good lives; we are striving toward a positive goal. Thus, the evil-avoiding aspect of morality is largely passive, while the good-approximating one is predominantly active. Of course, both aspects are required by any adequate moral tradition. But the justification of the different endeavors called for by the two aspects is also different. One reason for avoiding evil is to make good lives possible. One reason for pursuing good is actually to live them.

The asymmetry between the two aspects of morality also reinforces the pluralism of the eudaimonistic tradition I am defending. I have been denying that there is a *summum bonum*, a best life for human beings and, consequently, that morality can be made into a homogeneous system. One argument for pluralism is to point out the multiplicity and irreducibility of goods, an argument I shall take up in chapter 8. My present argument for the asymmetry of the two aspects of morality supports pluralism in a different way. It shows that morality cannot be a unified homogeneous system, because it has two unassimilable aspects, two functions, calling for two types of justification.

The distinction between the evil-avoiding and good-approximating aspects of morality does not coincide with the distinction between social and personal morality. Both social and personal morality have an evil-avoiding and a good-approximating aspect. My concern in this chapter has been with self-direction and its two aspects in the context of personal morality and the complex moral situations to which it typically gives rise. The complexity of situations is due to the constant necessity to balance the requirements of our personal aspirations and of the forms of intimacy we establish with others against the requirements of social morality. There can be no generally applicable principles for maintaining this balance, because one side of it depends on the individual characters and conceptions of good lives of the participating agents. Since we are bound to differ in these respects, we must each work out for ourselves just what to put in the balance on the side of individuality and how much of it is enough to avoid evil, act with decency, and pursue good lives. Self-direction is this process of weighing and balancing, and it can be done well or badly. I have discussed some of the ways in which it can be done badly, and the mistaken view of human nature partly responsible for it being done badly. How well it can be done depends on how good are the judgments of self-directing agents. In the next chapter, I shall continue to consider self-direction by examining what makes judgments good in complex moral situations.

CHAPTER SEVEN

Good Judgment

> [J]udgment is a peculiar talent which can be practiced only, and cannot be taught. . . . For although an abundance of rules borrowed from the insight of others, may indeed be preferred to, and as it were grafted upon, a limited understanding, the power of rightly employing them must belong to the learner himself. . . . [A]lthough admirable in understanding, he may be wanting in natural power of judgment. He may comprehend the universal *in abstracto*, and yet not be able to distinguish whether a case *in concreto* comes under it.
>
> —Immanuel Kant[1]

JUDGMENTS AND PRINCIPLES

Judgment may fail through ignorance of principles, through ineptitude in the application of principles to concrete cases, or through an inability to interpret complex situations in the absence of principles. The first two are less serious than the third, for in their cases there are principles available, and only the shortcomings of individual agents stand in the way of applying them to the situation at hand. The third source of failure, not knowing how to judge when there are no relevant principles, is much more serious than the others, because unless it is possible to judge without principles, we could not, in the end, judge on the basis of principles either. The reason for this is that principles, as we shall see, are expressions of patterns of concurring judgments. So principles presuppose judgments, and, consequently, good judgment cannot merely be the application of principles to situations. Good judgment consists primarily in finding the right interpretation of complex moral situations in the absence of principles.

There are four considerations in favor of the primacy of judgment over principle. First, before a situation could be judged in accordance with a principle, the principle must be formulated and accepted. How does this happen? The reasonable answer is that principles are ex-

---

[1] Kant, *Critique of Pure Reason*, A134.

tracted from particular situations that are judged to be alike in some relevant respects. The formulation of principles is the systematization of such judgments. And the principles, thus formulated, are accepted, because they prescribe what people have been doing about the relevant situations prior to the principles. Thus, principles are born out of the practice they subsequently guide, and they are born through the midwifery of judgment.

Second, potential principles are subject to judgment: they are to be rejected, accepted, or revised as we see fit. How could this be if principles were basic and judgments derivative? The answer, of course, is that principles are not basic, judgments are, and the fate of newly formulated principles depends on how well they reflect our prior judgments about relevant situations and tally with already accepted principles. But since these principles also had to conform to prior judgments, principles are parasitic on judgments.

Third, there is an unavoidable gap between principles and situations. For it is a question even for the clearest principle and the simplest situation whether the situation does indeed fall under the principle. In social morality, this question has an intuitive answer, precisely because the principles are clear, the situations simple, and the agents well trained. But, as we have seen even in this ideal case, the intuitions are still fallible. In personal morality, fallibility becomes a constant danger, because there are many variable conventions expressed as principles, and the situations are complex, because, typically, the agents are in the process of deciding which principles reflect their conceptions of good lives. Here, the gap between principles and situations cannot be bridged by intuition; it is bridged, if at all, by judgment. So not only does the formulation and acceptance of principles presuppose judgment, their application to complex moral situations does so as well.

Fourth, the application of a principle already presupposes an implicit judgment evaluating the situations that the principle is supposed to legitimate or prohibit. For situations must be recognized as coming under the jurisdiction of a principle before they can be viewed in its terms. I can follow the principle of paying my debts only if I judge that what I received from you makes me indebted to you. If I do not judge it so, then being given the principle will not help; and if I do judge it so, then it is not the principle, but the judgment that makes me acknowledge the obligation.

This, of course, is not to deny that principles are useful. They are effective as formulas that can be taught in the early stages of moral education, as reminders of already acknowledged obligations, and as a kind of shorthand like-minded people can use to communicate to each other the grounds of their moral approval and disapproval.[2]

In discussing good judgment, therefore, I shall concentrate on the interpretation of complex moral situations in which there are no clear principles to guide judgment. The judgment of other, less difficult, complex situations is derivative.

A STUDY OF COMPLEX SITUATIONS: JAMES'S *THE AMBASSADORS*

One complex situation is given to us by Henry James's portrayal of the relationship between Strether and Chad in *The Ambassadors*. Strether is the trusted friend of the leading family of the Massachusetts manufacturing town, Woollett. He is a shrewd, perceptive, middle-aged man, a Yankee through and through. He is the next thing to being engaged to Mrs. Newsome, a widow, who is the unquestioned head of the family. Strether's occupation, financial affairs, and personal loyalty are all bound up with the Newsome family. Mrs. Newsome dispatches Strether to Paris on the mission of bringing home her only son, a young man, Chad. Nobody in Woollett really knows what Chad has been doing in Paris during the past few years. There has been regular correspondence, but Chad has not been forthcoming, and his family has not been inquisitive. Mrs. Newsome and the others assume that Chad has been sowing his wild oats, and, while they are willing to put up with what they suspect is his youthful immorality, they want to keep it at arm's length. But Chad has been gone for a long time, the family business needs a head, and so Strether is to bring Chad back. Strether's task is to assert his undoubted moral authority, remind Chad of his responsibilities, put an end to his prolonged fling, and set him firmly on the road to the serious business of life, as Woollett sees it.

Strether is prepared to find an errant young man whose sensuality temporarily overwhelmed his better nature; this would be an understandable and forgivable weakness, best to be gotten out of systems prone to it at just about Chad's age. But Strether does not find what he thought he would. He finds a Chad who appears to have changed for the better. From the good-natured raw youth of Woollett, he seems to have been transformed into a civilized man of the world; he has become a gracious, discriminating, sensitive man.

Strether is understandably confused. He is an intelligent and perceptive man, and he entertains the possibility that Chad has greatly

---

[2] The general idea I here follow is in agreement with the more detailed discussion provided by Baier, *Postures of the Mind*, part 2.

improved. But he also sees that this improvement, if that is what it is, cannot be appreciated by the moral outlook of Woollett. Strether has come to apply the principles of Woollett and finds the situation too complex for it. With much help, Strether gradually comes to understand Chad, but as he goes through this process, so his way of seeing Chad changes. He begins with the perspective of Woollett and gradually shifts from it to the perspective that formed Chad. Strether has a moral task. At first, he thinks that it is the simple one of recalling Chad to his responsibilities. But as Strether grows in understanding, it becomes increasingly unclear to him that Chad's responsibilities lie in Woollett. Thus, Strether comes to realize that he cannot just apply his principles; first, he must perceive accurately the unexpectedly complex situation in which he finds himself. He sees that accuracy requires understanding the influences that transformed Chad and the moral possibilities the variable conventions of Paris opened up for Chad, and it also prompts Strether to weigh the variable conventions of Woollett against those of Paris.

All these add to the complexity of the situation. But what truly complicates matters is that as Strether is struggling toward accurate perception, which is the precondition of any reasonable judgment, so he, himself, is changing. He finds that his own moral perspective is shifting from Woollett's toward what he takes to be Paris's. The result is an enlargement of Strether's understanding of moral possibilities. These are first seen as possibilities in terms of which Chad's conception of a good life should be understood, but they slowly become possibilities of a way of life for Strether himself. As Strether tries to understand Chad's transformation, so he is being transformed himself. And as he is transformed, so he reinterprets the complex situation he faces and, consequently, changes his view of how to judge it. Thus, a large part of the complexity of such moral situations comes from the participation in them of the people who need to judge them. The ways in which they participate and judge are intertwined, they change together, and they reciprocally form each other.

What we need to understand is how to make good judgments in the sort of complex situations in which Strether found himself. There are two preliminary observations required about where we should *not* look for this understanding. The first reinforces the uselessness of searching for principles to guide judgment. Strether's trouble is not that he lacks principles. In fact, he is a highly principled man. His problem is that he cannot find a fit between his principles and the situation he is called upon to judge. What stands in the way is neither ignorance of the appropriate principles nor character defects handicapping him in applying known principles. He cannot find the fit because his principles seem to be increasingly inappropriate. They do not give clear guidance to the man he is becoming. To judge well, he must first take stock of himself, settle on some perspective on the situation, and then assess the relevant facts. Once he gets into the habit of judgment appropriate to the changes he has undergone, then, and only then, will principles readily present themselves.

The second observation follows a thread back to the defense of eudaimonism against voluntarism discussed in chapter 2. I argued there that the central moral notion is character, not choice or action. We can see how this applies to Strether. He makes no significant choices, he does very little, and he has no epiphany leading to a new fundamental commitment. True, he ends up advising Chad not to go home, he comes to see that he cannot marry Mrs. Newsome, and life at Woollett has become impossible for him. These changes would have been unthinkable before he arrived in Paris. But they are expected and flow naturally from his altered character. Strether's choices and actions are not significant in themselves; they derive their significance from his perception of the situation; and that perception reflects the changes in his character. The man Strether has become would not choose and act otherwise. His choices and actions follow with a kind of inevitability from the way he is, from his changed view of moral possibilities. His eventual judgment is the result of his more generous conception of good lives, not of any radical choice he has made. In trying to understand good judgment, therefore, we should concentrate on character and perception as they are formed through participation in complex moral situations and relegate principles, choices, and actions to a lesser place.

Objectivity

Moral agents have good judgment if they possess and are guided by the moral modes of objectivity, breadth, and depth in trying to find the right interpretation of complex moral situations in the absence of guiding principles.[3] I shall assume, for the sake of simplicity, that the facts relevant to the sought for interpretation are fully known. Thus, to revert to Strether's situation, he can ignore such possibilities as Chad having discovered in himself a great talent for painting, or that he realized that he hates his mother, or that he converted to Catholicism and is going to become a monk.

"[O]bjectivity [is] not . . . 'contemplation without interest' (which is

---

[3] For a suggestive exploration of good judgment in another area of life, see Beiner, *Political Judgment.*

a nonsensical absurdity), but . . . the ability to *control* one's Pro and Con and to dispose of them so that one knows how to employ a variety of perspectives and affective interpretations in the service of knowledge."[4]

To be objective in complex moral situations is to exercise the control of which Nietzsche speaks without distortion. I know of no more sensitive contemporary cataloger of the varieties and pitfalls of distortion than Iris Murdoch. She writes: "By opening our eyes we do not necessarily see what confronts us. We are anxiety-ridden animals. Our minds are continually active, fabricating an anxious, usually self-preoccupied, often falsifying *veil* which partially conceals the world."[5] Objectivity breaks through this falsifying veil. "The difficulty is to keep the attention fixed upon the real situation and to prevent it from returning surreptitiously to the self with consolations of self-pity, resentment, fantasy, and despair."[6] Self-centeredness and fantasy are the two main sources of distortion, the obstacles to objectivity.

Self-centeredness leads us to distort complex moral situations by attributing disproportionate importance to aspects that bear on us. If Strether's view of Chad is deeply colored by Strether's fear of disappointing Mrs. Newsome, or by envy for Chad for doing what he, Strether, missed out on as a young man, or if his pride gets involved in making Chad conform to his will, then Strether is distorting the facts. His self-centered feelings direct his attention in the wrong way. He is, then, primarily interested in his own feelings, which bear on Chad only incidentally.

Through fantasy, we construct scenarios that do have some grounding in the facts of the complex situations we have to judge; yet their point is not to guide accurate perception but to help us to come to terms with our own hopes and fears.[7] In this way, Strether may fantasize that Chad is the son he never had and that Chad sees him as the father he lost; or he may see himself as Virgil to Chad's Dante, conducting him through Purgatory, which is Paris; or Strether may inflate his own importance and suppose himself to be the pivot on which his world turns either toward Woollett or toward Paris. If

[4] Nietzsche, *The Genealogy of Morals*, III.12.

[5] For palpable illustrations, one should read her novels; I particularly recommend *The Nice and the Good* and *The Black Prince*. But here I shall make use of the essay "The Sovereignty of Good Over Other Concepts" in *The Sovereignty of Good*; the quoted passage is on 84.

[6] Murdoch, "Sovereignty of Good," 91.

[7] There is an important discussion of fantasy in Wollheim, *The Thread of Life*, especially chapters 3 and 4.

Strether allows his judgment to be clouded in these ways, his concern is not with the situation he faces but with his own reaction to it.

Now, Iris Murdoch's view is that "[o]nly rarely does one meet somebody in whom . . . one apprehends with amazement the absence of the avaricious tentacles of the self."[8] In this, I think, she is right. But when we ask about what makes it possible for the rare few to acquire objectivity, her answer is less convincing. She is looking for "anything which alters consciousness in the direction of unselfishness, objectivity and realism."[9] The way to improvement is progressive "unselfing,"[10] to be achieved through the experience of beauty, nature, love, or of the mysterious Platonic notion of the Good. No doubt, if we have these experiences intensely, they displace our habitual self-preoccupation, and, thus, the tentacles of the self have a looser hold on us. But the goal is much more than that, it is "acceptance of our own nothingness," the ultimate "unselfing" to be sought, because it "is an automatic spur to our concern with what is not ourselves."[11]

However, if meant literally, this cannot be right. The better we succeed in unselfing ourselves, the less there is left of us to act as moral agents, since our selves are the subjects of moral agency. And since the reason for making the attempt at unselfing in the first place is to become better moral agents, unselfing is a self-defeating strategy. It seems to me that the first step in the moral task of reaching objectivity is to develop a robust sense of the self. If it is sufficiently strong and confident, then we are much less likely to have corrupt judgments, since we are, then, not prone to anxiety, fantasy, or overcompensation. If we reach this stage, we can take the second step toward objectivity and guard against this strong sense of self nourishing selfishness.

But these criticisms of unselfing perhaps derive from taking literally what is really meant as a metaphor. If unselfing means the process of getting into the habit of not allowing selfishness to distort what we see, then it enters at the second stage of our progress toward objectivity, and we can agree with Iris Murdoch that it is morally necessary. My criticism, then, becomes only an insistence on there having to be a strong self capable of objectivity, before we can heed the call to unselfing, so that our strong selves will not intrude and corrupt our moral development.

Even if we reach objectivity, however, our moral task in judging complex situations is far from complete. For objectivity merely saves

[8] Murdoch, "Sovereignty of Good," 103.
[9] Ibid., 84.
[10] Ibid.
[11] Ibid., 103.

us from misinterpreting the facts. It does not help us to be aware of the many alternative, equally undistorted, equally objective interpretations, and it does not help us to find the right one among them. Lack of objectivity is just one, albeit great, obstacle to good judgment.

MORAL IDIOMS

In addition to objectivity, good judgment also requires breadth and depth. I shall understand these requirements through the notion of *moral idioms*. Imagine a composer setting down the score of a symphony. He writes note after note. Each note acquires significance from its place in the symphony. The symphony itself is the public result of a private creative effort: a long imaginative process involving the selection of variations, melodies, instruments. It is informed by the tradition, by the composer's own precepts and more or less clear conception of what the finished product should be, practical considerations about orchestration, the skill of musicians, the receptivity of the likely audience, and so on. The symphony, of course, *is* made up of notes. But it is the symphony that matters, not the notes.

Moral actions are like notes. They acquire significance from the lives of the agents who perform them. As symphonies, so also lives can be appreciated only by understanding the traditions forming their background, the practical options available to the agents, and the private worlds of which the actions are manifestations. The same actions may have vastly different moral significance. To concentrate on the actions, as voluntarists do, is to risk missing their significance.

The composer can be said to choose each note: no one forces him, and he could always use one rather than another. But to say this is to emphasize the wrong thing. For if all goes well, the choice of notes is dictated by the tradition, by his own precepts and conceptions, and by practical considerations. The emphasis on choice in morality is similarly misleading. Most actions most of the time follow from the character of the agent. People normally do just the sort of thing they would do. Choosing an action is only rarely and only exceptionally a conscious process of deliberation. We act as a matter of course, given our social and personal moralities, our perception of the situation, and practical exigencies. This is why concentration on choice and action obscures the texture of moral life. To appreciate that texture, we must start with how we perceive the situation in which we are to act.

Consider a list of terms connoting moral approval: forthright, unassuming, generous, faithful, considerate, trustworthy, modest, courageous, honest, pure, conscientious; and another list of condemnations: corrupt, cruel, treacherous, envious, petty, hypocritical, selfish, greedy, cowardly, overbearing, obsequious, arrogant. These approving and disapproving descriptions are moral idioms.

Our perception of complex moral situations depends, in the first instance, on the available moral idioms. They are provided by our social morality. Every social morality has moral idioms, and the lists culled from different social moralities contain very many of the same items. But this is not to say that their significance is also the same. This is true of many other words as well. I suppose most languages have words for family, stranger, peace, religion, and manhood. Yet, what these words suggest, their emotional force, and cultural connotations vary, of course, from context to context. Understanding another culture, society, or tradition involves understanding not just the surface grammar but also the deeper meaning such words have. And so it is with moral idioms. Courage and cowardice, for instance, were moral idioms in Alexandrian Macedonia, Confucian China, the Weimar Republic, and Roosevelt's Washington. But their significances were vastly different. The moral idioms we have available, thus, acquire significance partly from their context in social moralities.

It would be desirable to have a general definition of moral idioms. However, I cannot give it, I doubt that it could be given, and I think we can do without it. To appreciate the difficulty, consider what a comparable definition of legal, aesthetic, engineering, or medical idioms would be. One can give examples, and this I have done. One can rely on the usage of authorities, and this, too, can be done once we understand what having good judgment consists in. These considerations, however, will not decide how to add to the list of moral idioms or how to contest the inclusion of items on the list. I can go some way toward helping to decide, but, in the end, decision depends on intelligent and sensitive discussion of contested cases.

To begin with, the idioms are *moral*. They are intended to indicate concern for human welfare; with their help, judgments of good and evil can be expressed. Part of the reason why a definition is not available is that this territory shades into others. Our social morality shares with jurisprudence such terms as justice, fairness, impartiality. Charity, humility, faithfulness are as religious as they are moral. Purity, solemnity, sensitivity are on the borderline between aesthetic and moral considerations. Politeness, propriety, and dignity are claimed both by our social morality and by social customs, manners, and mores. Politics, commerce, psychology, and education claim yet other idioms. All in all, I doubt that there is a moral idiom with an exclusively moral use.

Moral idioms are *specific*, rather than general. There are general moral terms, such as good, right, obligation, and duty. If situations are described in these general terms, we remain uninformed about the characters of the agents or of the nature of their conduct. These general terms are abstract, while moral idioms give content to them. But moral idioms are not entirely specific either. For they themselves may be used in many different forms. Thus, their specificity consists in being more specific than the most general moral terms, such as right or good. But since interest in morality is both general and specific, some degree of generality is inevitable. Concentration on moral idioms seems to me to maintain the right balance between generality and specificity.

Moral idioms describe human character traits: dispositions to conduct ourselves in certain ways. When an action is described by the adverbial form of a moral idiom, the intention is to identify it as an episode instantiating a disposition. To behave courageously is to exercise courage. Of course, not every instance of courage exemplifies the disposition, and dispositions do not inevitably result in instantiating episodes. People can act uncharacteristically, but to do so calls for an explanation; that honest people act honestly does not. These character traits are virtues and vices. In the Aristotelian tradition, they are placed at the center of morality, and I agree that moral thinking should concentrate on these character traits. They are the components of character, and thus, according to eudaimonists, at the center of morality, they are the deeper structures of which actions are normally manifestations.

Moral idioms are *interpretative* rather than descriptive. This is a difficult contrast to draw, and I am not supposing that a sharp distinction can be defended. Yet there is a kind of argument about interpretation that is different from descriptive arguments, and it is the one involved in disagreements about the application of moral idioms. These are arguments about the significance of agreed upon facts, not about the facts themselves. They typically occur when there is agreement, not only about the relevant facts, but also about the purpose of the interpretation, and yet there is disagreement about the importance of the elements upon which the interpretation is to be based. These disagreements hinge on what is taken to be central, rather than marginal; novel, rather than banal; surprising, rather than routine; revealing, rather than obscure. Such disputes need not be public, for moral agents may be arguing with themselves.

Moral idioms are *morally interpretative*; they form a subclass of interpretations. Historical interpretations of wars, treaties, revolutions, anthropological interpretations of the significance of rituals and observances, interpretations of texts by literary critics need not carry with them moral evaluation. But if a moral idiom has been applied to characterize a situation, then those applying it are committed to evaluating the situation accordingly. If we describe Socrates' drinking the hemlock as honorable, we are thereby committed to a favorable moral judgment.

Lastly, moral idioms are *action-guiding*. This is not to say that, if we characterize a situation by an idiom, then we are committed to acting in a certain way. We frequently evaluate situations without any possibility of doing anything about them. Historical and fictional situations are the clearest cases in point. But even in actual and present situations, where we could conceivably act according to the assigned moral idiom, we often do not because it would be inappropriate. Yet moral idioms are action-guiding, because *if* we are called upon to act in a situation, moral idioms guide the way in which we ought to act. If someone asking for help is properly characterized as a conniving scoundrel, we are guided one way; if he is the victim of injustice, in another.

This is an important characteristic of moral idioms, for it shows why it is mistaken to regard the question of what ought we to do as central to morality. If we are satisfied by our characterization of a situation in terms of a moral idiom, then what we ought to do is usually clear. The action, then, need not be chosen, for we have already instructed ourselves about what we ought to do. If we perceive the person asking for help as a victim of injustice, and we can help, that is what we recognize as being what we ought to do. Of course, there are still problems. For knowing what we ought to do does not tell us how to do it, and how much of it, and at what cost to ourselves ought we to do it. But moral idioms do guide the kind of action we should perform.

Moral idioms, then, are specific, rather than general; they refer to virtues and vices instantiated in moral actions; they are morally interpretative, rather then descriptive; and they are action-guiding. Moral idioms have a central importance in both social and personal morality. For to characterize a situation by a moral idiom is to understand it in a certain way and to recognize what sort of response we are called upon to make. The question of what ought we to do has a straightforward answer once the situation has been understood to come under the provenance of a moral idiom. The selection of moral idioms, therefore, is a far more important and problematic matter in a moral tradition than the choice of action. And their selection depends on good judgment informed by moral breadth and depth.

BREADTH

Good judgment requires moral agents to be alive to the possible relevance of many undistorted interpretations of complex moral situations. Each moral idiom carries with it a load of interpretation, and in being aware of the possible relevance of competing interpretations, moral agents are aware of the applicability of competing moral idioms for describing the situations they face. When the judgments of moral agents are habitually informed by this awareness, they possess *moral breadth*. Its source may be familiarity with many different moral traditions from whose perspectives a particular situation may be judged. Accordingly, Strether may be aware of such alternative ways of understanding his relationship to Chad as are suggested by the relationship between Protagoras and Polus in *Gorgias*, between father and prodigal son in the New Testament, between journeyman and apprentice in a medieval guild, or between old warrior and young brave in Indian folklore. Knowledge of history, anthropology, and comparative literature can give this sort of breadth to moral agents.

But this is not the really important dimension of breadth, for knowledge of other moral traditions usually goes hand-in-hand with allegiance to our own tradition and its moral idioms. Strether was not seriously tempted by the moralities of fifth-century Athens, early Christianity, medieval guilds, or American Indians. He was firmly planted in the Protestant Ethic. The important dimension of breadth is produced by awareness that even within one and the same moral tradition there are genuinely different moral idioms according to which moral situations can be objectively interpreted. Thus, breadth rules out the search for the standpoint of an ideally objective judge from which the canonical interpretation of complex moral situations would follow. Breadth is the realization that there is no ideal judge. Within one and the same moral tradition, there are many possible and perfectly reasonable interpretations of complex moral situations.

This irreducible plurality of reasonable interpretations is due to the possibility that even though all the relevant facts are available, the respective importance attributed to the facts varies with the participants. The differences among alternative undistorted interpretations of the same facts are produced by the varied assessments of their significance, weight, and relevance. Moral agents who possess breadth are alive to this possibility, and their interpretations of complex moral situations, signified by the moral idioms they employ, are informed by them. In the apt phrase of W. B. Gallie, complex moral situations are *essentially contestable*;[12] to have breadth is to know that this is so.

The situation of Strether and Chad will again illustrate this. Strether's first task is to avoid distorting the facts. But assuming that he has

---

[12] See Gallie, *Philosophy and the Historical Understanding*, and my *The Nature of Philosophy*.

succeeded in that, his second task is to weigh the importance of un-distorted facts. And this will partly depend on the moral possibilities that the moral idioms available to Strether make him capable of en-tertaining. Accordingly, he may characterize Chad as an equal part-ner in the joint enterprise of arriving at a *modus vivendi* that would best satisfy everyone concerned and see the situation as a matter of balance, fairness, consideration, and compromise. Or he could re-gard Chad as a romantic hero struggling to free himself from the conventional constraints that permeate his life, and then the appro-priate moral idioms would be freedom, happiness, self-realization, and authenticity. Or Chad may seem to Strether to be immature, self-indulgent, undisciplined because he takes too far a passing phase in life that most of us go through. Or he may interpret the situation in terms of the moral idioms appropriate to the relationship between teachers and pupils, judges and the accused, men of the world, con-servative defenders of the *status quo* and radical reformers, and so on.

These, however, were not the moral idioms Strether adopted. But given his moral tradition, character, and circumstances, the ones he did adopt, had he been a real person, would probably have had to compete with these and others. In any case, the point is that if Strether adopts any of the moral idioms of which he is aware, he need not deny that the others are legitimate. He may even concede that they play a subordinate role in his own interpretation, and he may readily admit, being reasonable, that other people could regard as important features of the situation what he relegates to a lesser place. For even if others share his moral tradition, they are unlikely to be so like him in their characters and circumstances as to develop identical relationships with another person. Just so, Chad's mother, lover, friend, and brother-in-law had quite different interpretations of the situation. Strether's moral task was to find his own.

If moral agents have breadth, as Strether does, they are aware of alternative and yet equally reasonable moral idioms for interpreting complex moral situations. This awareness is at once necessary for good judgment and makes it seem very difficult. For the more clearly moral agents appreciate the complexity of the situations they encoun-ter, the more difficulty they will experience in finding the right one of the numerous undistorted interpretations. And herein lies the danger of breadth. It is undoubtedly a good thing to have in complex situations, but, at the same time, too much of it may paralyze judg-ment. It may do so through cynicism fed by the supposed arbitrari-ness of choosing among the many reasonable moral idioms; or the paralysis may be due to having despaired of our ability to justify the moral idioms we have adopted. This shows, I think, that not even the combination of objectivity and moral breadth is sufficient for good judgment.

DEPTH

Thus we arrive at the third component of good judgment: moral depth. Together with objectivity and breadth, depth enables moral agents to find the right interpretation of complex moral situations. Depth consists in a growing appreciation of the available moral idioms. This appreciation is both personal and impersonal. Its impersonal aspect makes it possible to understand that underneath apparently disparate moral responses there is often a discernible unity that a particular moral idiom may capture. It is to appreciate that Robinson Crusoe creating a miniature civilization for himself, Thomas More resisting his king's insistent bidding, Antigone pitting herself against Creon, Spinoza following his own light as an outcast thrice over, and countless mothers, political prisoners, and long-suffering patients carrying on with their deadly routines are different manifestations of the same moral excellence: courage. Through depth we can come to see that the unity of these superficially different forms of conduct is provided by steadfast adherence to one's conception of a good life in the face of adversity. And as we realize this, so we come to a deeper understanding of the significance of one moral idiom. But this understanding needs also to be translated into personal terms. We not only admire lives of courage from the outside, we want also to live them ourselves, in our own context. The personal aspect of depth is the appreciation of the meaning of moral idioms in our own conceptions of good lives. It is developed through reflective transformation of our own aspirations in the light of a growing appreciation of moral idioms. The impersonal aspect of depth is cultivated through imaginative understanding of how others interpret complex moral situations.

Strether's struggle to see Chad accurately will again help us to understand this. Strether has to make up his mind about Chad. The easy part for him is to recognize that identical moral idioms mean different things in Woollett and in Paris. This is a question of breadth, and Strether's intelligence stands him in good stead here. His serious difficulties begin when it occurs to him that the improvement in Chad is in part at least due to his having replaced the significance attributed to the same moral idioms by Woollett with those they have in Paris. He faces the possibility that the Parisian interpretations of moral idioms are better. Chad is the living testimony that the conception of good life Paris offers to him may be superior to

Woollett's. That Strether entertains this possibility is an indication of his growing depth. But it grows in two directions: Chad's and Strether's own.

As far as Chad is concerned, Strether's understanding improves. He comes to see that where Woollett is common, blunt, indiscriminate, vulgar, Chad has become civilized, refined, sensitive, a man to whom standards of excellence, unheard of in Woollett, are now second nature. Thus, new moral possibilities open up for Strether. His growing depth makes him see these alternatives as real possibilities, not just as something foreigners or expatriates may do, but as possibilities for himself. And this imaginative capacity leads him to his most serious difficulty: forming a view of how these possibilities should affect him.

So the question of how to see Chad recedes, and the question of how Strether should change, if at all, comes to the fore. This is really the fundamental question, for Strether's response to Chad, and to everything else, depends on a deeper appreciation of the moral idioms in which are couched the moral possibilities he is considering making his own.

Depth must be achieved without outside help. Objectivity and breadth can be taught, but depth cannot be. For it requires the reflective transformation of our appraisal of moral possibilities from what we used to have to what we aspire to having. This transformation is the driving force of personal morality. But one is driven by it in two different directions: outward and inward. They are inseparable from a practical point of view, but they are different all the same.

Strether asks, Is Chad corrupted or refined? These idioms have one meaning in Woollett and another in Paris. To understand this takes breadth. To adopt one rather than another in the light of this understanding is an aspect of depth. It requires having reflected on human possibilities, and on Chad's possibilities, and having come to the judgment that one idiom is more fitting than another. The selection of idioms, of course, calls for appropriate action. If Chad is corrupted, Strether should make him go home; if he is refined, he ought to be encouraged to stay. This is the outward aspect of depth.

The inward aspect is the realization that the idiom Strether judges to be fitting depends on what *he* thinks of as corruption and refinement. The mere fact that he hesitates shows that he is becoming aware of new moral possibilities for himself. And that he comes to see Chad this way rather than that indicates that he himself has changed. For he has passed from Woollett's view of corruption and refinement, through a realization that they take different forms in different contexts, to an appreciation that behind these forms there is, after all, a common element. It is corruption, if it is an exercise in the clever manipulation of minute discriminations; it is refinement, if it leads to a more sensitive appreciation of the good life to which Chad aspires. But that Strether is capable of judgment of this sort is a sign of his growing depth.

Moral idioms, then, gain significance from their social context and from their transformation by individual moral agents into meaningful personal terms. The better we appreciate the significance of moral idioms, the better are our judgments of the complex moral situations characterized by them. My claim is that good judgment is the capacity to find the right interpretation of the complex situations in which we are called upon to act, and these interpretations depend on objectivity and on the breadth and depth of our appreciation of the moral idioms we derive from our social morality. This is one main concern of personal morality.

But we encounter here a major problem. How can there be a right interpretation, the object of good judgment, when we deny that there can be a canonical interpretation? Now, a canonical interpretation, if *per impossibile* there were one, would be the interpretation all reasonable moral agents would arrive at, once they had freed themselves from distorting self-centeredness and fantasies and had duly weighed the comparative importance of the relevant facts. If it is true that there could not be such an interpretation, because the weight given to the facts varies with the moral idioms the agents have adopted, then what could be a right interpretation? What is the difference between the canonical interpretation, which we cannot have, and the right one, which good judgment supposedly yields?

The canonical interpretation of a complex moral situation would be analogous to the true scientific interpretation of an empirical situation. But the analogy between empirical and moral situations founders on a crucial difference: scientific observers only accidentally and unintentionally interfere with the situations that engage their attention (I ignore the complications of quantum mechanics), while it is essential to being a moral agent that we play an active role in the situation we encounter. It is true that we may occasionally merely behold moral situations as uncommitted observers and not as agents, but I shall ignore this, too, since it is an elliptical way of saying how we would act if we were called upon to do so. The crucial difference is not merely that scientific judgments are only contingently action-guiding, if at all, while moral judgments are essentially connected to action. An even deeper difference is that in typical moral situations, moral agents partly create the situation through their participation in it, while typical scientific observers merely attend to, but do not aim to influence, what they find.

In typical complex moral situations, two agents respond to each other in the framework of their social morality to which they both feel at least some allegiance. I have been illustrating this in the case of Strether and Chad. But the relationships between married couples, parents and children, physicians and patients, teachers and students, superiors and subordinates, lovers, siblings, and friends also bear out my point. In complex situations, social morality provides only a general outline of the form the relationship ought to take. What counts as friendship, marriage, being colleagues, etc., is established by the social morality in the background. But the type of marriage, friendship, or collegiality two people develop within the social framework depends on their personal morality as formed by their history, character, mutual influence, and interpretations of the complex situations in which they encounter each other. This is why moral agents participating in complex moral situations necessarily play an active role in creating their situations. Since their personal moralities, formed of their character, history, etc., will differ, and since appropriate responses require interacting moral agents to take account of each other's personal moralities, reasonable moral agents will interpret the same sort of situation differently.

Thus, the fundamental reason why there could not be a canonical interpretation of a complex moral situation is that what the situation is partly depends on what the participating agents make of it and of each other. Since moral agents are different, and since they perceive and respond to each other differently, there cannot be an interpretation that all agents would arrive at if they were sufficiently reasonable. Interpretations of complex situations are essentially influenced by the variable individual qualities and interactions of the participating interpreters. This is why it is a mistake to try to assimilate interpretations of complex moral situations, which are necessarily personal, to scientific interpretations, which aspire to complete impersonality.

But from the unavailability of the canonical interpretation, the unavailability of the right interpretation does not follow. Just because there is no interpretation of particular situations that all reasonable moral agents would reach, if they were objective enough and had sufficient breadth and depth, does not mean that there is no right interpretation for a particular agent in a particular situation. How, then, can moral agents decide which is the right interpretation among the many reasonable interpretations that their objectivity, breadth, and depth make available to them? They can do so through moral reflection, the topic of the next chapter.

CHAPTER EIGHT

Moral Reflection and Conflict

> By our continual and earnest pursuit of character . . . we
> bring to our own deportment and conduct the habit of
> surveying ourselves, as it were, in reflection, which keeps
> alive all the sentiments of right and wrong, and begets, in
> noble creatures, a certain reverence for themselves as well as
> others, which is the surest guardian of every virtue.
> —David Hume[1]

PLURALISM, REFLECTION, AND CONFLICT

The rejection of the possibility of a canonical interpretation of complex moral situations is a consequence of the rejection of the *summum bonum*. For the interpretations follow from the moral agents' conception of good lives, and since there are many equally reasonable conceptions, there are also many conflicting interpretations of complex moral situations. The task of moral reflection is to lead moral agents to find the right interpretations among the many conflicting ones.

Moral reflection is "the habit of surveying ourselves" in order to "bring our own deportment and conduct frequently in review." It is a difficult process in any case, but it is especially so if the pluralism I have been defending is correct. For, in that case, we must realize that the difficulties of moral reflection are not produced merely by having to take a realistic view of ourselves but also by there being conflicts among the conceptions of good lives that we may adopt and from which the conflicting interpretations follow.

There is an emerging consensus in contemporary moral thought that once we reject the *summum bonum* and embark on moral reflection, conflicts become absolutely central to morality. As a result, it becomes difficult to see how reasonable choices could be made between conflicting conceptions of the good life and between the interpretations they suggest. If choices on this deep level involve arbitrary commitments, then pluralism leads back to the voluntarism I have rejected in chapter 2. I think that this emerging consensus is mistaken. My aim in this chapter is to give an account of moral reflection

[1] Hume, *Enquiry*, 225.

and to show that, while it may lead to conflicts, conflicts rarely prevent reflective moral agents from finding the right interpretations of complex moral situations.

Let us begin by defining the common ground among pluralists who insist on the centrality of conflicts and those, like myself, who attribute lesser importance to them. It is agreed by all that morality makes different types of claims on reasonable moral agents. These claims are based on duties, rights, virtues, personal and social ideals, and so on.[2] Moral agents recognize the force of these claims, because they regard the various duties, rights, etc., underlying them as good. Now, the essential thesis of pluralism is that these admittedly good things are not reducible to each other, because they are incommensurable.

As Williams puts it: "[T]here is no common currency in which . . . gains and losses of value can be computed, that values, or at least the most basic values, are not only plural but in a real sense incommensurable."[3] Hampshire expresses the same point: "[T]he presupposition that there is a natural and normal harmony between conflicting moral requirements becomes questionable. How could there be a guaranteed harmony . . . if . . . human nature is always overlaid by some specific moral requirements . . . which are known to be diverse?"[4] Or in Nagel's version: "I do not believe that the source of values is unitary—displaying multiplicity only in its application to the world. I believe that value has fundamentally different kinds of sources, and that they are reflected in the classification of values into types. Not all values represent the pursuit of some single good in a variety of settings."[5]

My reconstruction of what pluralists mean by goods being incommensurable is as follows.[6] Two or more goods are incommensurable if and only if

1. there is not some one type of good in terms of which other goods are analyzable without serious loss; e.g., not all goods are analyzable in terms of pleasure or duty or the general welfare; and
2. there is not some one way of ranking different types of goods such that one type will always take justifiable precedence over the others; e.g., duties do not always count for more than the general welfare, and vice versa; and

[2] For a list of these claims and for arguments about their differences, see Nagel, "The Fragmentation of Values," and Williams, "Conflicts of Values."

[3] Williams, "Conflicts of Values," 76.

[4] Hampshire, *Morality and Conflict*, 142.

[5] Nagel, "The Fragmentation of Values," 131–32.

[6] The clearest statement of what pluralists mean by incommensurability is Williams, "Conflicts of Values," 77–80. My account is close to his.

3. there is not some neutral medium in terms of which different types of goods can be compared; e.g., duty and happiness are not comparable in terms of utility.

The reason why there cannot be a *summum bonum* is that there are many ways of ordering and balancing various incommensurable goods in a single human life. As a result, human lives can be good in many different ways. I take this to be the essential thesis of pluralism.

This pluralistic thesis is consistent with holding, as I do, that morality makes some universal claims equally binding on all moral agents, as well as claims that vary from one moral tradition to another. The universal claims are based on the facts of the body, self, and social life from which deep conventions are derived, and the claims that are binding only within particular moral traditions are based on the strongly held variable conventions of various traditions. These claims establish the minimum content of any acceptable moral tradition, as I have argued in the first five chapters.

This minimum is necessary but insufficient for good lives, for "human nature, conceived in terms of common human needs and capacities, always underdetermines a way of life, and underdetermines an order of priority among virtues, and therefore underdetermines the moral prohibitions and injunctions that support a way of life."[7] Acceptable moral traditions include the minimum and go beyond it. The pluralistic thesis is not merely that there is diversity of moral traditions but also that there is diversity within particular moral traditions and that it is good to have both kinds of diversity. "[T]he consciousness of the plurality of values is itself a good. . . . [O]ne who recognizes the plurality of values is one who understands the deep creative role that these various values play in human life. . . . [O]ne is prepared to try to build a life around the recognition that these different values do each have a real and intelligible human significance, and are not just errors, misdirections or poor expressions of human nature." "The deep error" is "supposing that all goods, all virtues, all ideals are compatible, and that what is desirable can ultimately be united into a harmonious whole."[8]

Beyond this point, the general agreement among pluralists ceases, because many go on to suppose that it follows from the incommensurability of goods that conflicts among them are a central feature of morality. The reasoning behind this supposition is that since there is a multiplicity of incommensurable goods, and since, given our cir-

---

[7] Hampshire, *Morality and Conflict*, 155.

[8] Williams's introduction to Berlin, *Concepts and Categories*, xvi–xviii. I rearranged the order of passages.

cumstances, we must choose among them in living a good life, we are inevitably involved in conflicts. We can and should be guided in resolving them by reflection and a realistic appraisal of ourselves. But, it is maintained, these gestures toward rationality are ultimately unavailing.

MacIntyre explains why this is so: "[U]nderlying each moral judgment there is a choice that the agent has made—a type of choice in which the individual is at the most fundamental level unconstrained by good reasons, precisely because his or her choice expresses a decision as to what is to count as a good reason for him or her."[9] The result, according to many pluralists, is that "[o]ur everyday and raw experience is conflict between contrary moral requirements at every stage of almost everyone's life,"[10] and "it is my view . . . that value-conflict is . . . something necessarily involved in human values, and to be taken as central by any adequate understanding by them,"[11] and "[h]uman beings are subject to moral . . . claims of very different kinds. This is because they are complex creatures who can view the world from many moral perspectives . . . and each perspective presents a different set of claims. . . . Conflicts between [them] . . . cannot, in my view, be resolved by subsuming either point of view under the other, or both under a third. Nor can we simply abandon any of them."[12]

What exactly is the kind of conflict these pluralists have in mind? First, it is a conflict within individual moral agents; not between two or more moral agents; nor between different conventions within a moral tradition; nor between different moral traditions. No doubt, these latter types of conflicts do occur, but they do not concern pluralists in this context. "We know that we in fact have essential divisions within us as persons and we experience moral conflicts arising from them";[13] and "[t]he type of conflict that will concern us is one-party conflict; and will take that as one-person conflict. . . . [S]ome one-person conflicts are expressions of a complex inheritance of values";[14] and "[w]hen faced with conflicting and incommensurable claims we still have to do something—even if it is to do nothing."[15]

Second, the conflict within individuals is not between the claims of morality and something else but between moral claims themselves.

[9] MacIntyre, *Revisions*, 8–9.
[10] Hampshire, *Morality and Conflict*, 151.
[11] Williams, "Conflicts of Values," 72.
[12] Nagel, "The Fragmentation of Values," 134.
[13] Hampshire, *Morality and Conflict*, 155.
[14] Williams, "Conflicts of Values," 72–73.
[15] Nagel, "The Fragmentation of Values," 134.

But moral claims can conflict in different ways. One is to have conflicting moral claims of the same type: two obligations that cannot both be honored, virtues that cannot be cultivated simultaneously, components of the general welfare so related that the more we have of one the less we can have of the other. Conflict-centered pluralists do pay some attention to these kinds of conflicts, but they are still not the most important sorts. The central conflict that concerns them is between different types of moral claims. "Human beings are subject to moral . . . claims of very different types . . . individual, relational, impersonal, ideal, etc. Conflict can exist within each of these sets, and it may be hard to resolve. But when conflicts occur between them, the problem is still more difficult";[16] and a "person hesitates between two contrasting ways of life, and sets of virtues, and he has to make a very definite, and even final, determination between them. The determination is a negation, and normally the agent will feel that the choice has killed, or repressed, some part of him."[17]

Third, the conflicts are not between types of individual goods but between the ways of life of which the goods are constituents. The reason for this is that within a particular way of life conflicts between different types of goods can always be settled, at least theoretically, by assigning priorities to them on the basis of their respective importance to that way of life. To people dedicated to social reform, rights and social ideals are usually more important than virtues and personal ideals, while deeply religious people tend to hold the reverse; duties normally rank high in the lives of soldiers, but for artists they are likely to be less important.

The emerging consensus among many pluralists, then, is that, as a consequence of the incommensurability of goods, one central feature of moral life is that individual moral agents experience frequent conflicts between the different ways of life that incorporate these goods. This is the mistake I shall now proceed to argue against.[18]

SIMPLE MORAL SITUATIONS WITHOUT REFLECTION AND CONFLICT

As a first step of this argument, let us recall that there is a very large area of our moral tradition, social morality, from which the type of conflict upon whose ubiquity these pluralists insist is largely absent. Simple moral situations, characteristic of social morality, are simple, because moral agents accept the prescriptions of their society and they usually find no difficulty in seeing their relevance to the situa-

---

[16] Ibid.

[17] Hampshire, *Morality and Conflict*, 155.

[18] See also Pincoffs, *Quandaries and Virtues*.

tions in which they have to act. Our typical experience in the domain of social morality is that of having a large repertoire of intuitive, frequently unarticulated moral reactions. Our moral education makes us see simple situations in a certain light, and, as a result, we do not agonize over the morality of everyday life. We know what is good or bad, right and wrong in that context, and we act accordingly. We get a bill, we pay it; a friend asks, we help; it is part of our job, we do it; we made a promise, we keep it. Of course, we sometimes knowingly violate the prescriptions of social morality. But even this tends to be a rather banal backsliding. Our desire was too strong, doing the right thing was too hard or embarrassing; we count our small gain for more than someone's big loss; we are thoughtless, lazy, or stupid. And even if these episodes of immorality are frequent and significant, their occurrence is not due to the type of conflict these pluralists have in mind. They are signs of conflict between moral requirements and selfishness, weakness, or inattention, but not between contrary moral requirements.

Thus, as we noted earlier, social morality consists of undramatic acts of common decency, and immorality is a similarly pedestrian affair, provided the social morality is not disintegrating. Disintegration is not just change. A healthy social morality is always changing in some ways, because the social conditions in which it has to guide conduct are changing. In social morality, therefore, there are always likely to be areas of uncertainty and doubt, as there are now in ours, for instance, about sex. But we have no comparable doubts about promises, contracts, honesty, burglary, courage, cruelty, love, murder, and countless other aspects of our moral existence. Moreover, our attempts to resolve uncertainties and conflicts are made by delving deeper into our social morality for guidance. We approach conflicts about sex by arguing in terms of equality, fairness, freedom, and responsibility, and thereby we pay tribute to more fundamental aspects of social morality.

Change could, however, become so radical as to produce disintegration. If this happens, conflicts do become ubiquitous. Many pluralists write as if this were the usual state of morality. I have argued in the first five chapters that it is not. Conflicts occur if social morality is disintegrating, if deep and variable conventions are routinely inconsistent, or if considered opinions about simple moral situations often clash. But these are infrequent and atypical occurrences. We all have vested interest in keeping them so, because they undermine social morality—the framework within which we may live good lives. Moral crises, great decisions, tragic confrontations, then, rarely occur in this context. To suppose that "our everyday raw experience is conflict between contrary moral requirements,"[19] or that "value-conflict is . . . central"[20] is to falsify our moral experience in the domain of social morality.

Conflict-centered pluralists may acknowledge that many people live their lives in the manner I have described and that it may be proper to do so in the domain of social morality and in simple moral situations. But they would go on to argue that people should not live like that in the context of personal morality and complex moral situations. And in this I agree with them. What is at issue, then, is whether personal morality and complex moral situations are indeed riven by the kinds of conflicts I have just described.

The outcome of this issue depends on which of two ways of thinking about moral reflection is correct. My opponents' view is that reflection enables us to decide what we really want, as independent, autonomous individuals and, then, to go on to try to extract it from our surroundings. If moral reflection were like this, then conflicts would indeed be central to morality, for moral reflection would lead moral agents, as it led Oedipus, to an adversary relationship with their moral tradition, and they would be warring within themselves as well. The conflict with the moral tradition would occur because moral agents would be bound to regard moral prescriptions as restrictions on what they may do in order to get what they want. And internal conflicts would also be inevitable, since insofar as moral agents have internalized their moral tradition, they would be acting against their own convictions as well. Thus, moral reflection is taken to involve unceasing battles, initiated by incompatible wants and constrained by morality.

This view is not false or inconsistent, rather it is incomplete and unbalanced. The incompleteness comes from regarding human beings as ensconced in the fortress of their minds, reflecting on what they want, and then conducting forays into the hostile world to get it. The truth is that our minds and wants are formed by the conventions into which we are born. Conventions are not the traditional gloss upon our wants; wants are given form and articulation by couching them in the moral idioms our tradition provides.

To say this is not to diminish the importance and value of individuality but to explain its source. To be individuals is to construct our moral perspectives that enable us to identify our important wants by expressing them in appropriate moral idioms. We thereby make ourselves into what we have learned to value from our moral tradition. But if this is so, conflicts need not be a central part of our nature.

[19] Hampshire, *Morality and Conflict*, 151.
[20] Williams, "Conflicts of Values," 72.

Many conflicts occur because the conventions forming us are inconsistent or because we misinterpret their intimations. And conflicts are eliminable, then, by being judicious in our receptivity to conventional influences and by correcting our misinterpretations of them. In neither case need conflicts be the raw material of our moral experience. What is wrong with the view that places conflicts at the center of morality is that it lacks appropriate recognition of the formative influence of conventions and it mislocates the source of moral conflicts. As a result, it becomes unbalanced by attributing far greater importance to conflicts than they have in our moral experience.

The view of reflection I propose to substitute in place of this incomplete and unbalanced one begins by noting that our normal situation is that we are born into a moral tradition. We learn from it to articulate our wants, to identify the wants whose satisfaction is morally permissible, and to find acceptable ways to go about satisfying them. The moral tradition provides for us the framework and the guidance for the lives we lead. But the fit between the tradition and individual lives in it is imperfect. The tradition is much richer, it provides many more conceptions of good lives, composed of many different combinations of goods than we can try to achieve in a lifetime. So we must choose among them. These choices, however, are difficult, because it is not always obvious what our wants are or whether we have the capacities required for satisfying them. Consequently, it is unclear how the conventions of our moral tradition apply to our own cases. Also, there is a reciprocal process between our growing awareness of what we are about and the opportunities for realizing our aspirations provided by the conventions. We find out what we are about by considering our limitations and possibilities, and many of them are defined by our conventions. As I understand it, the main role of moral reflection is to overcome the imperfect fit between individual lives and the moral tradition; it is to help develop our individuality by giving form to such inchoate, unarticulated wants and capacities as we may have. Moral reflection does not have as its object the discovery of what we are independently of the tradition that has and is forming us; rather, it guides the way in which we subject ourselves to the formative influences of the tradition. The way moral reflection accomplishes this is by concentrating on limitations and possibilities.

MORAL REFLECTION ON HUMAN LIMITATIONS: TOLSTOY'S IVAN ILYCH

Moral reflection is a cognitive process: it is a kind of knowledge of our limitations and possibilities. In this section, I shall discuss knowledge of our limitations by considering a man who lacked it: Tolstoy's Ivan Ilych.[21] Ivan Ilych was "a capable, cheerful, good-natured and sociable man, though strict in the performance of what he considered to be his duty; and he considered his duty to be what was so considered by those in authority" (105). He spent his life as an official "easily, pleasantly and correctly" (118). But he had found himself with a recurrent pain, and it grew worse. "Suddenly he felt the old familiar, dull, gnawing pain, stubborn and serious. . . . His heart sank, and he felt dazed. . . . A chill came over him, his breathing ceased, and he felt only the throbbing of his heart" (129–30). And so "Ivan Ilych saw that he was dying, and he was in continual despair. In the depth of his heart he knew he was dying, but not only was he not accustomed to the thought, he simply did not and could not grasp it" (131). "The syllogism he had learnt in Kiezewetter's Logic: 'Caius is a man, men are mortal, therefore Caius is mortal,' has always seemed to him correct as applied to Caius, but certainly not as applied to himself. . . . Caius really was mortal, and it was right for him to die; but for me, little Vanya, Ivan Ilych, with all my thoughts and emotions, it's altogether a different matter. It cannot be that I ought to die. That would be too terrible" (131–32). There was a sense in which Ivan Ilych knew that he would die, but in another, he did not know.

What kind of knowledge did Ivan Ilych lack of his death? Well, it was not information; the trouble was not his ignorance of actuarial statistics. The knowledge involved in moral reflection is not descriptive. Nor is it knowledge of finding one's way in the world. Ivan Ilych did not lack cleverness, he had the worldliness needed to get along in life well; but knowing the ways of the world was not enough for him, and it is not enough for us either. To know how to find means to our ends is useless, and may actually be harmful, if the ends themselves are not good.

The beginning of the answer is that the object of this knowledge is finding good ends at which we may reasonably aim. This kind of knowledge is interpretative. In descriptive knowledge we know facts; in interpretative knowledge we know the significance of descriptively known facts. The facts whose significance we know through the kind of interpretative knowledge that is involved in moral reflection concerns our conceptions of good lives. For it is these conceptions that embody the ends we aim at.

What, then, are these significant facts? They are among the "massive central core of human thinking which has no history—or none

[21] Tolstoy, *The Death of Ivan Ilych and Other Stories*; numbers in parentheses refer to the pages.

recorded in histories of thought; these are the categories and concepts which, in their most fundamental character, change not at all. Obviously, these are not the specialities of the most refined thinking. They are the commonplaces of the least refined thinking; and yet the indispensable core of the conceptual equipment of the most sophisticated human beings."[22] They are the facts of the body, self, and social life. Knowledge of them is knowledge of the limits of human possibilities.

The limits these facts set are moral, not logical or empirical. They must be taken into account by all adequate conceptions of good life. The failure to do so makes good life, according to that conception, impossible. These limiting facts are among the most elementary forms of descriptive knowledge, possessed by all normal human beings. Although in our knowledge of them "there are no new truths to be discovered, there are old truths to be rediscovered."[23] The object of interpretative knowledge of limitations is the rediscovery for ourselves of these old truths. In coming to know them, we come to understand their significance for living good lives. Everybody has descriptive knowledge of them, but not everybody has interpretative knowledge of their significance. Ivan Ilych, for instance, had the first but not the second.

Ivan Ilych despaired as he was dying. "His mental sufferings were due to the fact that . . . the question suddenly occurred to him: 'What if my whole life has really been wrong?' It occurred to him that what had appeared perfectly impossible before, namely that he had not spent his life as he should have done, might after all be true. . . . 'But if that is so,' he said to himself, 'and I am leaving this life with the consciousness that I have lost all that was given me and it is impossible to rectify it—what then?' " (152). Well, then his life had been wasted, because he failed to realize that death sets a limit to it, and he must find the things important to him and not waste time with trifles. The significance of death is not only that it terminates our lives but also that the decisions about what to do with our lives should be made in the light of the knowledge that death curtails the time we have at our disposal. And this, Ivan Ilych did not realize.

Death is only one example of the limitations moral reflection should take into account. Another is the changing seasons of life. Youth, maturity, and old age set limits by altering our physiological, psychological, and intellectual capacities. If we try to live without accommodating our aspirations to these inevitable changes, our lives are bound to be disappointing, for we shall want to accomplish either

22 Strawson, *Individuals*, xiv.
23 Ibid.

more or less than what our capacities permit. And then there is the limitation imposed by having to balance the short- against the long-term significance of satisfying or frustrating our wants. If we live only in the present, our future will be bad; but if we care about the future only, our lives will be without satisfactions, for the future is always ahead.

Part of what reflective people know, then, are the limitations adequate moral perspectives must take into account. This knowledge is not esoteric, for it is within everyone's reach. Nor does it require high intelligence or special talent, for it concerns limitations that have been the same for everyone since time immemorial. Speaking colloquially, we can say that those who have this knowledge know what's what; and speaking to echo Arnold's homage to Sophocles, we can say that they see life steadily and see it as a whole. Contrariwise, the characteristic we must ascribe to those who conspicuously lack this knowledge is foolishness.

Ivan Ilych lived a foolish life because he knew, descriptively, that he would die, but he did not know, interpretatively, the significance of this. He was preoccupied with trivial pursuits, and he failed to find out what was important in his life. And so Ivan Ilych wasted his life; but at the end he became tragic. The tragedy was that by the time he came to see his life steadily and see it as a whole, it was too late to do anything about it. Ivan Ilych is emblematic of the human situation, because his case shows that we do not get a second chance to put right the shortcomings of a wasted life. (I am not convinced by Tolstoy's wavering about it being otherwise.)

Moral reflection is corrective,[24] because it guards against foolishness by reminding us of what is significant and what is trivial in our lives. Thinking of moral reflection in this way runs the risk of what I shall call the Polonius syndrome. Polonius seems like a foolish old man, and yet he speaks what are perhaps the wisest lines in *Hamlet* when he advises Laertes about how he should live (act 1, scene 3). In reciting to his respectful but impatient son these precepts, Polonius stands in a long tradition. All the major religions have texts encapsulating similar pieces of advice, and folklore, in the form of proverbs, is full of them. Yet these fruits of wisdom are frequently embarrassing because they seem to be nothing but clichés. The reason why Polonius seems foolish in that scene is that he appears to be mouthing platitudes. To avoid the Polonius syndrome, we must ask, How are thoughtful reminders offered by morally reflective people different from platitudes?

The same sentence can express a thoughtful reminder and a plati-

---

[24] Foot, *Virtues and Vices*, 1–18.

tude. What distinguishes them is their psychological background. *I shall die* was a platitude in Ivan Ilych's mouth before he was actually dying; and if he had recovered and gone on living, but with an appreciation of the significance of his mortality, then *I shall die* would have expressed a thoughtful reminder. Similarly, Polonius said, To thine own self be true . . . , and so on. Whether we take this as a sign of moral reflection depends on whether Polonius was repeating the tedious platitudes his father delivered on a no less awkward occasion or whether Polonius was giving his son the hard-earned results of his own moral reflection. We have to know about Polonius to decide how to take what he said. What transforms a platitude into a thoughtful reminder is the utterer's recognition that it expresses a significant truth about the human condition.

We may wonder, however, about what point there could be to these thoughtful reminders. To the foolish, they will seem fatuous, and for the morally reflective, they will be gilding the lily. The answer is that they are addressed to the very large majority that is neither foolish nor sufficiently reflective to have no need of them. Most of us are a mixture of some degree of foolishness and reflectiveness. In cool moments, we see moral reflection as a good thing and foolishness as bad. Although not even the most authoritative reminders can take the place of moral reflection, they may nevertheless spur us to engage in it and consider the facts whose significance we need to realize.

Moral and intellectual shortcomings may handicap moral reflection, prevent us from acquiring knowledge of our limitations, and doom us to frustration. But whatever handicaps us, it is not the kind of conflict many pluralists think of as being central to morality. We do not fail to take account of our limitations, because we vacillate between contrary moral requirements, because we feel equally strongly the prescriptive forces of rights, duties, virtues, ideals, and individual or general happiness. Whatever forces these prescriptions exert on us must occur within the area defined by human limitations. We know what they are, we may be foolishly ignorant of them, or we may struggle toward making the degree of knowledge we have inform our lives. In any case, it is not conflicts but our shortcomings that stand in the way.

Moral Reflection on Human Possibilities

So far we have established that conflicts between equally reasonable interpretations do not play a central role either in the context of social morality or in that of moral reflection about human limitations. In the former case, simplicity minimizes conflicts, while in the latter, there is little scope for decision. The requirements of morality, in these contexts, are based on facts that we ignore at our peril. But good lives require more than a hospitable society and reckoning with limits that would be foolish to ignore. Good lives also depend on realizing some of our possibilities. The identification and selection of these possibilities is the other function of moral reflection. These possibilities vary from person to person, because our wants, characters, and aspirations vary, and because in civilized circumstances, for normal people, there are usually many possibilities. Hence, moral reflection cannot appeal here to common human considerations; it must recognize individual differences and different possibilities within individuals. If anywhere, this is where conflicts between equally reasonable interpretations may be central. It may be thought that the task of moral reflection is precisely to resolve the conflict individuals experience among their moral possibilities. My view is that conflicts do occur in this context and moral reflection does have as one of its objects the resolution of these conflicts. But not even here are conflicts central. In order to show that this is so, we need to consider the second kind of knowledge involved in moral reflection: knowledge of our possibilities.

As before, in the case of limitations, the possibilities involved in moral reflection are moral, not logical or empirical; they concern what we can do, given our characters and circumstances, to make our lives good. And once again, the knowledge of our possibilities involves interpretation of the relevant facts. Both knowledge of limitations and possibilities are action-guiding, because in each case we know something important about the good lives we want to have. But knowledge of limitations is action-guiding negatively; it acts as a corrective by reminding us of limits we should heed. Knowledge of possibilities, on the other hand, is action-guiding positively; it actually spurs us to realize such possibilities as we incorporate into our moral perspectives.

Let us now look at an illustrative instance of Ivan Ilych's moral reflection. He is in great pain, and he is struggling toward the realization that he is dying. "It occurred to him that what had appeared perfectly impossible before, namely that he had not spent his life as he should have done, might after all be true. It occurred to him that his scarcely perceptible attempts to struggle against what was considered good by the most highly placed people, those scarcely noticeable impulses which he had immediately suppressed, might have been the real thing, and all the rest false. And his professional duties and the whole arrangement of his life and of his family, and his social and official interests, might all have been false. He tried to defend all these things to himself and suddenly felt the weakness of what he was defending" (152).

In this moral reflection, Ivan Ilych is taking stock of what he has made of his possibilities. Before his illness, in his own eyes and in the eyes of the world, he was successful. He opted for the possibilities held out by the life of an ambitious and rising official, and he got what he wanted. But the life he had been living changed him. "Very soon, within a year of his wedding, Ivan Ilych had realized that marriage, though it may add some comforts to life, is in fact a very intricate and difficult affair towards which in order to perform one's duty, that is, to lead a decorous life approved by society, one must adopt an attitude. . . . And Ivan Ilych evolved such an attitude towards married life. He only required of it those conveniences—dinner at home, housewife, bed—which it could give him, and above all that propriety of external forms required by public opinion" (110). His work affected him the same way: "[T]he thing was to exclude everything fresh and vital, which always disturbs the regular course of official business, and to admit only official relations with people, and then only on official grounds. . . . [He] would observe the courtesies of life. As soon as official relations ended, so did everything else" (117–18). And so in his illness, came "that loneliness in which he found himself as he lay facing the back of the sofa, a loneliness in the midst of a populous town and surrounded by numerous acquaintances and relations . . . that terrible loneliness" (149). In that loneliness came the conclusion of his moral reflection: "It is as if I had been going downhill while imagining I was going up. And that is really what it was. I was going up in public opinion, but to the same extent life was ebbing away from me. And now it is all done and there is only death" (148). Ivan Ilych realized that he had wasted his life, because he had pursued the wrong possibilities. His reflection on his possibilities came too late. In his last moments, he made such amends as he could, but, although Tolstoy intimates otherwise, they could not undo the pattern of a lifetime.

What should Ivan Ilych have done, and what should we do, to prevent moral reflection on our possibilities from going wrong? To begin with, we should realize that moral reflection is a process whereby we consciously change some of our psychological states. For instance, we may weaken our inclination to be argumentative if we come to believe that it is due to sublimated aggression; we may cease to feel jealous of a person if we find him pitiful; or we may undermine our belief in God by constantly reminding ourselves of how great and widespread is human suffering. Thus, moral reflection acts to strengthen or weaken the action-guiding force of our psychological states.

Second, we should realize that moral reflection not only guides our actions but also modifies us. In normal lives, there are countless episodes in which we consciously alter our psychological states. One episode rarely causes significant changes in us. But episodes accumulate, and they make or break dispositions. And developing or curtailing dispositions does significantly alter us. Our characters depend on our dispositions, and dispositions are fostered or thwarted by episodes. If we realize this, we have taken an important step toward keeping moral reflection from going wrong. We shall, then, reflect not only on what we want to do then and there but also on the effects acting or refraining has on the shaping of our characters. We shall ask ourselves, Do I want to become the sort of person who does that sort of thing? Ivan Ilych did not ask the second question, so he did not see that doing what was required to live "easily, pleasantly and correctly" (118) would make him into the sort of person whose life is "not real at all, but a terrible huge deception" (152).

Assuming that we are alive to the dual significance of moral reflection, what forms should that aliveness take? The beginning of the answer, which will be completed in the next chapter, is that it will involve clarity about our possibilities. The further our wants are from being physiological, the less clear it is what would satisfy them. We want love, enjoyment, respect, security, an interesting life, and we want to avoid pain, hostility, contempt, fear, and boredom. But each of these objects is quite general: by wanting them, we do not yet know which of a vast array of goods possible in our moral tradition we actually seek. Is our wanting to be loved, at this stage of our lives, a longing for parental, comradely, filial, or sexual love? Is it that we want it from our friends, spouses, colleagues, children, or students? To get clear about these, and countless other wants, is to understand specific instances as manifestations of our deeper, more general dispositions. And to understand the unspecific dispositions in the background is to come to know what particular episodes do and do not instantiate it. In reaching this knowledge, however, we are trying to find out what our range of relevant possibilities is and what possibilities, within that range, would satisfy the wants we have. But the wants become articulated and specified in terms of the possible satisfactions provided by our moral tradition. So the clarity involved in moral reflection is not a process of self-divination but an attempt to match our individual wants and the traditional possibilities into which we could comfortably fit.

Finding the right fit calls for sensitivity. This is a mode of imagination directed at the future; its objects are our own future states of being and acting. These states, however, are imagined from the inside, from the point of view of ourselves as agents experiencing them. We try to imagine how we would feel about being in that state and act accordingly; we try to gauge whether the future state would provide the anticipated satisfactions or the amelioration of frustrations. Sensitivity, like clarity, is inseparably connected with the available possibilities. For if we were to imagine, for instance, what it would be like to have great influence, we would have to do so in terms of the opportunities provided by our tradition. Being a politician, a journalist, or an author are options in our society; being a king, a prophet, or a shaman are very remote possibilities. Sensitivity, therefore, supplements clarity as a form of moral reflection directed toward trying to construct a life for ourselves out of our wants and capacities that we articulate, form, satisfy, and exercise in terms of the possibilities provided by our moral tradition.

Through clarity and sensitivity, moral reflection focuses on wants and capacities individually, but in good lives wants and capacities cohere, because we order them and establish priorities among them. This requires maintaining a balance between simultaneous wants, between short- and long-range satisfactions, and between wants and prevailing conventions. The extent to which we maintain this balance is the extent to which we have succeeded in imposing coherence on our lives. And how good our lives are is partly determined by how well we are able to sustain this balance.

Given this understanding of moral reflection, my dispute with conflict-centered pluralists can be stated more sharply. They think that moral reflection, thus understood, inevitably produces the relevant sort of conflicts, and I disagree. The issue is not whether conflicts may occur in our lives; I acknowledge this obvious truth. What I am disputing is that conflicts must occur to all full-fledged moral agents, and that they are persistent and central features of our moral lives. This dispute is not about the fundamental pluralistic belief that it is necessary for a healthy moral tradition that it should contain a plurality of incommensurable possibilities seen as good. I share the belief that moral traditions should be like this. My claim is that it does not follow, and it is not true, that incommensurable possibilities must always or even frequently produce conflicts in individual lives. The very function of moral reflection is to find a fit between the possibilities a moral tradition offers and individual lives, and thus remove the source of conflicts. I am disputing the view that "[a]s soon as it is recognized within a moral theory that human beings reflect on their own distinguishing desires and interests, and on their actions . . . a duality opens up, which, once opened, cannot be closed; it must infect the whole of moral theory: . . . a whole range of different complete lives is represented as normal . . . the capacity to envisage conflicts between norms for a complete life, conflicts of ends and values, is natural in human beings."[25]

At the very early stages of moral development, there usually occur conflicts between inclinations and conventions. These conflicts, however, are not the kind that are supposed to be central to pluralistic morality. For they do not stem from moral reflection about a multiplicity of incommensurable possibilities regarded as good but from the clash between two kinds of prereflective inclination: the aggressive or self-centered primitive ones and the promptings of our second nature formed by moral education. And when our moral education prevails, we do not feel a loss but a sense of achievement enhanced by the approval of others.

As our moral development continues, we begin to reflect and look critically at the prereflective deliverances of our second nature. We come to understand that the moral possibilities open to us are richer than we could explore and realize in a lifetime. If conflict-centered pluralists are right, this is the context of ubiquitous moral conflicts. But the moral experience of reflective moral agents does not support them.

Let us take, first, people thoroughly successful in their moral reflections. They have achieved clarity about their wants and possibilities; they are sensitive to how the realization of various possibilities would affect their characters; and they maintain a balance between their wants, capacities, and moral tradition. For such people, the surfeit of riches provided by their moral tradition presents no problems, for, having successfully reflected, they know what possibilities suit best their characters and circumstances. The mere fact that there are such people—Marcus Aurelius, Bach, Montaigne, and Einstein—among us shows that conflicts need not be ever present in moral life.

It may be said, however, that exceptionally few people are thoroughly successful in their moral reflection, and while they may not be prone to conflicts, for the rest of us, the vast majority, who reflect but stumblingly, conflicts are ever present. Upon examination, however, this claim also turns out to be overstated. The failure of moral reflection that most of us suffer from shows itself either as lack of clarity or as dullness of sensitivity or as a breakdown of the balance between our aspirations and possibilities.

Lack of clarity means that we are unsure of what we want. The symptom of this uncertainty is confusion, not conflict. Our situation is not that several possibilities appear strongly and equally attractive

[25] Hampshire, *Morality and Conflict*, 145.

to us and we do not know which one to try to realize. Rather, we are uncertain about the attraction of available possibilities. The source of our uncertainty may be failing to know what kind of life we want or whether a way of life is appropriate to our characters and circumstances. This kind of uncertainty, however, does not appear as conflict. We do not know which possibilities we want, not because there are several we want equally, but because we have unclear wants.

Failure of sensitivity about our possibilities does not lead to conflicts either. We usually suffer from this defect because we fail to enter imaginatively into a way of life and envisage what it would be like to live it. As a result, we fail to explore our possibilities and live an empty life of rule-following decency. We give no thought to changing circumstances, to other possibilities, or to the availability of other ways of seeing than what habitually occurs to us. More than anything else, this was Ivan Ilych's fault. Fear, laziness, habit, comfort, stupidity make most of us morally hidebound at least some of the time. But whatever can be said in criticism of this defect, it is the very opposite of conflict-producing. For its essence is to ignore, minimize, or to be blind to alternative possibilities.

Moral reflection may also fail through our inability to maintain a balance among our wants and possibilities. This failure does allow for the kind of conflict conflict-centered pluralists have in mind. In these conflicts "one is fairly sure about the outcomes of alternative courses of action, or about their probability distribution, and even though one knows how to distinguish the pros and cons, one is nevertheless unable to bring them together in a single evaluative judgment, even to the extent of finding them evenly balanced. An even balance requires comparable quantities."[26] But why is it supposed that we cannot balance them? Because "considered and thoughtful moral attitudes, accompanied by strong feelings . . . typically come into conflict with each other."[27] The claim of conflict-centered pluralists is that we are so constituted that our considered moral attitudes routinely conflict with each other. The typical conflict is supposed to be that our considered moral attitudes favor two ways of life that we want equally strongly and equally reasonably. I emphasize that our conflicting wants must be roughly equal in strength, because otherwise the stronger would prevail as a matter of course. And the objects of the conflicting wants must be ways of life, because conflicts within a way of life can usually be settled by opting to satisfy the want that is judged to be more important to that way of life.

[26] Nagel, "The Fragmentation of Values," 128.
[27] Hampshire, *Morality and Conflict*, 152.

I think that considered moral attitudes could and do conflict in these ways in complex moral situations. But should we conclude that morality has its source in these conflicts, that the typical moral problem is the resolution of conflicting moral attitudes? I do not think so.

Where in our moral experience do we find conflicts such as these? We find them in people with more than one great talent, in women divided between conventional motherhood and a career, in corrupt and disintegrating societies where conscientious people have to consider whether to continue to participate in the hope of improving things or leave for another country and culture. These are wrenching conflicts, and there is no doubt that people experience them. But the conflict-centered pluralist thesis goes far beyond this. It is that morality necessarily involves this sort of conflict and that it occurs, for all or most of us, not once or twice in a lifetime, but routinely. I have argued that we must reject this as false to our moral experience.

The majority of people live more or less self-directed lives without such wrenching conflicts. For them, morality consists in doing their jobs, raising children, being good husbands and wives, helping those in need, not abusing such power as they have, giving others their due, and, if things go badly, facing misfortune steadfastly. Of course, sometimes it is difficult to live in this way, but only rarely is the difficulty that there is a fundamental conflict between incommensurable ways of life. Usually, the difficulty is that selfishness, unclarity, insensitivity, or indifference stand in the way of us doing what we recognize we should do. As a result, we feel guilty, ashamed, resolve to improve, and try to make amends; or we deceive ourselves, pretend ignorance, harden our hearts, and invent spurious justifications.

If physicians misdiagnose illness, scholars overlook relevant evidence, politicians lose contact with their constituents, violinists give slipshod performances, we do not automatically assume that conflicts lie at the source of their failure. Nor should we do so when moral failures occur. The mistake conflict-centered pluralists make is to inflate the importance and exaggerate the frequency of one kind of conflict and attempt to assimilate the whole of morality to one rare pattern.

Thus, there are several good reasons for rejecting the thesis of conflict-centered pluralists that moral reflection inevitably leads to conflicts between incommensurable ways of life. First, morally reflective people may have sufficient clarity and sensitivity to know which of several possible ways of life best suits their characters and circumstances. Second, even if moral reflection fails, it need not be that conflict is responsible for it. The failure may have its source in unclarity about what is wanted or in insensitivity to what it would be like to have it. Third, there are two very large areas of morality in which there is no scope for this sort of conflict: social morality and knowledge of our limitations. For what is at stake in these areas is the prior question of what would make any form of good life possible. Only if that question is satisfactorily answered can we engage in the possibly conflict-producing worry about choosing among our options.

Through moral reflection we seek the right interpretation of the complex moral situations we encounter. This process is not arbitrary, because it is guided by our limitations and possibilities that, in turn, are established by such balance between our moral tradition and individuality as we are capable of maintaining. Finding the right interpretation depends on good judgment, and how good our judgments are depends partly on the extent of objectivity, breadth, and depth we possess and on how well we reflect. But it also depends on the recognition that how we judge particular situations has a formative influence on our characters. For judgment involves moral reflection, and through it we consciously modify our psychological states, and, consequently, our dispositions and characters. This modification is guided by our conceptions of good lives. We aim to change ourselves to become what we think we should. These conceptions of good lives provide our moral perspectives. Thus, good judgment also depends on possessing an adequate moral perspective. I shall consider moral perspectives next and then their adequacy.

CHAPTER NINE

Moral Perspectives

> He . . . has discovered himself who says, '[t]his is *my* way;
> where is yours?'—thus I answered those who asked me 'the
> way.' For *the* way—that does not exist.
>   —Friedrich Nietzsche[1]

COMMITMENTS AND THEIR STRUCTURE: THOMAS MORE

The relationship between individuals and their moral tradition can
be described from an external and an internal point of view. Jointly,
they provide a full characterization of the relationship. The external
account stresses how social morality provides moral possibilities.
These possibilities are at once liberating and restricting. They are liberating, because they appear both as manifold forms good lives can
take and as various options within particular forms of life. But the
possibilities are also restricting, because the variety they provide is
limited and they set the requirements of the various forms. The contents of these moral possibilities are the deep and variable conventions of the social morality surrounding individuals. The external
view leaves room for, but does not furnish, an account of how individuals grapple with their possibilities. The internal view concen-
trates on this process—the process of self-direction. By exercising
their options, individuals develop allegiance to the conventions that
guide the realization of some selected possibilities. When individuals
form such an allegiance, they have, as I shall call it, made a *commitment*. Since there are many conventions, there are also many possible

---

[1] Nietzsche, *Thus Spoke Zarathustra*, 306–7. The account of moral perspectives I am
about to give resembles Nietzsche's in many ways. The extremely illuminating interpretation of Nietzsche by Nehamas, *Nietzsche: Life as Literature*, is particularly close to
my view. I should, therefore, note that there are two crucial respects in which I differ
with Nietzsche. First, I stress, while Nietzsche denies, the existence of objective good
and evil; he recognizes no counterpart to deep conventions based on the facts of the
body, self, and social life. Second, I think that the test of whether lives guided by moral
perspectives are indeed good is the enjoyment of external and internal goods, see
chapter 10. Nietzsche thinks that his own test, eternal recurrence, is inconclusive because the possibility of self-deception cannot be ruled out; see Nehamas, *Nietzsche*, 162–
63.

commitments, and they differ in strength. When our commitments cohere and form a hierarchical structure ranging from strong to weak ones, we have a *moral perspective*.

The intermediate goal of self-direction is the development of a moral perspective, while its ultimate goal is a good life consisting in the realization of the possibilities inherent in the conventions to which agents have thus committed themselves. The impetus for self-direction is provided by the universal wants we all have due to the facts of the body, self, and social life, and by the individual wants created by our personal aspirations and the various forms of intimacy we wish to have or to maintain. The satisfaction of these individual wants typically occurs in complex moral situations whose identity is partly determined by how the participating agents interpret them. Reasonable interpretations require good judgment, and how good judgments are depends on our moral perspectives. Thus, in the notion of a moral perspective, self-direction, good judgment, and the aspiration toward a good life are all intermingled. The domain of personal morality is this complex aspect of our lives. My aim in this chapter is to understand what it is to have a moral perspective through understanding the structure of commitments that compose it and to consider some of the differences between more and less adequate moral perspectives.

Commitments, then, are *to* conduct according to specific deep and variable conventions. Depending on their strength, commitments may be unconditional, defeasible, or loose.[2] To discuss them and their differences, I shall consider the character of Thomas More, as portrayed by Robert Bolt.[3] Bolt writes of More that he was "a man with an adamantine sense of his own self. He knew where he began and left off, what area of himself he could yield to the encroachments of his enemies, and what to the encroachments of those he loved. It was a substantial area in both cases, for he had a proper sense of fear and was a busy lover. Since he was a clever man and a great lawyer, he was able to retire from these areas in wonderfully good order, but at length he was asked to retreat from that final area where he located his self. And there this supple, humorous, unassuming and sophisticated man set like metal, was overtaken by an absolutely primitive rigor, and could no more be budged than a cliff."[4]

The key to understanding More's "adamantine sense of self" is to understand his commitments. As Bolt tells it, More was prepared and

---

[2] My discussion of commitments is indebted to Hampshire, *Morality and Conflict*.

[3] Bolt, *A Man for All Seasons*.

[4] Ibid., xiii.

eventually did go to his death, because he would not take an oath falsely. The details are irrelevant, but I mention in passing that More was required to confer legal and moral legitimacy on Henry VIII's wish to marry Ann Boleyn, and More, having run out of evasions, would not do so. He had unconditionally committed himself, and he was unwilling to take an oath, not even to save his life, that would have involved violating his commitment. More had many other commitments as well, and from these he retreated, when pressed, in "wonderfully good order." Thus, some commitments matter more than others, and unconditional ones matter more than anything else.

Unconditional commitments are the deepest, the most serious convictions we have; they define what we would not do, what we regard as outrageous and horrible; they are fundamental conditions of being ourselves. Unconditional commitments need not be universal, for they may vary from person to person. Nor are they categorical, for we may decide to violate them. But if through weakness, fear, or coercion we do violate them, we inflict grave psychological damage on ourselves, for the integrity of our characters depends on them.

More was a hero and a saint, and he died rather than violate his unconditional commitment. Most of us are made of softer stuff than More, but the violation of unconditional commitments is no less damaging to weaker people. There is a crisis, we do something that dishonors such a commitment, and we realize that we cannot come to terms with our act. If we had been what we conceived ourselves as being, we would not have done it, so we are not what we took ourselves to be. An abyss opens up at the center of our being; we disintegrate, go mad, or carry on in a desultory way looking in vain for a chance to undo the dreadful thing we have done.

One example of what happens when unconditional commitments are violated is Conrad's Lord Jim, who spent a lifetime expiating for his cowardice. Another is the guilt felt by many survivors of concentration camps who suspect that they survived at the expense of those who did not because they accommodated themselves to unspeakable evils that the dead, their betters, rejected. Other cases in point are Othello and King Lear, whose character flaws caused them to injure those who loved them most.

Many people have no unconditional commitments, and since having them renders us vulnerable, we may well wonder why we should be like More, or Antigone, and create in ourselves the potential to be driven to this state of "absolutely primitive rigor." If we take nothing *that* seriously, we are less prone to lasting psychological damage, we fashion ourselves with greater suppleness, and thus become better able to withstand the inevitable buffeting we suffer in life's treacherous waters. But this easy way out will not work. To show the need for unconditional commitments, I shall contrast them with defeasible ones.

Defeasible commitments are the stuff of everyday life in personal morality. They guide us in our intimate relationships and in whatever forms our personal aspirations take. The way we raise our children, the kind of marriage we have, how we respond to our friends, our attitude to the work we do, the direction in which ambition takes us, the fears we fend off, and the hopes that sustain us are all guided by the conventions we have adapted to our lives. But our commitments to these conventions are defeasible, because each could be reasonably overridden, if sufficiently strong considerations are found to weigh against them. The difference between them and unconditional commitments is that nothing we recognize as a good reason could override the latter, because our judgments of what reasons are weightiest are dictated by our unconditional commitments. They are the standards by which we measure, and unless we abandon our yardstick, there could not be rational considerations inclining us to reject conclusions properly derived from them.

As Bolt describes him, More was deeply in love with his wife, and he loved his children no less. Yet his commitments to marriage and parenthood were defeasible, because his religious commitment was deeper. When it came to the point, More honored his religious commitment and went to his death, while leaving his family to fend for themselves as well as they could. Someone else in More's position could have taken the oath falsely, because he had no unconditional commitments at all, or because he had it to marriage and parenthood and not to the dictates of his religion. Yet that could only have been done by a person More perhaps could have been but was not. More was what he was because his religious commitment took precedence over his other commitments.

It is conceivable for people to live good lives just by living up to their defeasible commitments. Lucky circumstances, phlegmatic temperament, intellect not given to reflection and self-analysis, the absence of political upheavals or glaring injustice, the enjoyment of robust health, a busy life, a happy family, and many good friends may make it possible for people not to have to ask themselves the kind of fundamental questions that, if answered at all, lead us to our unconditional commitments. For most of us, these questions do arise, because our defeasible commitments conflict and the conflict can be resolved only on a more fundamental level; because the lives we lead are hard or unsuccessful or unrecognized; because we waver in our defeasible commitments; or because we grow older and wonder whether the lives we live are the ones we should live. These questions force us to go deeper, and this is how unconditional commitments are connected with depth.

Not to have unconditional commitments is to lack depth. Without depth, we cannot arrive at the right interpretation of complex moral situations that the vast majority of us routinely encounter in the personal aspect of our lives. In these situations, unconditional commitments guide our interpretations. We judge well when we interpret complex situations in terms of the moral idioms suggested by the conventions to which we have committed ourselves. And the structure of our commitments ultimately rests on the few unconditional commitments; they provide the ultimate standards of our judgments. Thus, the cost of not having unconditional commitments is to be incapable of good judgment.

This incapacity may handicap us in different ways. One is through the lack of a strong sense of self. To have such a sense is to have made unconditional commitments, for the more defeasible commitments are, the more easily they are given up; but the more strongly we hold to our commitments, the firmer is our sense of identity. If we lack this strong sense of self, we face complex situations with uncertainty and doubt. We do not know how to interpret them, because we do not know how we, ourselves, enter into these situations. We lack objectivity, because we are unclear about what we are. The psychic space left empty by the absence of unconditional commitments is, thus, occupied by fantasy, fear, anxiety, and overcompensation, all of which color our selection of moral idioms and corrupt our interpretations.

Another way the lack of unconditional commitments handicaps us is through our incapacity to resolve conflicting interpretations suggested by defeasible commitments. Breadth acquaints us with the moral idioms of our social morality. When we defeasibly commit ourselves to some more limited range of them, we leave room for the possibility that our commitments may be overruled. But in the absence of unconditional commitments, we lack standards for establishing what could count against honoring defeasible commitments. And if honoring them is difficult, then, our weakness being what it is, we shall be tempted to count the difficulty itself as a countervailing reason. If our commitments are only defeasible, it becomes impossible to distinguish between strong and weak reasons for abandoning them. Unconditional commitments are needed partly because they can be appealed to in determining what should count as strong reasons for us. Thus, unconditional commitments are necessary for depth, as depth is necessary for good judgment.

Loose commitments are on the outer fringes of personal morality. Usually, their objects are the variable conventions regarding the local forms of deeper conventions to which we have unconditionally committed ourselves. More was a patriotic man, with a defeasible commitment to England. The form his patriotism took was fealty to his king, but obedience to his monarch was for More a loose commitment. The author of *Utopia* understood that the demands of patriotism are historically and socially conditioned.

Loose commitments are comparable to aesthetic style, to the manner in which creative artists express themselves and performing artists express their interpretations. If style is to be more than idiosyncrasy, it should be a vehicle suited for the expression of substance. Similarly for moral agents: their unconditional and defeasible commitments must be expressed, so there must be loose commitments giving form to their expressions. But some forms are more hospitable than others. When there are titles and honorifics, it is easier to express respect; before oaths and curses were cheapened into clichés, they were reliable indicators of serious resolve and enmity; when kisses and embraces were not indiscriminately bestowed on pets, children, and casual acquaintances, they were meaningful signs of love.

Hume called loose commitments "a kind of lesser morality,"[5] and Jane Austen called them "the civilities, the lesser duties of life."[6] Clearly, adherence to form is not a particularly praiseworthy moral achievement. Nevertheless, there need not be only a superficial connection between the forms of personal morality, embraced by loose commitments, and the substance of personal morality, to which we unconditionally or defeasibly commit ourselves. Ours is not a ceremonious age, and we are given to suspecting that attention to form is prompted by hypocritical attempts to disguise lack of content. But in societies more homogeneous and less mobile than ours, there is a seamless continuity from unconditional to defeasible to loose commitments. In such contexts, forms have a natural affinity with content. It is true that the occasional hypocrites may, then, take advantage of the reasonable presumption of having deeper commitments indicated by their observance of the forms, but most people do genuinely have them. There is not much point in regretting that our society is not like that. But even the most earnest scourge of hypocrisy must recognize that it is easier to live good lives when there are generally recognized and available forms they may take.

[5] Hume, *Enquiry*, 209.
[6] Austen, *Sense and Sensibility*, chapter 46.

UNCONDITIONAL COMMITMENTS AND DEPTH

The hierarchical structure of our commitments constitutes our moral perspectives. As we proceed from loose toward unconditional commitments, so we go in the direction of increasing depth. In discussing good judgment, I stressed the importance of depth but left incomplete the explanation of what it is. I did say that finding the right interpretation of complex moral situations, and thus selecting the appropriate moral idioms for characterizing them, depends, in addition to objectivity and breadth, also on depth. I can now add to this the explanation that depth consists in becoming aware, through moral reflection, of the hierarchical structure of our commitments—of our moral perspectives. But since reflection may reveal the absence of commitments or a jumble of incoherent commitments, it is insufficient for depth. And since we may have a coherent hierarchy of commitments without being aware of it, perhaps because we are unreflective or have never been forced to ask what really matters to us, the mere possession of a hierarchy of commitments is also insufficient for depth. Both the hierarchy, ranging from loose to unconditional commitments, and having become aware of it through moral reflection are required for depth.

As we have seen, this sort of reflection requires clarity and sensitivity. Both involve fitting our wants into the conventional possibilities available for their satisfaction. Because we have more wants than we can satisfy, and because there are many conventional ways of satisfying them, the fit between wants and conventions is imperfect. Through reflection we clarify what the available conventional possibilities are, and we become sensitive to what commitment to them would entail. Both involve a growing appreciation of moral idioms.

Clarification is articulation. As we leave behind simple moral situations in which social morality is an adequate guide, we encounter complex situations to which we must respond by finding out what our own hopes, fears, ambitions, desires, strengths and weaknesses are and what kind of close personal relationships we want and do not want. We begin with inchoate feelings of importance about some things; they seem fine or horrible, noble or base, but we do not really know why. Our aspirations impel us to find out, for only if we do so can we have a chance of achieving one and avoiding the other. We must make distinctions; put questions to ourselves; look at other people's lives and compare them to ours; ask and answer why their lives seem exciting or boring, admirable or wasted, inviting emulation or disgust. We do this, if at all, in terms of our moral idioms. Clarification is to learn to express in the moral idioms available to us what our moral possibilities are.[7]

Sensitivity is to gain imaginative entry into these possibilities, to understand them, as it were, internally. It is to discover the emotional reality behind the moral idioms with which breadth acquaints us. The object of this discovery is not merely the denotations and connotations of moral idioms but also understanding what it would be like for us to be the kind of person who sees a complex moral situation in this rather than in those terms.

Adopting a moral idiom for characterizing a complex moral situation always has a dual significance. On the one hand, we participate in the situation in a particular way and thus transform it. On the other, each interpretation we give adds its weight to our commitment to respond in certain ways. Thus, our interpretations transform us, as Strether's interpretation of whether Chad is being corrupted or refined has transformed Strether.

As we reflect, aiming for clarity and sensitivity, we are forced to ask ourselves about our commitments. For we answer the question of what moral idioms we should employ in terms of commitments to the conventional possibilities that suggest the idioms. And since there are alternatives, we must choose between them. As we understand and appreciate our options, so we reflect on the possibilities that best represent the kind of person we want to be.

Once again, More's life illustrates this. He was a reflective man of great depth. Thus, he knew where he stood. He was aware of many different ways of characterizing his situation, but he did not hesitate among them. What made his decision the only one possible for him was the hierarchy of his commitments. He saw life ultimately in terms of unconditional commitment to his God. The moral idiom that perhaps best fits him is faithfulness. There were other options and, of course, temptations. If he had perceived his situation primarily in terms of patriotism, he may have felt compelled to choose his allegiance to his country over allegiance to Rome. Or, he may have characterized it primarily in terms of love, and then the happiness of his wife and children would have dictated taking the oath falsely. Alternatively, he may have suspected himself of pride, of putting too high a value on his own word, and then humility would have required him to deceive. But he rejected all these interpretations and the moral idioms they suggested. He was aware of them, but they did not express his unconditional commitment. Robust, happy, hungry for life

[7] For a discussion of this difficult subject, see Taylor, "Responsibility for Self."

though More was, he gave it all up because, like Antigone, he knew that being what he was, was more important than boons.

More of the drama is a moral hero. Heroes are important to morality, because they inspire us and they embody in a clear form the virtues we may aim to cultivate in ourselves. More's dramatized life illustrates what it is to have a clear sense of ourselves through reflection on the structure of our commitments, how this reflection guides our selection of moral idioms, how actions flow naturally from what we are and in terms of what moral idioms we interpret complex moral situations, and, thus, how moral perspectives may issue in good judgments.

THE STRUCTURE OF COMMITMENTS AND THE STRUCTURE OF CONVENTIONS

Up to now in this chapter, I have been concentrating on an internal account of the relationship between individuals and their moral tradition. I have been trying to understand the elements responsible for the complexity of complex moral situations from the point of view of individual participants in them. This is, indeed, the concern of personal morality. But the relationship between individuals and their moral tradition is also shaped by social morality with its deep and variable conventions. Thus, we need to discuss a further feature of complex moral situations, this time from the external point of view, from the point of view of the conventions, which adds yet another dimension of complexity to already complex moral situations.

Corresponding to the hierarchical structure of commitments forming individual moral perspectives, there is also a structure inherent in the conventions of the social morality from which individual moral perspectives are derived. This latter structure is also hierarchical, and it is composed of strongly and weakly held conventions. Of course, it is still individuals who hold these conventions strongly or weakly, but I am interested here in the aggregate formed of these individual attitudes, rather than in the attitudes themselves. This aggregate allows one to make general statements about the moral outlook implicit in a social morality. The outlook depends on how strongly or weakly particular deep and variable conventions are generally held. As we have seen, in a healthy social morality, deep and some variable conventions will be strongly held, while other variable conventions will be weakly held. If deep conventions are weakly held, the minimum conditions for good lives are in jeopardy; if all variable conventions are weakly held, the society is threatened with disintegration; and if very many variable conventions are strongly held, the social morality will tend to be rigidly orthodox and, thus, lacking in flexibility to accommodate inevitable moral changes.

The question I want to consider now is the relationship between these two structures: the structure of commitments made by individuals and the structure of conventions prevailing in a social morality. What should be the relationship between the unconditional, defeasible, and loose commitments of individuals' moral perspectives and the strongly and weakly held deep and variable conventions of the social morality in which individuals live?

The first point to note is that commitments are to actions in accordance with conventions, so the relationship between commitments and conventions is bound to be intimate. The structure of conventions appears to individuals as the framework of their moral possibilities. The commitments individuals make represent a more or less conscious decision to try to realize some of these possibilities and to ignore others. Such decisions are guided by self-direction whose ultimate goal is the achievement of good lives.

The second point is that whether good lives are achieved partly depends on the congruence between the strength of individual commitments and the strength with which the conventions to which individuals commit themselves are generally held. If the unconditional commitments of individuals are to conventions weakly held by other people around them or if strongly held conventions elicit only loose individual commitments, then the people whose commitments these are will feel alienated from their social morality.

Morally speaking, this may be a good or a bad thing, depending on the moral standing of the social morality in question. If the moral credentials of a social morality are in order, as described in chapter 5, then alienation from it is at once morally suspect and stands in the way of good lives. It is morally suspect, because the strongly held deep and variable conventions do indeed protect everyone's well-being, and those who have only loose commitments to these conventions are likely to undermine the conditions for everyone's well-being. It also stands in the way of good lives for those who are thus alienated, because they are undermining the conditions of their own well-being by violating the requirements of decency, and thus, they live in a state of hostility with others in their context.

But alienation from social morality may be a good thing if the social morality is morally faulty. If individuals are unconditionally committed to deep conventions that ought to be strongly held in their social morality but are not, then they have the making of the kind of heroism the lives and deaths of Antigone and More illustrate. And if individuals have only loose commitments to variable conventions that, for no good moral reason, are strongly held in their social morality, then they may appear, in retrospect, as moral reformers with a sound sense of proportion, much as people who refused to be outraged by sexual experimentation a generation or two ago may appear to us now. However, although alienation may have excellent moral credentials, it still stands in the way of good lives if it spreads to several aspects of people's contact with their social morality. For, justifiably or not, they will still be morally at odds with their fellows, and so one element required for good lives will be absent from theirs.

The burden of these remarks is that there could be conflicts between personal and social morality, and the fault may lie on either side. The pursuit of good lives may be jeopardized, on the personal side, by faulty moral perspectives and, on the social side, by inhospitable social conditions. The world being what it is, the chances of correcting faulty moral perspectives are very much better than the chances of improving society. For the influence of individuals over their own moral perspectives is often decisive and always considerable, while their influence on society is almost always negligible. This should not stop us from exerting what little influence we have, but it should not blind us either to how little it is. The fact is that we are much more at the mercy of whatever the conditions happen to be in our social morality than at the state of our personal morality. This suggests the reasonable strategy for improving our lives. Correcting the faults of our moral perspectives, however, depends on recognizing the faults, and so I turn to the discussion of how more or less adequate moral perspectives can be distinguished.

MORAL PERSPECTIVES AND THEIR ADEQUACY

Our hierarchically structured commitments constitute our moral perspectives, and they, in turn, define our individual conceptions of good lives. To understand lives, both our own and others', is partly to understand the moral perspectives, the moving forces behind them. This understanding is derived from what we and others do or refrain from doing in many varied situations, including situations in which we characterize our own conduct. Actions, therefore, matter a good deal for understanding our moral perspectives. But, as Hume says, they matter "as signs or indications of certain principles of mind and temper."[8] The identical actions of different people may have vastly different moral significance, because they may indicate differ-

[8] Hume, *Treatise*, 573.

ent principles of mind and temper, that is, different moral perspectives.

In one sense, everybody has a moral perspective, because we have all made more or less conscious and more or less strong commitments to some of the conventions of our social morality. The possession of moral perspectives, in this sense, is like learning our native language. It is a necessary part of human education, but it is not a difficult achievement; only its lack is notable. As we grow in understanding and take charge of our lives, we transform these initial moral perspectives into increasingly personal points of view. We are forced to do this, although most of us also want to do it, because the moral perspectives with which we start are inadequate guides in complex moral situations. We must respond to complex situations, because we unavoidably participate in them and our responses are guided by what we are and want to be. As we reflect on the present and on the desired future, we go beyond our initial moral perspectives and begin the process of their transformation in the direction of greater maturity and more pronounced individuality.

Of course, this transformation can yield more or less adequate moral perspectives. We can derive from the arguments thus far presented certain minimum conditions adequate moral perspectives must meet if they are to lead to good lives. In discussing these conditions, I assume, for the sake of simplicity, that the social morality in the background is healthy. The complications introduced by the failure of this assumption will be discussed later. Given this assumption, moral perspectives should foster the satisfaction of universal wants, created by the facts of the body, self, and social life, by conforming to the deep conventions of the social morality prevailing in the society. They should also include commitments to some variable conventions and, thus, satisfy the requirements of decency. We can add to these conditions the requirement discussed earlier in this chapter, namely, that the commitments should form a hierarchical structure and, thus, have *order*.

A further requirement of adequate moral perspectives is *coherence*. Commitments should cohere, but failure to do so is a serious defect only if it occurs among unconditional commitments. Incoherence is a symptom of incompatible commitments; they result in conflicting interpretations of complex situations and in inconsistent prescriptions of how to act in them. If the incompatible commitments differ in importance, then their conflict is easily removed, for, obviously, the more important commitment should take precedence. Nor is the conflict serious if it occurs between loose commitments or between defeasible ones, for these conflicts can also be resolved by appealing to the standards set by deeper commitments. But what happens if the conflict is between unconditional commitments?

Consider, for instance, a young man who has unconditional commitments to social activism and scholarship. He is motivated in one direction by a passionate sense of social justice and a consequent feeling of obligation to do what he can for it. But he is also a historian convinced to have found reasons for the radical reinterpretation of his period, and his intellect, ambition, and curiosity provide powerful impetus for hard work. Both commitments draw on his energy, and neither social justice nor the revisionary thesis will be secure in the near future. He is young and energetic, and so far he has managed to honor both of these unconditional commitments. It is clear, however, that even though he has done respectably in both areas, he has not done as well as he could have if he had concentrated only on one. The danger signals are already there. As time goes on, he will age and have to slow down; he can plod on in both directions, but the cost will be increased frustration and the inability to do what he thinks he should in either area. Alternatively, he can give up one or the other and devote his energy to what he decides is the more important of the two. If he wants to have a good life, he must shift his moral perspective by demoting one of his incompatible unconditional commitments to a lesser rank.

The necessity of making our moral perspectives coherent is contingent on wanting to have good lives. We may not want that, because we have resolved on self-sacrifice, resigned ourselves to deep frustration, or given up the struggle to make ourselves better. The issue is well posed by this question: "[D]o you think that one can sell one's soul in a good cause?"[9] The answer is yes. My point here is that provided we have not done that, and we do want to have good lives, our moral perspectives should be coherent.

Adequate moral perspectives should be *rich* enough to guide our interpretations in a sufficient variety of familiar complex moral situations and also in hitherto unencountered ones. It is difficult to be precise about the optimal range of variety. The desirable range is a mean between the indiscriminate acceptance expressed by the slogan, nothing human is foreign to me, and the kind of systematic exclusion of the foreign and the unpleasant that characterized the morality of Woollett.

In one of those ghastly situations philosophers are fond of inventing, Jim walks into a South American village just in time to observe the preparations for the execution of many people. The man in

[9] Drabble, *The Needle's Eye*, 379.

charge of the proceedings offers Jim a choice: if Jim kills one of the people, the rest will be reprieved; if he does not, all will be killed as planned. What should Jim do?[10] My view is that our moral perspectives are not at fault if they are not rich enough to guide us in such fantastic situations. A moral perspective should be an adequate guide in circumstances we are likely to encounter. For the vast majority, this does not include the pros and cons of taking a hand in South American executions. If our lives normally, or even occasionally, involved such situations, moral perspectives should guide our conduct in them. As it is, most of us have the opportunity to deplore barbarism at many removes.

The point of these stories, of course, is not to represent a realistic situation but to test, in the light of difficult cases, what our commitments dictate if pushed to the extreme. But there are extremes and extremes. Reasonable ones to consider are those that we, living in civilized conditions, might encounter. Suicide, euthanasia, capital punishment are such; compulsory organ transplants, lifeboat situations, and the morality of dealing with extraterrestrial beings are not. It is a sign of the brutality of our times that conduct in concentration camps has become a borderline case.

The pursuit of good lives can be considered negatively and positively. The aim, viewed negatively, is to remove impediments that make good lives impossible or extremely hard to achieve; violations of the conditions set by the facts of the body, self, and social life are such impediments. But I am considering here the prospects of good lives positively, where the impediments do not exist and we have the energy, leisure, and opportunity to become self-directed. The kind of extremes in which moral perspectives developed in this context need not provide guidance take us back into the context in which we must contend with barbarism. And the kind of extremes that adequate moral perspectives should be rich enough to handle are those we can reasonably suppose to occur in civilized contexts.

Richness is a mean between indiscriminate inclusion and narrowminded exclusion. I have discussed the limits of inclusion, but what can we say about exclusion? How far can we reasonably go in the direction of restricting our moral perspectives? One example of going too far is provided by Kant. He writes: "[I]f nature has put little sympathy in the heart of a man, and if he, though an honest man, is by temperament cold and indifferent to the sufferings of others, perhaps because he is provided with special gifts of patience and forti-

---

[10] The case is Williams's in Smart and Williams, *Utilitarianism: For and Against*, 98–99.

tude and expects or even requires that others should have the same
. . . would not he find in himself a source from which to give himself
a far higher worth than he could have got by having a good-natured
temperament? . . . [I]t is just here that the worth of character is
brought out, which is morally and incomparably the highest of all: he
is beneficent not from inclination but from duty."[11] Kant recommends as the best moral perspective one characterized by the exclusion of all unconditional commitments, except the one to duty.

A fictional portrayal of the Kantian ideal is Mrs. Solness in Ibsen's
The Master Builder. She is a dutiful monster. With grim resolve, she
bends her will to do her duty. Her bitterness, resentment, and cold
fury are just bubbling under the moral exterior, but she has them in
control. She is determined to do what she thinks is right, even if it
kills her; and, in a way, it does, for as a feelingful, fallible, searching
human being, she is dead. The moral perspective from which she
views life allows her concern only for one thing: the Kantian ideal of
duty.[12]

What is wrong with this perspective is that it excludes almost everything that we normally need for good lives. It is clear that self-direction requires the deliberate frustration of some of our wants. But the
Kantian prescription goes further, and much too far, in calling for
the frustration of all wants as the highest ideal. It even suspects wanting to do our duty: we should do what is right, not out of inclination
but because we are compelled by the categorical imperative. So I conclude that moral perspectives should be rich enough to allow for the
satisfaction of more wants than the Kantian ideal does. But how
much more?

We can approach this question through the recognition that adequate moral perspectives must be *realistic*. By this I mean that our
perspectives must fit us and our situations. They can fail in this and
thus be unrealistic for many reasons. One kind of unrealism is inherent in perspectives that depend on character traits the agents do not
have or have only to an insufficient extent. Imagine, for instance, a
principled man of considerable strength of character who is morally
fastidious and unwilling to compromise what he thinks is right. Suppose, further, that he is an American and he is led by his convictions
to become a politician. He is unconditionally committed to political
work for the common good, as he sees it. Given this man's character,
and politics in America being what it is, he cannot but be frustrated.

[11] Kant, *Foundations of the Metaphysics of Morals*, 17–18.
[12] Another fictional treatment of the Kantian idea is Fontane, *Effi Briest*; see also the
discussion of it by Annas, "Personal Love and Kantian Ethics in *Effi Briest*."

I think that Woodrow Wilson was such a man, as the public calamity of Versailles and the private tragedy of his own disintegration show. His life as a politician was doomed from the start, because his moral perspective did not fit his character and circumstances. There was nothing wrong with his character; in fact, he was rather admirable, in the Presbyterian mold. Nor can we fault the morality of his political goals; they were certainly among the few reasonable options then current. The trouble was the combination of the political goals and the character. This man of straight thinking, simple moral certitudes, imbued with the manners and mores of Princeton, should not have been closeted with such masterful manipulators as Lloyd George and Clemenceau and be expected to escape with his purity intact. And when he finally emerged, soiled as he became, to have as his duty to sell the damaged goods he had been sold to a skeptical American public was beyond human endurance. That man, in that position, should not have had that moral perspective; it was psychologically unrealistic.

A moral perspective may be free from psychological tensions and yet be unrealistic, because the social context makes it difficult to come anywhere close to realizing the aspirations implicit in it. The classic example here is Don Quixote. The pursuit of courtly love, single combat, the fealty of servants, and knightly honor cannot succeed at a time when lovers, enemies, subordinates, and peers are guided by entirely different considerations. But harking back to a disappeared past is only one form lack of realism may take. Another is the perfectionist vision that rejects the supposedly evil present in the name of a projected idyllic future. The trouble with this is not only the idealization of a fantasized future but the rejection of the present. By casting this perspective upon the world, what actually surrounds us appears to be so corrupt that only very drastic change of it can make good lives possible. Perfectionists may differ on whether this change should be brought about by revolution, divine grace, the Second Coming, or by a return to the simple goodness of a pastoral state of nature. But they are at one in seeing the present as evil. And so they bring about their own death to escape corruption, as Simone Weil did; or advocate and commit horrible crimes to hasten the dissolution of the *status quo*, as various terrorists did and are doing; or they brutalize themselves by rejecting the benefits of civilization for which the less fortunate majority of mankind yearns, as many hippies turned dirt farmers are doing. They are all for the destruction of the present and, in being so, deprive themselves of the possibility of good lives. Their unconditional commitments are either to various forms of naysaying or to a chimerical future so distant as to be beyond their, and their children's children's, reach.

Another source of lack of realism is perhaps the most common of all. Many people have commitments capable only of transitory satisfaction, and these yield asymptotically diminishing returns. The lives of many gourmands and sexual conquistadores are characterized by intensely satisfying early peaks, followed by doldrums and then, the flesh being what it is, by incapacity. It requires no great sagacity to see that the longer such lives last, the more frustrating they are likely to be.

Moral perspectives may avoid the pitfalls I have so far discussed and still not permit good lives if they fail to *appeal* to us. We may dutifully follow our moral perspectives, and yet our lives may still be unfulfilling because there is no joy or excitement in them. Margaret Drabble in *The Needle's Eye* contrasts two people: both have unconditional commitments, both live according to fairly clear moral perspectives, but one does and the other does not appeal to the people who have them.

Here is Drabble's barrister talking: "I have a strong sense of obligation. It is on this sense of obligation that I have conducted my life. It is very destructive of the emotions. Had I ever trusted my emotions, I would have led a far less admirable existence, I can assure you." He is asked, "But in what sense, then, can you say that your existence has been admirable?" And he answers, "It has been admirable in that I have fulfilled my obligation. As I said, I've spent most of my time, I think, doing what on balance seemed I ought to do, not what I might have wanted to do, and now there isn't much that I do want to do."[13] Occasionally, this decent, drab, upright man finds someone whose life has what his lacks. And then, like a child against the candy store's window, he presses his nose, hoping to get a vicarious taste.

He is wistfully observing the life of a dowdy woman, no longer young, born rich, who has, for no very good reason, given away her wealth to a cause she now knows to be useless. She is clumsily trying to raise three children in largely self-inflicted squalor and messiness; she is not beautiful, not particularly intelligent, indeed, rather lacking in grace. And she says, " 'I've given up public causes . . . I think I ought to sit here at home and keep quiet and dig my own garden. Literally dig it, actually. Now that's the kind of activity that used to seem sublimely useless, and now at my age seems a good thing to do. . . . It's a privilege, to be able to learn the lessons I've learned. The

[13] Drabble, *The Needle's Eye*, 108.

lessons of the privileged. But that does not mean that I can't learn. I refuse to believe that I was damned from birth, you know. It would be rather hard, not to allow people to learn. I can't really believe all that once a lady always a lady.' . . . She smiled, suddenly cheerful. A sudden ripple of energy want through her, as she sat there: she lifted up a hand, and held it there, the fingers spread out, mocking, smiling, serious. 'All alone,' she said, 'I arrest the current of nature. I arrest it. I divert the current.' "[14]

This is the contrast I want: between "Now there isn't much that I do want to do" and "I arrest the current of nature . . . I divert the current." She is inspired; he is not. She is excited by life, he dutifully plods on. She lives in discomfort, clutter, poverty; he in decorous comfort. Yet, her life pleases her, and his life fills him with quiet desperation. Being that sort of English, they both carry on, of course, regardless. But with what a difference.

Moral perspectives must have *latitude* for change. By this I do not mean that we should be ready to change our commitments. Indeed, it is one of the conditions of good lives that if we have made a reasonable commitment, we should hold to it steadfastly. Furthermore, the more important the commitment is, the more damaging the change is likely to be. Yet, it is possible to make inappropriate, silly, vicious, or self-destructive commitments, and, in these cases, we would be better off if we changed them. To get clear, then, about what I mean by latitude for change, we should recognize that change may occur in two different contexts. In one, we are engaged in developing a moral perspective; in the other, the perspective has matured into a settled outlook on life.

The attempt to develop a moral perspective is the process of becoming self-directed. Trying here begins with the recognition that we have many wants, that not all of them are capable of satisfaction, and that some that might be satisfied should not be. At this stage, we begin to consider our aspirations and proceed, as it were, by trial and error. We try out roles, and we fantasize about them. Change is essential to this process, for it is essential to experimenting with commitments. Some people get stuck at this stage, cultivate roles, poses, personas, and lack serious commitments. Thus, they do not know what they really want and, as a result, cannot satisfy their wants. There is a time in life when commitments should be questioned and everything is still possible. And there is a time when we should have answered the questions and decided which possibilities to try to realize.

In the second context, after a moral perspective has become "a du-

---

[14] Ibid., 111–12.

rable principle of the mind," change still has an essential role, but it differs from its role in the first context. Moral perspectives should allow for change, but the rate of change has considerably slowed and what is changing has also altered. The change is not in our commitments but in our attitudes to them. The changing attitudes do not affect the strength of commitments either, for, in the context of a moral perspective, their respective importance is established; that is just what having a moral perspective means. The changing attitudes concern rather the connection between our commitments and our lives. There are seasons in life and our attitudes should change accordingly.

When our moral perspectives are new and we have just settled on the direction in which we want to go, the important things are in the future. The past is seen as something well left behind with its childishness, irresolution, and unclarity of purpose. The future is full of promise and risks, and our attitude to it may be hope, doubt, ambition, resolve, fear, confidence, optimism, and often a combination of several of these. The perspective is untried, like the first staging of a new play. On the other hand, in successful mid-life, when we possess a well-established perspective, the present, broadly understood, is the most important. We are engaged in doing what we want. These are the years when our perspectives are truly tested. If our commitments are defective, we shall bear the consequences. The future, old age, is seen as holding inevitable decline, ameliorated perhaps by the enjoyment of having achieved what we wanted or exacerbated by failure. And the past may be viewed wistfully as a time of great energy and enthusiasm, or a period of foolish innocence when the wrong or silly choices, now producing their bitter harvest, have been made. Finally, in old age, the future holds nothing at all. The time for summing up has come, and the best we can hope for is the continued satisfaction of seeing what we have, liking it, and having perhaps the greatest reward of all: the conviction that if we could do it all again, we would not do it very differently.

The rate of change is slow in these shifting attitudes toward the importance of the past, present, and future. Each phase may take decades. And, of course, the length of these phases is strongly influenced by the particular perspectives we have adopted. The rate for athletes is different from the rate for historians. Explorers are one thing; statesmen, another. I doubt that anything general can be said about the appropriate rate for change or about when it is fitting to change our attitudes. But I do think that a moral perspective failing to allow for changes is defective. For the old people who still live in the future, the middle-aged ones who believe that all is either before or behind them, and the youths who cultivate an air of settled opinions and sober judgment all fail to take notice of the passing seasons and the attitudes and sensibility appropriate to them.

To conclude, a moral perspective conforms to minimal standards of adequacy, and it will foster good lives if it satisfies the wants created by the facts of the body, self, and social life, prompts the observance of the appropriate deep and variable conventions of a healthy social morality, and if it has order, coherence, richness, realism, appeal, and latitude. Conformity to these minimal standards is necessary but not sufficient for the justification of eudaimonistically conceived moral perspectives. In chapter 11, I shall discuss the additional requirements of justification.

The reasons for seeking justified moral perspectives are the benefits derivable from them. These benefits maximize the chances of successful self-direction and, thus, the realization of personal aspirations and participation in desired intimate personal relationships. The means by which this is accomplished is the development of good judgment, enabling us to arrive at the right interpretations of the complex moral situations we inevitably encounter. Good judgment depends on objectivity, excluding the misinterpretation of complex situations through self-centeredness and fantasy; on breadth, acquainting us with our moral possibilities; on depth, involving conscious allegiance to hierarchically structured commitments; and on moral reflection, informing our objectivity, breadth, and depth with knowledge of our possibilities and limitations. In the realm of personal morality, this is what we can do to make our lives good. And in the realm of social morality, we can strengthen the framework that creates a hospitable setting for the efforts required by personal morality.

CHAPTER TEN

The Goods of Good Lives

> Everyone who has the power to live according to his own
> choice should . . . set up for himself some object for the
> good life to aim at . . . by reference to which he will do all
> that he does, since not to have one's life organized in view of
> some end is a sign of great folly.
>
> —Aristotle[1]

EXTERNAL AND INTERNAL GOODS

Moral perspectives may be thought to contain the legislative and judicial branches of good lives. Their task is to decide which wants are
to be satisfied and in what manner and to judge which interpretations
of complex moral situations are right. But these branches must be
conjoined, in the spirit of the metaphor, with the executive one, for
the object of decisions and judgments is to obtain the goods that
make life good, and this requires action. These goods may be external or internal,[2] and my purpose is to discuss the roles they play in
good lives.

Every good life is a way of life: an amalgam of personal projects
and various intimate and impersonal relationships conducted in the
context of a social morality. Goods are external or internal *to* such
ways of life. Internal goods are satisfactions involved in being and
acting according to our conceptions of good lives. External goods are
satisfactions derived from possessing the means required for living in
the ways we do and from receiving appropriate rewards for it. Typically, understanding, good judgment, clarity, and sensitivity are internal goods, while security, honor, prestige, and influence are external goods.

Philosophical discussion of external and internal goods faces a

---

[1] Aristotle, *Eudemian Ethics*, 1214b.

[2] The distinction between external and internal goods is Aristotle's; see especially
Nicomachean Ethics, book I. Aristotle's account is brief and obscure; my discussion derives from it, but I do not claim to be faithful to it. I am indebted to Cooper, *Reason
and the Human Good in Aristotle*, part 3, and "Aristotle on the Goods of Fortune," and
also to MacIntyre, *After Virtue*, chapter 14. I have adapted both Cooper's and Mac-
Intyre's discussions to my own purposes.

methodological problem. If such a discussion is to illuminate moral experience and be helpful in living good lives, it must have sufficient generality to transcend the confines of individual lives. Yet the further it goes in the direction of generality, the more it loses the concreteness required for illuminating individual experiences. "How could it be that a *subject*, something studied in universities (but not only there), something for which there is a large technical literature, could deliver what one might recognize as an answer to the basic questions of life? It is hard to see how this could be so, unless . . . the answer were one that the reader would recognize as one he might have given himself. But how could this be?"[3] Bernard Williams, who asks these questions, gives a discouraging answer and talks about the limits of philosophy.

But I do not think that we need to be discouraged. We know that philosophical discussion can illuminate individual experience because it has done so. Sensitive readers of Plato, Aristotle, Spinoza, Hume, Kant, and Mill come to appreciate the moral visions that permeate their texts, and they come to perceive them as moral possibilities, even if they do not choose them as their own. Nor is the concreteness of literature without general implications. How else could we recognize the permanent significance of Oedipus, Antigone, King Lear, Anna Karenina, or Ivan Karamazov? So the problem is not whether generality and concreteness can coexist, since they obviously can, but rather how to discuss good lives in a manner that unites these necessary concerns.

Such a discussion must go beyond giving merely a formal account of external and internal goods; it must become substantive. Thus, the requirements of the Kantian life of duty; the life of impartial benevolence advocated by utilitarians; the Christian imitation of Christ; the Enlightenment ideals of liberty, equality, and fraternity must be expressed in concrete social and personal terms if they are to mean anything to people exhorted to conform to them. The first step toward giving a substantive account is to include in it satisfactions universally required for all good lives, regardless of the contexts in which they are lived. These are the satisfactions of the wants created by the facts of the body, self, and social life; they are universal, primary, or necessary goods. No human life can be good unless it has a sufficient supply of them. But to know that prolonged starvation, exhaustion, and torture are incompatible with good lives falls very far short of knowing wherein consists the goodness of lives that escape brutalization and have the required comforts. So in giving a substantive ac-

[3] Williams, *Ethics and the Limits of Philosophy*, 1–2.

count of external and internal goods, we must go beyond universal goods and consider particular ones. My intention in doing so is not to recommend particular goods but to illustrate how they function as constituents of good lives.

With this in mind, consider the role particular external and internal goods may play in the lives of exemplary contemporary philosophers when all goes well for them. The external goods their lives yield are, among others, the salary they receive; the status they have at their university; the respect of their students and colleagues; the prestige they enjoy in the profession; and the influence their opinions carry. The internal goods are the satisfactions of having understood another philosopher's outlook; of knowing that they got a difficult argument just right; of having succeeded in presenting persuasively their own thoughts about a problem; of observing themselves gradually growing in understanding how philosophy illuminates the human condition, finding that it informs their lives and makes them more thoughtful and, perhaps, wiser persons; of feeling at home in a noble tradition. The general point this particular case suggests is that internal goods are satisfactions involved in the successful exercise of some of our dispositions in the context of a way of life to which we have committed ourselves, while external goods are satisfactions involved in possessing the means to their exercise and in receiving various forms of recognition for doing well.

One recurrent theme in philosophical discussion of this topic is that good lives should be independent of the vicissitudes of luck.[4] Thus, Nussbaum writes: "I shall use the word 'luck' . . . closely related to the way in which the Greeks themselves spoke of *tuche*. I do not mean to imply that the events in question are random or uncaused. What happens to a person by luck will be just what does not happen through his or her agency, what just *happens* to him, as opposed to what he does or makes."[5]

I shall not follow this usage because luck connotes chance events (see any dictionary), and the obstacles to good lives are natural events, not random or uncaused ones. What does not happen through our own agency need not happen by luck. Obstacles to good lives only seem like a matter of luck to us, because we lack the capacity to understand and control them. It is, therefore, more perspicuous to refer to the *contingency* of human lives than to their being subject to luck.

---

[4] For a historical account, see Cioffari, "Fortune, Fate, and Chance"; for a contemporary discussion, see Williams, "Moral Luck," and Nagel, "Moral Luck," and Nussbaum, *Fragility of Goodness*.

[5] Nussbaum, *Fragility of Goodness*, 3.

The recurrent theme, then, is that the good-making components of our lives should be our own contributions, dependent on our own efforts and not on the state of the world around us. This is the reason why Socrates could seriously claim that the good man cannot be harmed and that virtue is its own reward. Of course, he did not deny that we can be treated unjustly and be injured, but he thought that these sorts of injustice and injury are irrelevant to the goodness of our lives. For their goodness depends on what we are and do and not on what is done to us. The importance of this for the present discussion is that it is a natural extension of the Socratic view to suppose that since internal goods depend on exercising our dispositions, while external goods depend on circumstances beyond our control, good lives require only internal goods. I think that this is one of the great mistakes in moral philosophy, and I shall be arguing against it throughout this chapter. It will suffice to note here that we can trace to it the dangerous idea that moral purity requires turning inward, working for one's salvation while ignoring as much as possible the soiling, corrupting influence of the world. It is to overcome this danger that Plato has his philosophers return, inexplicably, to the cave; that Jesus advises, in a rare gesture toward prudence, giving Caesar his due; and that Kierkegaard preaches, misguidedly, as we shall see in the last chapter, purity of heart.

The Contingency of Goods

Let us approach external and internal goods through the distinction between moral and natural goods. Moral goods are benefits produced by human beings, while natural goods are benefits enjoyed without appreciable human intervention. Possessing innate talents, escaping injury in accidents or natural disasters when others around us are killed or maimed, being constitutionally immune to prevalent illnesses are natural goods; living in a stable society, cultivating one's talents, being loved are moral goods. External and internal goods are moral, because they are due to human agency. One difference between them is that in the case of internal goods, the human agency is primarily oneself, while external goods are benefits conferred on us by others and frequently by others acting on behalf of institutions.

Internal goods are achieved only as a result of personal effort. They are due to the cultivation of our talents, to working hard at some endeavor, to becoming proficient at the skills required by our way of life. Internal goods are the result of reasonable self-direction that proceeds in accordance with adequate moral perspectives. Internal goods are not accidental, because they require considerable effort; they do not come from the outside, because they are the by-products of our own activities; and they cannot but be deserved, because the agents are always responsible for achieving them. When technique becomes effortless for violinists; when historians are so familiar with their period that it seems much like lived-through experience; when mothers, through deep love, are intuitively attuned to the needs of their children; when teachers communicate to students the importance, excitement, and complexity of their subjects; then some of the internal goods necessary for making good these ways of life are present.

By contrast, individual effort is neither necessary nor sufficient for obtaining external goods. It is not sufficient, for we can be worthy and deserving of prestige, honor, respect, security, or influence, and yet they may elude us, because their distribution is unjust, or because our merits are unrecognized. Nor is personal effort necessary, for external goods may be given unfairly to the undeserving, and passing fashions, stupidity, or perversity may corrupt the distributing institutions. External goods should depend on the appreciation of merit, but the hard fact is that merit may be unappreciated, the distribution of external goods is a fickle affair, and their possession need not signify desert.

Nevertheless, it does not follow that the possession of external goods is entirely a contingent matter or that good lives depend only on our own efforts to gain internal goods. The possession of internal goods is also, in part, a contingent matter of luck, because it depends on natural goods, and the possession of natural goods is contingent. Internal goods involve the successful cultivation of our talents and capacities; and this, of course, requires effort. But the effort presupposes that we have the talents or the capacities to cultivate, and whether we do depends on the outcome of genetic lottery. So internal goods are not the pure products of human endeavor.

Furthermore, although external goods are often capriciously distributed, they need not be. The institutions and people in whose power it is to give or to withhold them may be just or unjust. In the long run, it is in everybody's interest that they should be just, because what they reward, then, are achievements that contribute to making lives better. Just distribution is not due to contingency but to the recognition of merit and to the general support of the institutional framework in which people produce and enjoy the relevant benefits. It is natural and expected to use some of the external goods one possesses for strengthening the institutions that justly distribute them. One of the uses of honor, influence, etc., is to defend and improve the future distribution of these rewards. The reason for doing so is not to perpetuate the *status quo* but to do our share in strengthening the endeavor in which we participate and from which we and others benefit. And since the general framework for these various endeavors is social morality, here is yet another reason why personal morality, involving participation in these endeavors, is inseparable from social morality, protecting the endeavors.

Thus, internal goods are not free of contingency, and external goods need not entirely depend on it. Both external and internal goods are required for good lives, for reasons I shall now go on to give, and so the goodness of lives is, to some extent, a contingent matter—the Socratic denial notwithstanding.

MIXED GOODS

Some things are good in themselves, others are good as means to something else, and yet others are good in both ways. I shall refer to these goods as intrinsic, instrumental, and mixed. In agreement with Plato,[6] I think that mixed goods are the best. External and internal goods are mixed. Insofar as they are good in themselves, they are constituents of good lives, and insofar as they are means, they help to bring good lives about.

In an autobiographical passage, Virginia Woolf wrote: "Perhaps this is the strongest pleasure known to me. It is the rapture I get when in writing I seem to be discovering what belongs to what; making a scene come out right; making a character come together. From this I reach what I might call a philosophy; at any rate it is a constant idea of mine; that behind the cotton wool is hidden a pattern."[7] The discovery of the hidden pattern was one of the internal goods of her life. It was intrinsically good because she wanted it for itself. It and her writing were inseparably intertwined; she did not write in order to get this "strongest pleasure," and the pleasure was not the reason for further writing. Her way of life and this internal good were related as a whole is to one of its constituents. However, this constituent was not a detachable part but more like the shade of a color, the mood of an experience, or the style of a monument. One permeates the other; it is integral to it. Just so was the pleasure of the discovery of the hidden pattern intrinsic to her life. She lived the way she wanted, she was being and doing what she reflectively and reasonably decided to be and to do, and she found it satisfying. That satisfaction, experienced in that way, is what makes this internal good intrinsically

[6] Plato, *Republic*, 357–58.
[7] Woolf, *Moments of Being*, 72.

good. But it is also instrumentally good, because it was required for making her life good. Its instrumentality, however, is not a means-end connection but one of participation, composition, or constitution. Whether her life was, on the whole, good, I shall not venture to say; but it was certainly good insofar as it had this internal and mixed good.

Generally speaking, internal goods are indications that our lives are going well. They are not infallible indications, because the satisfactions they give us may be outweighed by frustrations encountered in other aspects of our lives. Nevertheless, internal goods are enjoyed as a result of living according to our commitments. Thus, they are doubly satisfying: as confirmations that the supposed good lives we are directing ourselves toward are indeed good and as genuinely enjoyable experiences of satisfying our important wants. They come to us when we are living and acting as we think we should, and they give us reasons to believe that we are correct in so thinking.

External goods are also mixed. The instrumental part of their mixture consists in being direct means to internal goods and, thus, indirect means to good lives. Internal goods are produced by the exercise of our talents and capacities. External goods are means to internal goods, because they play a necessary role in establishing the conditions in which talents and capacities can be exercised. The optimal conditions for the appropriate activities differ from endeavor to endeavor and from person to person engaged in the same endeavor. Athletes require one thing, scholars another; some athletes and scholars function best when seriously challenged; others need to be unruffled to do well. If we are engaged in an endeavor, we must be able to cope with adversity, for the conditions are rarely optimal. But adversity can grow so strong as to undermine the conditions in which even the most steadfast of us can carry on. When scholarship is politicized and scholars' lives depend on the conclusions they reach; when war or revolution wrecks the society in which creative artists work; when lifelong brutalization leads a mother's children to become vicious; when soldiers are forced to fight against their convictions in an unjust war; when circumstances compel statesmen continually to have to choose between recognized evils; when students contemptuously jeer at the traditional values teachers aim to impart; then the internal goods these endeavors normally yield recede beyond reach. And even if they are achieved against such heavy odds, their enjoyment must appear to be morally suspect, given the context. They will seem like fiddling while Rome burns, and the corruption of the satisfaction thus derived is not mitigated by the fiddler not having started the flames. When the conditions for living any kind of good life are undermined, the appropriate response is to strengthen the conditions rather than feast on the remaining dregs.

The dissolution of society is one way in which the lack of external goods can jeopardize the achievement of internal ones. Another is personal misfortune, which can handicap us even in societies hospitable to our endeavors. Extreme poverty; poor education; recurrent physical or psychological abuse; not being taken seriously by fellow participants in our endeavors; systematic discrimination; having to earn a living by doing a soul-destroying job; happening to be out of step with the dominant fashion and, thus, receiving no recognition may make it impossible to do whatever our ways of life call for with sufficient concentration and energy to derive the internal goods more fortunately situated people can enjoy.

It may happen that people are deprived of external goods through their pride, bitterness, stupidity, timidity, pettiness, self-doubt, or envy. But the lack of external goods often has nothing to do with character defects. Poverty, crime, discrimination, and injustice frequently handicap people through no fault of their own. In any case, the general point, put negatively, is that external goods are instrumental to internal ones, and if people lack the first, whether culpably or not, they cannot have the second. More positively, we can say that at least some degree of physical and financial security, justice, and respect are external goods necessary for continued engagement in our endeavors and, hence, for the enjoyment of internal goods derivable from these endeavors.

But external goods are also intrinsically good, if they are rewards for our achievements. Security, prestige, respect, and status make our lives better. They are good in themselves, because they are indications that our achievements are valued. Those who contribute to the well-being of others ought to receive recognition, and external goods are these recognitions. They are intrinsically satisfying in two ways. First, as justly earned rewards they are public confirmations that we are doing well at our ways of life. They provide an objective corollary to the enjoyment of internal goods our activities yield by showing that others appreciate what we are doing. And second, external goods are intrinsically good also as specific contents that forms of appreciation have. They confer privilege because their recipients receive a greater share of scarce goods than others. If the system of distribution is just and if the goods received enhance the recipients' enjoyment of their lives without injuring others, then there is nothing objectionable about such privilege.[8] It is fitting and proper that a great violinist

---

[8] On this point, see Vlastos, "Justice and Equality," section 4.

should have a Stradivarius to use; that parents who raise their children well should be especially respected by them; that administrators responsible for the smooth functioning of organizations should have greater influence than others have; that first-rate scientists, artists, or scholars should have the prestigious task of evaluating the performance of others; or that great actors should have the first pick of roles.

Of course, this rosy picture assumes that the distribution of external goods is just, so that reward is commensurate with achievement and that justly received external goods will not be misused. Both assumptions can and often do fail. And because they do, deserving people may be deprived of good lives. But this is not an acceptable reason for denying that external goods are both intrinsically and instrumentally good. On the contrary, it should act as a spur for assuring that people should receive the external goods that are their due.

Thus, external goods make our lives better, if we have them, and worse, if we do not. But since the distribution of external goods is an unreliable affair, the question of whether and to what extent we can do without them often arises. The Socratic answer is that we should learn to do without them altogether, and if we fail to do so and are made miserable by their lack, we are to be blamed. For it is the beginning of wisdom to understand that in trying to live good lives, we can count only on our own efforts; everything beyond them is in the domain of contingency. Now we have a further reason for rejecting the Socratic answer. Just as natural goods are both necessary for internal goods and beyond our control, so, often, are external goods. Hence internal goods, and consequently, good lives, cannot be freed from the influence of contingency.

However, the Socratic answer has long survived, and it would not have, unless it had some important truth to it. My account of external goods as being both intrinsically good, as rewards, and instrumentally good, as means to internal goods, makes it possible to identify what is true and what is false in the Socratic answer. The truth is that good lives are possible without external goods as rewards; but this does not mean, as it has been falsely supposed, that good lives are possible without external goods as means. We can live enjoyable and morally meritorious lives without basking in the wealth, respect, status, prestige, and influence that a juster distribution would bestow on us. And many otherwise good lives have been ruined by the resentment, anger, envy, jealousy, and bitterness produced by the frustrated expectation of just rewards. Socrates is surely right to warn us against this danger. Nevertheless, social instability, physical insecurity, extreme poverty, personal misfortune, living in the midst of war or revolution do jeopardize and often make impossible the enjoyment of internal goods. The external goods from which these misfortunes deprive us are often beyond our control. Yet, by being means to internal goods, they are, *contra* Socrates, required for good lives.

THE ENJOYMENT OF GOODS

External and internal goods, then, are alike in being moral, mixed, and, in their different ways, necessary for good lives. But there are also important differences between them. External goods come to us from the outside, internal goods are the by-products of our own activities. External goods are given by institutions or people, and they are received by individuals. The process is public, and it can be seen by all who care to look. It may be more difficult to perceive the respect or influence people enjoy than it is to observe financial rewards, but the difficulty is routinely overcome by historians, novelists, and anthropologists. It is otherwise with internal goods. People's possession of them can be observed by others, but the possibility depends on those enjoying them letting on that they do so. The greater privacy of internal goods is due to their origin. They are the satisfaction involved in doing well at our endeavors; the enjoyment of being and doing what we set out to be and do. Two people can engage in the same activity, do equally well at it, but one may and the other may not derive satisfaction from it, because the satisfaction depends on the place of the activity in the two lives. A scholar and an ideologue can both penetrate to the core of a system of ideas, but the understanding they share may be an internal good for the scholar and anathema for the ideologue. An amateur mountain climber and a professional rescue worker may attain the same difficult peak, but what is an exhilarating experience for one is merely a demanding day's work for the other. Internal goods depend on the relation between activities done well and the moral perspectives of the agents; external goods depend on the relation between the activities of the agents and the public regard for them. As a result, we can enjoy internal goods without, or even in opposition to, existing institutions, while external goods are inseparably connected to them.

The relation between internal goods and the agents possessing them is direct, while that between external goods and their recipients is indirect. The direct relation is due to the absence of any mediating agency between people and internal goods. Internal goods are related to activities as being amused by an anecdote is to hearing it, finding a short story subtle is to reading it, regarding an argument as elegant is to understanding it. As amusement, subtlety, and elegance are not fully explicable in terms of the objects that occasion them, so also the enjoyment of internal goods is not derivable solely from the activities of which they are by-products. As amusement, subtlety, and elegance require agents to bring discrimination to appropriate objects, so the enjoyment of internal goods requires agents to view their activities from their moral perspectives. In the case of internal goods, the objects we find satisfying are our own activities. Thus, we shall not fail to find satisfaction in them, provided our moral perspectives are adequate, for the satisfaction comes from the sense that our lives are going as we wish. When we come to external goods, however, the objects that satisfy us are only contingently connected to what we have done. The relation between external goods and their recipients is indirect because there stands between them some distributing agency or another.

External goods are competitive; internal goods are not. The more some people have of money, status, influence, prestige, the less is left for others. External goods depend on our standing in a hierarchy that is maintained by an institution, part of whose function is to compare and rank achievements and distribute the scarce external goods. Universities and professional organizations, like the Modern Language Association or the International Olympic Committee, are clear examples. Museums, editorial boards of publishers, personnel officers in large corporations, the consensus of literary or art critics are less well defined institutions. And families, schools, and neighborhoods are looser still. The salient fact is, however, that if external goods were not scarce and competitive, they would not be the rewards they are.

It is tempting to be knowing and cynical about this, but the temptation should be resisted. If an institution is functioning moderately well, the distribution of external goods is by and large just, and the endeavor, the *raison d'etre* of the institution, is beneficial, then the competition for scarce goods serves everyone's interest. To know how institutions function and to enjoy external goods is not to be corrupt. Corruption is to use that knowledge and external goods to manipulate the institution or to fail to use them to improve the institution when it is needed.

Understanding what we or others regard as internal goods always has a kind of importance that a similar understanding of external goods has only exceptionally. For to know what count as internal goods for people is to know what their conceptions of good lives are and, thus, to know what they are about. It is to understand the roots of their actions, the hierarchy of their commitments, their moral perspectives. To understand ourselves in this way is essential to living a good life, for, as we have seen, depth and good judgment presuppose it. Understanding the place of internal goods in other people's lives is, in turn, necessary for establishing intimate relationships with them. For part of intimacy is to know what matters to others and to know whether their lives are going well or badly.

By contrast, normally we can be close friends with others or love them deeply without needing to know much about the external goods they possess. I say this holds only normally, because exceptional rewards or deprivations clearly make a difference to how good lives are. But if the exceptional does not happen, then how the world regards our friends or those we love is not an important aspect of our relationships with them. What counts is how they think they are doing at what matters to them and not what others think. Only if the intrusion of the world seriously influences their enjoyment of internal goods does it become a matter of concern. This, of course, is just another way of saying that since the connection between internal goods and good lives is much closer than it is between external goods and good lives, intimacy requires paying more attention to the former than to the latter.

MORAL MERIT AND PERSONAL SATISFACTION

There are several ways of misinterpreting the distinction between external and internal goods. One is to confuse it with the distinction between public and private goods. In one sense, both external and internal goods are private. For part of what makes them good is that they are satisfactions, and satisfactions are private experiences. In another sense, internal goods are often private and external goods are public, because the objects of the satisfactions involved in them are usually private and public in their origin. The usual objects of satisfaction, in the case of internal goods, are our own activities, while for external goods, they are the high regard others have for us. But the activities that may occasion our satisfactions need not be always private. It may be that the activities we find satisfying are our growth in understanding, aesthetic appreciation, or depth, and these are indeed private. However, the activities may also be performing in a first-rate chamber music group, playing an excellent game of chess, or putting a case so persuasively as to change the opinions of many people. Hence the private-public distinction cuts across the distinction between external and internal goods.

The reason for stressing this point is to make clear that lives made good by the possession of external and internal goods need not involve the kind of self-realizationist inwardness that makes us turn away from the world. Good lives could, I suppose, take that form, but usually they involve participation in the world. For the satisfying activities often essentially involve others, require cooperation with them, and depend, for success or failure, on the effect they have on them. Thus, self-directed lives need not be self-centered.

Another, closely related, misunderstanding fuels the suspicion that the pursuit of external and internal goods is a form of selfishness. It may be objected to the search for good lives I have been describing that it is search for selfish lives; the satisfactions are self-satisfactions; and the goods sought benefit ourselves, not others. The truth in this charge is that the lives made good are indeed ours and that they are made good by the satisfactions we seek and enjoy. Yet the accusation of selfishness is unfounded, because the activities that make our lives good and occasion our satisfactions may be altruistic. Part of what may make the lives of physicians, teachers, mothers, statesmen, novelists, and fire fighters good is that they benefit others. These people, and others, want good lives and satisfactions for themselves, but achieving them depends on promoting other people's welfare. Thus, wanting good lives for ourselves is not only compatible with wanting them for others but often presupposes it.

The aura of selfishness, however, may continue to linger. Self-direction can involve benefiting others, but, it may be objected, benefiting them comes from mixed motives. Caring about their welfare is a means to our welfare, so we do not care for them genuinely, but only as a condition of our own good. I think that there is a sense in which the motives of self-directed people are usually mixed. But I do not think that the mixture is bound to be one of selfishness and altruism, nor that mixed motives are bound to be less genuine than unmixed ones.

It will be recalled that self-direction typically occurs in complex moral situations where the requirements of morality can be discovered only by good judgment. And good judgment involves interpreting complex moral situations from the point of view of our moral perspectives. Assume for the sake of simplicity that these moral perspectives are adequate. Each judgment, then, unites two concerns. The immediate one is to interpret the situation correctly and act accordingly. The more reflective one is to understand how the interpretation and action bear on the moral perspective in the background. The moral perspective is composed of a hierarchy of commitments, and these commitments are dispositions to interpret complex moral situations in certain ways and to act on the interpretations. Thus, each interpretation and each action strengthens or weakens the commitments in the background and thereby leaves its mark on the moral perspective. The more fully people realize the dual significance of each act of judgment, the more self-directed they are; that is, the more aware they are of the moral process of transforming themselves from what they are to what they think they ought to be, the more likely it is that they will succeed in this endeavor.

If moral judgments are understood in this way, we can see that they have indeed two concerns: an immediate one, bearing on the situation at hand, and a long-term one, bearing on moral self-improvement. One can describe these two concerns as constituting mixed motives, but the description does not deserve the stigma usually attached to it. Wanting to become morally better is something we want for ourselves, but what we thus want is to have, among other things, due regard for the welfare of others. The confusion giving rise to the charge of selfishness involves an unwarranted inference from the correct observation that self-direction is centrally concerned with making good lives for ourselves to the incorrect supposition that making good lives for ourselves is bound to be selfish, that it is bound to exclude concern for the welfare of others.

A third confusion about the distinction between external and internal goods is due to ignoring that both are intrinsically and instrumentally good. The confusion is to think of internal goods as the true satisfactions, while external goods are merely conditions, perhaps grudgingly admitted to be necessary conditions, of the satisfactions internal goods may give us. This is doubly mistaken.

First, external goods are not only means to internal goods; they can be good in themselves. It is hypocritical to deny that the security, comfort, prestige, or honor we justly receive are intrinsically enjoyable. Of course, we do not merely bask in them but put them to various uses. However, I see no good reason for supposing that having uses is incompatible with being intrinsically enjoyable. Why could not a recipient of the Nobel Prize both find it satisfying in itself and make use of the money?

Second, internal goods are also instrumental, and, if the distributing institutions are just, they are instrumental to external goods. For, in that case, external goods are rewards given for the very activities whose enjoyment constitutes internal goods for the agents. The goodness of the lives of violinists, poets, scholars, and inventors consists precisely in finding satisfaction in the activities for which just institutions may reward them.

All three of these misinterpretations of the distinction between external and internal goods are traceable to the supposition that moral merit and personal satisfaction are at odds with one another. If moral merit is thought to consist in controlling our base urges, of not doing what we want to do, then it is indeed hard to reconcile it with personal satisfaction; for how could it be satisfying to frustrate ourselves? And, of course, it would be wrong to deny that we have base urges that ought to be controlled. But if moral merit is understood only in this negative way, then it becomes incomprehensible why reasonable people wish to have it. It is readily understandable why people or society would demand moral merit from others, but not why those who are not duped by this insidious coercion would fall in with it.

The alternative is to recognize that moral merit has to do, not only with the avoidance of harm to others, but also with the achievement of benefits both for ourselves and for others and with the avoidance of harm for ourselves. Given this recognition, it becomes obvious that reasonable people wish to live morally meritorious lives, because they wish to have the benefits and avoid the harms; that, since benefits for ourselves normally involve engagement in activities that benefit others, reasonable people are not selfish; and that moral merit and personal satisfaction coincide, because it is personally satisfying to have the benefits morality makes possible. This is the reason why eudaimonism requires good lives to be both morally meritorious and personally satisfying. The contribution of this chapter has been an account of the nature of the sought for benefits in terms of external and internal goods.

We began with the blunt claim that good lives depend on doing what we reasonably want to do. I have been engaged in making it less blunt by exploring the significance of the limitation reason imposes on us. We may say now, in a summary way, that these limitations require that we should conform both to the deep conventions of our moral tradition and to some of the variable ones, that our moral perspectives should be adequate, and that we should have a sufficient amount of external and internal goods in our lives. If our lives are lived within these rational limits, then we have done all we can to make them good.

I shall close with three observations about the eudaimonistic conception of good lives. One is that although good lives partly depend on contingency, they also depend on effort. The element of contingency enters, because the external and natural goods we need are often beyond our control; they may elude us even if we do all we can to possess them. The various forms of effort we can make to achieve good lives, eudaimonistically understood, is what I have called self-direction. If we fail at it, we shall fail to make our lives good in this way. Thus, provided we want to have the sort of lives I have been describing, there is no alternative to self-direction, although not even successful self-direction guarantees its achievement.

Another observation is that each of the requirements mentioned in the penultimate paragraph presupposes social morality and decency, although they do so in different ways. The first, because social morality protects the social context within which good lives are possible; the second, because the possibilities we aim to realize through self-direction are provided by social morality; and the third, because the justice of the distribution of external goods, necessary as means and as rewards, depends on decency prevailing in our society. Consequently, social and personal morality are inseparably connected, and both are required for good lives.

The last observation is a reminder that I am discussing good lives from the point of view of a particular moral tradition: eudaimonism. This tradition is pluralistic and, thus, recognizes that good lives may take many different forms, both eudaimonistic and others. Thus, I have no intention of excluding the possibility of other conceptions of good lives. But they need to be argued for, as I am trying to argue for the eudaimonistic one. A successful argument of this sort would not, of course, detract from the goodness of lives eudaimonistically interpreted.

CHAPTER ELEVEN

The Justification of Eudaimonism

> Moral philosophy is the examination of the most important
> of all human activities, and I think that two things are
> required of it. The examination should be realistic. Human
> nature has certain discoverable attributes, and these should
> be suitably considered in any discussion of morality.
> Secondly, since an ethical system cannot but commend an
> ideal, it should commend a worthy ideal. Ethics . . . should
> be a hypothesis about good conduct and about how this can
> be achieved.
>
> —Iris Murdoch[1]

PLURALISM AND JUSTIFICATION

If there is no *summum bonum*, then there are many different good
lives possible. And if that is so, it follows that, beyond certain minimum requirements, there are no statable limits on the forms good
lives may take. But if there are no such limits, then the specification
of the requirements for good lives cannot consist in a complete list of
necessary and sufficient conditions. For, first, an unspecifiable variety
of circumstances external to lives may prevent them from being
good, and, second, good lives require the development of individuality that depends on features different from life to life.

It is a further consequence of pluralism that we cannot specify even
all the necessary conditions of good lives. For, if moral possibilities
are indeed open-ended, then existing good lives need not exhaust the
possibilities. We cannot tell whether the necessary conditions we can
enumerate now are all the necessary conditions there are, because we
cannot test the completeness of our list against untried possibilities.
And since this will always remain so, it is pointless to seek completeness. Can we say, however, that *any* of the conditions I have discussed
are actually necessary for *all* good lives? I shall argue that we can say
this of some conditions. But beyond these, there are some additional
conditions that eudaimonistically conceived good lives must meet. My

---

[1] Murdoch, *The Sovereignty of Good*, 78.

aim in this chapter is to discuss these conditions and show how the eudaimonistic conception of good lives can be justified.

The fundamental claim of eudaimonism is that good lives depend on maintaining a balance between our moral tradition and individuality. We find our lives good if we succeed in satisfying our wants. But since some wants are trivial, and their satisfaction does not matter, while others are destructive, and their satisfaction is harmful, this short answer needs to be expanded to explain how important wants are identified and what satisfactions are reasonable to seek. My explanation appeals to personal and social morality, for they provide the possibilities and limitations of good lives. Since many of these possibilities and limitations exist independently of the particular lives that conform, or fail to conform, to them, they also provide the independent standards by which lives can be objectively judged. Thus, provided that our subjective judgments about the goodness of our own lives are made reasonably, that is, by taking our possibilities and limitations into account, they actually presuppose objective judgments regarding the conformity of our lives to independent standards. So the relationship between subjective and objective judgments about the goodness of our lives is not that objectivity imposes additional and stricter requirements than mere subjectivity does; rather, the reasonability of subjective judgments is inseparable from concurring objective judgments. Thus, objective justification is required by the good lives we seek, not by misplaced epistemological fastidiousness.

The ultimate test of the goodness of our lives is whether they involve the lasting possession of external and internal goods and whether the satisfactions derived from their possession outweigh, in quantity and quality, such hardship and suffering as we experience. Only lives with deep roots in personal and social morality can pass this test. For the lasting possession of these goods presupposes that we have a conception of a good life for ourselves and we engage in activities appropriate to it; that we find these activities satisfying in themselves and we receive for them the various forms of public recognition that we need and are our due; and that our society and its institutions are hospitable to our endeavors.

One contribution we can make toward passing this test is to become self-directed, with all that it entails. We need to construct an adequate moral perspective for ordering our commitments; develop our characters in the direction of greater objectivity, breadth, and depth; master the moral idioms of our tradition; and improve our reflection in complex moral situations. We need, in short, to acquire good judgment. The other contribution required of us is to conduct ourselves decently by observing the deep and some of the variable conventions of our social morality, provided the social morality is healthy, or to do what we can to improve it if it is defective.

Self-direction is reasonable because it is constitutive of good lives, while decency is reasonable because it protects the conditions in which good lives can be lived. We derive self-direction from our personal morality, and we learn about decency from our social morality. Thus it is that good lives presuppose both personal and social morality, not as superimposed external standards, but as standards to which reasonable people would wish to conform.

SUBJECTIVISM AND OBJECTIVISM

The problem of establishing what judgments about good lives are reasonable, however, goes deeper than I have so far indicated. The requirement that objective judgments, concerning independent standards, and subjective judgments, concerning the satisfaction of our wants, should concur remains vacuous unless the belief that they concur is itself reasonable. And when we ask what would make this latter kind of belief reasonable, the dichotomy between objective and subjective ways of judging their reasonability confronts us once more. For one answer to the question of what makes it reasonable to believe that both independent standards and the satisfaction of wants support the judgment that particular lives are good is that the people living these lives sincerely hold this belief. The other answer is that the belief is reasonable only if we go beyond what the people in question sincerely believe and find that their beliefs have independent grounds. As we have seen, the first answer is given by subjectivists, the second by objectivists. I shall now consider them further.

Subjectivism, then, is the view that if people believe that they possess the external and internal goods they reasonably seek, then there is nothing further that can or needs to be given by way of additional support for their beliefs. When all is said and done, according to subjectivism, we ourselves are the final judges of the goodness of our lives.

Objectivism requires more. Subjective justification is necessary but not sufficient for the reasonability of the belief that our lives are good, because we may be mistaken in believing in the goodness of our lives. This belief is reasonable, from the objective point of view, only if the likelihood of its being mistaken is eliminated. Objective justification calls for going beyond what we believe, to ascertain the correctness of our beliefs. Subjectivists deny and objectivists assert that this can be done.

My view is that objectivists are right in this dispute. But objectivism has two versions, and only one of them is correct. The difference between the two versions hinges on the nature of the grounds to which we appeal in trying to eliminate mistaken subjective judgments. One version of objectivism is that these grounds are ontological; the other is that ontological grounds permit only minimal objectivity and that we must appeal to epistemological grounds as well. I shall call these two versions *ontological* and *eudaimonistic* objectivism, and I shall defend the latter.

The ontological objectivist argument derives from a conception of human nature. According to it, human beings are essentially alike. The differences among us are secondary elaborations. Human lives consist in activity in accordance with our essential nature. This is our function. Good is for us what aids the exercise of this function; bad is what hinders it. The goal of human lives is to realize the potentialities inherent in human nature. The extent to which lives are good depends on the extent to which this is done. This presents an objective ground for judging whether our beliefs about the goodness of our lives are justified. The best life is the complete realization of all essential possibilities. This ideal may be unattainable, but human lives can still be compared and evaluated on the basis of how closely they approximate it. A life is better, and it is more rational than another, if it comes closer to the ideal. I have sketched ontological objectivism roughly in an Aristotelian vocabulary, but a closely similar conception is held by Plato and many Christian moralists. So ontological objectivism has impressive credentials.

Nonetheless, I find it seriously flawed, for the connection between human nature and good lives is not as ontological objectivists suppose. Human nature includes benign and vicious characteristics, rational and irrational tendencies, the capacities for selfishness and altruism, stupidity and intelligence, love and aggression. If good lives depend on realizing the potentialities in our nature, then some irrational and immoral activities will be part of it. From the fact that human nature potentially is in certain ways, it does not follow that it ought to be in those ways. In fact, trying to live good lives must include repressing some human potentialities. The question of which parts of our complex nature we should curb or foster is crucially relevant to good lives. But it cannot be answered by reference to human nature, for it is our nature that prompts the question.

Subjectivists see this problem clearly. Their position follows from what they take to be the impossibility of objective grounds for justifying good lives. Human nature does not provide such grounds and, according to them, there is no reason for supposing that any other grounds are available. In the light of this, subjectivists conclude that the best policy for human beings is to make a decision about how they want to live. The decision is a leap in the dark, but without it, we shall certainly waste our lives, while taking it holds out the possibility of lives that we may find good. If our decisions lead to such lives, they have been justified to the fullest extent possible. This justification, however, is subjective, for it is based on how we regard our lives. To hope for more is an illusion. Subjectivism is the position of emotivists and of many egoists and existentialists.

The central difficulty with subjectivism is that it overlooks two considerations: one about human nature and the other about the possibility of mistaken subjective judgments. Subjectivists are correct in supposing that we cannot infer from human nature what lives are good. What they fail to see is that we can infer from human nature what lives cannot be good. There are certain conditions all lives must meet, if they are to be regarded as being even subjectively good; these conditions follow from human nature. Meeting them does not guarantee good lives, but failing to meet them guarantees bad lives. Since these conditions are independent of what anyone believes, and since they apply to all human lives, they are objective. The other consideration overlooked by subjectivists is that objective justification is needed, because we may be mistaken about the goodness of our lives. We may believe that we are satisfied with them and be wrong. Since satisfaction is something we all seek, it is in everyone's interest to eliminate errors.

My argument will proceed in two stages. First, I shall argue against subjectivism by showing how subjective judgments could be mistaken. And then I shall argue for eudaimonistic objectivism by showing how reasonable objective judgments about the goodness of lives can be made.

SUBJECTIVE JUSTIFICATION

We need to understand how we could be mistaken about the goodness of our own lives. How could it be that when we reasonably and honestly survey our lives and sincerely believe that they are good, we are, nevertheless, mistaken? Who, if not we ourselves, are the authoritative judges of whether we have satisfied our wants? As they stand, these questions are ambiguous. They may mean, How could we doubt the reasonable and sincere beliefs of people that they actually find something satisfying? And, of course, the answer is that doubt has no scope here, provided the beliefs really are not hasty, insane, feverish, or insincere. But the questions posed above may also mean, How could we doubt that the satisfactions, the objects of reasonable and sincere beliefs, actually add up to good lives? And the answer to this may well allow for doubt, for it is not our beliefs about our own experiences that are open to question but our judgments about the significance of our experiences. Many satisfactions may not make lives good. Reflecting on our lives, we may think otherwise and be mistaken. This possibility presents one serious objection to subjectivism.

Whether our many satisfactions add up to good lives depends on the place these satisfactions have in our moral perspectives. But moral perspectives may or may not be adequate, as we have seen in chapter 9, and if they are inadequate, they will stand in the way of good lives. And this remains true quite independently of what we think about our satisfactions or about the adequacy of our moral perspectives. The difficulty for subjectivism is that moral perspectives may prove inadequate in their own terms. Moral perspectives are supposed to enable us to judge complex situations well; but if they are inadequate, we shall misjudge what intimate personal relationships and our own aspirations call for. As a result, our personal morality will fail to yield the external and internal goods required by our own conceptions of good lives. This possibility is open, even though we may temporarily have many satisfactions.

If our moral perspectives are inadequate, although we believe otherwise, then the defects must be disguised from us. We have no reason to suppose that there are defects, because the satisfactions we presently have obscure them. Nevertheless, the defects are there and the satisfactions cannot last. There are many ways in which this may happen, but I shall sketch only a few to illustrate the general point.

One possibility is that there are hidden incoherences in our moral perspectives. These may occur because the moral perspectives contain incompatible commitments. The incompatibility could remain hidden due either to inadequate reflection or to lucky circumstances that so far prevented the incompatibility from manifesting itself in actual conflicts. Consider, for instance, people with strong commitment to independence who live in a tightly organized institution requiring obedience from participants, such as an army or a religious order. If advancement is swift, the rewards considerable, the institution embattled, then the incompatibility may not surface for a long time. Or, if the people are busy, not given to thinking about their lives or monitoring themselves, and humility or stoical temperament makes them temporarily ready to put up with frustration, then, once again, the incompatibility of their commitments may not become evident. In such cases, things may seem, on the surface, to be going well, and the people may sincerely believe that they are satisfied with their lives. But the satisfactions are unlikely to last, and in the long run their lives will probably suffer.

Another disguised defect may be the unrecognized impoverishment of moral perspectives. This occurs when our commitments are too meager. If moral perspectives have no place in them for some love and the appreciation of beauty; if they give no scope to creativity, playfulness, and imagination; if they make no demands for discipline and effort; they are extremely unlikely to lead to satisfactory lives. Of course, we may still be satisfied with such lives as we have. A differently placed Robinson Crusoe, without Friday and liberation, may have lived out his life lacking in personal relationships and reciprocated love. It is conceivable that he may have come to terms with his solitary lot and have developed a kind of resigned equilibrium. He may have said to himself that, given his circumstances, he was satisfied with his life. However, the satisfaction would not come from the presence of many good things in his life but from having succeeded in making the most of what his misfortune left him. He could have readily specified what would make his life better.

Having a meager set of commitments is a defect, however, only if we could have richer moral perspectives and yet lack them. We want certain external and internal goods; circumstances may stand in the way, and we can still make do. However, if we ourselves create the circumstances in which we are deprived of satisfactions, then occurs the defect I am describing. Of course, we can, do, and sometimes ought to make choices leading to lives less satisfying than they could be. But that is not the situation I have in mind. I am thinking of people who aim to have satisfying lives, no external obstacles stand in the way, and through lack of reflection or misguided reflection allow an important part of themselves to lie fallow.

The symptoms of this self-imposed deprivation are the uncultivated capacity to love, often manifesting itself in an inability to express affection; an undeveloped sense of beauty, leading to a vulgar knowingness of the price of everything and the value of nothing; lack of playfulness, producing stolid people without a sense of humor; untrained discipline, making it impossible to be seriously engaged in any endeavor; and the lack of imaginative life, resulting in dreariness and boredom. The effect of all this is to diminish the goods moral perspectives may yield and, thus, stand in the way of satisfaction.

Lack of realism is another internal defect; it makes lives futile. This may be disguised from us for quite some time, but eventually it leads to lives wasted in their own terms. Futility results from an unrealistic appraisal of the suitability of moral perspectives for our characters and circumstances. One way this can come about is by having commitments whose realization requires talents or temperament we lack. Clumsy people should not try to be craftsmen; irritable and irascible ones will fail as teachers; someone needing a great deal of solitude should not have a large family; physical cowards will be poor war correspondents; and righteous, dogmatic people will not do well as negotiators. Furthermore, although moral perspectives may be right for us, they may be unsuitable to our social or historical contexts. In another age and country, General MacArthur would not have had to wait until old age to find a task large enough for his talent, and he would not have been treated with proper democratic suspicion and distrust.

Finally, there is the internal defect of rigidity. Moral perspectives may be well constructed, coherent, sufficiently rich for our characters and context, and yet fail through being incapable of adjustment to inevitable changes. The cult of youth and the abhorrence of old age breed much frustration. We all wrinkle, sag, droop, lose resiliency, tire more easily, and have diminishing capacities. Moral perspectives that suit only one period of a normal human life are bound to be unsatisfactory, no matter how well things go for us during the appropriate period.

In all the cases I have described, the moral perspectives are defective in their own terms. Although they could yield many external and internal goods, they will not continue to do so. The defects are obscured from us because we have not reflected sufficiently well. Provided we want to have good lives, we shall want to eliminate hidden incoherence, unrecognized impoverishment, too meager or unrealistic commitments, and rigidity. However, since we may not be aware of the presence of these defects, we may be satisfied with our lives over all and yet be mistaken. For this reason, subjective justification is not sufficient to make it reasonable to believe that our own lives are good. If we are indeed reasonable, we shall seek objective justification as well to eliminate disguised defects from our moral perspectives.

The difficulties of ontological objectivism and of subjectivism set the stage for eudaimonistic objectivism. I shall defend the possibility of objective justification, in opposition to subjectivism. But, in opposition to ontological objectivism, I shall greatly weaken the connection between objective justification and the ontology of objectivism.

EUDAIMONISTIC OBJECTIVISM

Ontological and eudaimonistic objectivists agree that reasonable beliefs about the goodness of lives require that there be standards for eliminating, or, at least, minimizing the occurrence of the sort of mistakes I have just described. They disagree, however, about the nature of the standards. Ontological objectivists think that universal facts about human nature provide the required standards. Eudaimonistic objectivists think that universal facts about human nature, that is, the facts of the body, self, and social life, do provide some of the required standards, but they are insufficient. For good lives, and the moral perspectives that lead to them, are much richer in content than the requirements derived from these facts would lead us to believe. The possibility of going beyond them does not depend on further facts about human nature, as ontological objectivists believe, but on the rational appraisal of moral perspectives and of the beliefs they suggest. This appraisal involves appeal to epistemological, not to ontological, standards. Thus, ontological and eudaimonistic objectivists agree in regarding the requirements set by the facts of the body, self, and social life as some of the standards on which the reasonability of moral perspectives and beliefs about the goodness of our lives can be judged. It is unreasonable to regard any moral perspective as adequate, unless it recognizes that the requirements set by the facts of the body, self, and social life must be satisfied. Beyond this point, however, disagreement between ontological and eudaimonistic objectivists begins.

Eudaimonistic objectivists hold that the distinction between objectivity and subjectivity has been poorly drawn by both ontological objectivists and subjectivists. To improve it, they replace the traditional twofold distinction by a fourfold one. This suggests the following scheme for the relevant standards:

	Subjective	*Objective*
Ontological	made by personal decision	exists independently of personal decision
Epistemological	acceptance or rejection depends only on personal decision	acceptance or rejection can be rationally judged independently of personal decision

Ontological objectivists think that reasonable standards for judging moral perspectives must be both ontologically and epistemologically objective. This means that the goodness of our lives can be reasonably judged only by standards that exist independently of what we think or do. Subjectivists think that the goodness of our lives can be judged only by ontologically and epistemologically subjective standards; that is, the standards are what we decide to make them and they cannot be justified with reference to anything that exists independently of them. Eudaimonistic objectivists think that the standards, beyond those set by the facts of the body, self, and social life, are ontologically subjective and epistemologically objective. In other words, although the standards are made by us, they can, nevertheless, be reasonable or unreasonable independently of what we think or do. This is the view I shall defend.

The claim that we make our own standards for judging moral perspectives is still ambiguous. Moral perspectives are composed of hierarchical structures of commitments. Commitments, in turn, have two distinguishable but inseparable components: an act, summoning up a resolve, and the object of the resolve. The object is an external or an internal good. These goods not only inspire us, but they also act as standards for judging our moral perspectives. For the more we enjoy these goods, the better we should find our lives. And if we fail to get the goods, although circumstances are not adverse, or if we get them but fail to enjoy them, then the moral perspectives are at fault. The component of standards we always make is the act, not the object. Unless we make the resolve, we cannot be said to have made a commitment. Without the resolve, we may be obedient, habit-ridden, coerced, indoctrinated but not committed. On the other hand, the object of the commitment, the particular good, is not made by us. Thus, making our standards is making the resolve to seek some goods, but it is not making the goods themselves.

If we have imposed a moral perspective on our lives in accordance with the standards set by external and internal goods we seek, then the standards are ontologically subjective; they exist only because we have committed ourselves to seeking certain goods. But they are epistemologically objective because they can be justified independently of what we do. If the justification succeeds, then the moral perspective is adequate and the judgments following from it are reasonable; if the justification fails, then the moral perspective is inadequate, regardless of what we judge to be the case.

The defense of eudaimonistic objectivism depends on showing what independent justification can render epistemologically objective judgments about moral perspectives. There are two such justifications: the elimination of some faulty moral perspectives by specifying the conditions all good lives must meet and the employment of tests for identifying good lives.

THREE CONDITIONS OF ADEQUACY

There are three conditions all adequate moral perspectives must meet. It is not enough if we merely believe that they have met them; moral perspectives are adequate only if the beliefs are true. So the three conditions I am about to discuss are objective. This is not to deny that we can decide to live lives that violate the conditions. We can, and such decisions may be reasonable and have high moral credentials. However, they cannot lead to lives enabling us to satisfy our important wants by achieving the external and internal goods we seek. It may be reasonable and morally praiseworthy to abandon the pursuit of these goods out of love, self-sacrifice, or duty; but if we do want to achieve them, these conditions must be met. I take it as a fact about us, human beings, that we normally want to have good lives. There may be circumstances in which we cease to want them, or cease to work for them, and then the conditions need not be met. However, since normalcy, by definition, is what prevails most of the time, there is a presumption in favor of meeting these conditions. If the presumption is justifiably overruled, as it may be, then there must be an explanation in terms of unusual circumstances. Furthermore, the conditions are universal: they apply to all moral perspectives, everywhere, always; they are historically constant, socially invariant, and independent of psychological differences. So my claim is that moral perspectives cannot be adequate and, thus, cannot lead to good lives, unless they meet these objective, presumptive, and universal conditions.

The first such conditions is that the wants created by the facts of the body, self, and social life must be at least minimally satisfied. Unless they are satisfied, we die or are irreparably damaged. Exactly what items and how much of them should be included in a complete list of these requirements is a scientific question to which I do not have the answer. The important point for my purposes is that there are such specifiable requirements, I have specified many of them, and unless they are met, we cannot have good lives.

My claim is compatible with the undeniable fact that some people deprive themselves of the required satisfactions. Parents may starve themselves to save their children from starvation. In doing so, they nobly sacrifice their own chances for good lives for the sake of their children. Such cases strengthen rather than weaken the necessary link between minimal satisfactions and good lives.

But what about ascetics who connect self-mortification with good lives? If they do that, they are still committed to the minimal satisfactions of their requirements, for otherwise not even lives of self-mortification can go on. Suppose, however, that they believe that earthly existence is only a brief episode and the goodness of their lives is connected with their souls rather than their bodies. The first thing to notice about this is that there are extremely few people who genuinely do not care about their bodies. But there are some, and they raise the question of whether the presumption in favor of the satisfaction of this requirement for the adequacy of moral perspectives could be reasonably overruled. The answer depends on what is reasonable to believe about nonbodily existence. In the unlikely event that ascetics are right, they have presented one of those rare instances in which the presumption in favor of minimal satisfactions is reasonably overruled. And that does not defeat the claim that normally the presumption holds.

The second condition of adequacy for moral perspectives is that they must observe the *prima facie* case for conforming to the prevailing social morality. I have argued in chapter 5 that this requires, in the first instance, conformity to deep conventions. Second, it requires conformity to such variable conventions as provide the historically and socially conditioned forms deep conventions take in a particular social morality. These deep and variable conventions jointly define simple moral situations in that social morality. Decency is to conduct oneself in accordance with these conventions. Thus, moral perspectives are adequate only if they prescribe decency.

The justification for this condition is that social morality provides the possibilities and limitations for all forms of life. Thus, conformity to social morality is necessary for protecting the possibilities and limitations without which there can be no good lives. Unless this condition is generally observed, and decency prevails, so that social morality fosters rather than prevents good lives, the society will be unstable. Stability is in the interest of all people for whom good lives are made possible by the social morality.

The relevant conventions of social morality guarantee the possibility of good lives partly by establishing the many forms good lives can take and partly by setting limits to these forms and to what is morally permissible to do in order to achieve them. If the conventions accomplish this, conformity to them benefits both ourselves and others. If they fail to accomplish it, it is in our and other people's interest to do what we can to improve them.

The justification I am offering for this second condition of adequacy for moral perspectives is prudential. This needs emphasis because it is widely supposed that the justification can be moral. Thus, people appeal to natural or human rights, respect for others, the categorical imperative, the greatest happiness principle, the Golden Rule, loving one's neighbor, and the like. But I do not see how a moral justification of social morality could avoid begging the question, and so I doubt that moral justification could succeed here. If I am mistaken, the prudential justification I offer may be strengthened by a moral justification. In either case, however, the prudential justification stands.

The third condition for the adequacy of moral perspectives is that we must be subjectively justified in believing that the lives we live according to our moral perspectives are good. Such beliefs are subjectively justified, if they are held on the ground that we believe that our important wants are being satisfied, because we are possessing the external and internal goods we seek. I have argued that subjective justification is not sufficient for the reasonability of these beliefs. I shall now argue that it is necessary. What is necessary for the adequacy of moral perspectives is both that we should believe that our lives are good and that our beliefs should be subjectively justified.

Holding these beliefs does not require that they be expressed either publicly or privately. We may not even be conscious of them. We hold them in the sense that if we were asked whether we are satisfied with our lives, we would answer affirmatively. And if others were to observe our conduct, it would be reasonable for them to infer that we like our ways of life, we do not look for basic changes, we are satisfied with our work and intimate relationships, and we are not deeply frustrated on their account.

But we may hold these beliefs with or without appropriate grounds, and subjective justification requires appropriate grounds. This condition is not always met, because our satisfaction with our lives may be based on carefully nurtured self-deception or on taking perverse delight in our own frustration, due to feelings of guilt or shame, or on having been so crushed by circumstances that satisfaction is produced by our own deterioration and fast approaching death. The beliefs are subjectively justified only if they are based on what we take to be the satisfaction of our important wants. Of course, as I have argued, these beliefs may be false, and that is why subjective justification is only necessary and not sufficient for the adequacy of our moral perspectives and for the reasonability of the beliefs that our lives are good.

It may be objected, however, that our lives may be good even if we believe them to be otherwise, and if so, subjective justification is not even necessary. But our beliefs about our wants, satisfactions, and enjoyment of external and internal goods have a special authority. For the wants, satisfactions, and the enjoyment of goods are experienced by us and by no one else. We are, therefore, particularly well placed to form beliefs about them. Furthermore, the satisfaction of wants and the enjoyment of external and internal goods requires, as I have been arguing, at least modest self-direction and hospitable circumstances. So if we come to believe that our important wants are not being satisfied and we do not enjoy the goods we seek, we do so, provided we are reasonable, either on the grounds that we have failed in self-direction or because we are frustrated by our circumstances. Given our special authority, there is a presumption in favor of the reasonability of such beliefs. And it is hard to know what could defeat the presumption. Thus, if we believe, on reasonable grounds, that our lives are not good, our judgments should be accepted, unless it can be shown that we are mistaken about our wants, satisfactions, enjoyment of goods, or self-direction.

My general point is that our reasonable beliefs about the goodness of our lives have a crucial bearing on the objective justification of the judgment that our lives are good. If we are dissatisfied with our lives, on reasonable grounds, our lives are not good. For their goodness depends on the satisfactions of important wants, and we know best about them. On the other hand, if we are satisfied with our lives, on reasonable grounds, they may still not be good, partly because we may be mistaken about the adequacy of our moral perspectives. Therefore, subjective justification is necessary, but not sufficient, for the adequacy of moral perspectives.

This completes part of my defence of eudaimonistic objectivism. My claim so far is that what makes it reasonable to regard moral perspectives as adequate is that they meet the three conditions discussed above. So we can say that if a moral perspective does not meet the requirements set by the facts of the body, self, and social life; leads to the violation of the deep and the relevant variable conventions of social morality; fails to be subjectively justified due to its own inadequacy; then it cannot lead to a good life. Furthermore, whether a moral perspective conforms to these conditions is independent of what anybody believes, apart from the belief that it is subjectively justified. The conditions, therefore, are objective. They are also universal, in that they hold of all moral perspectives. And they are presumptive, rather than logically or causally necessary, because they hold normally, in the vast majority of cases; if critics claim to have found an exception, the burden is on them to show why the putative exception should be accepted. But meeting these conditions does not permit the conclusion that moral perspectives conforming to them will lead to good lives. For not even the conjunction of these three necessary conditions is sufficient to guarantee the goodness of lives.

THREE TESTS OF GOOD LIVES

In addition to the three conditions that must be satisfied by any adequate moral perspective, there are also three tests. If a moral perspective passes these tests, it is reasonable to suppose that it will lead to a good life, provided circumstances are favorable. In the order of justification, therefore, the conditions come first and the tests second.

Passing the tests is neither necessary nor sufficient for adequate moral perspectives and, thus, for good lives. It is not sufficient because moral perspectives may pass the tests and yet not lead to good lives, due to adverse circumstances that may stand in the way of even the most adequate moral perspectives. Nor are the tests necessary, for they are not conclusive. The adequacy of moral perspectives normally requires passing the tests, but there may be unusual circumstances in which the tests do not apply. It is unclear what, if anything, may make lives good on spaceships, deserted islands, or in concentration camps. Another reason why the tests are not necessary for good lives is that, unlike the conditions, they are not universal. The tests, in conjunction with the conditions and favorable circumstances, do identify moral perspectives that will lead to good lives, given the moral tradition of eudaimonism. But there are other moral traditions and other conceptions of good lives. My argument should not be construed as an attempt to exclude them. One can describe, recommend, and justify a moral tradition without denying the possibility that there may be others. What conceptions of good lives other moral traditions offer and whether they are justifiable are questions I intend to leave open. The possibility that there may be good lives that do not pass the tests does not undermine the objectivity of the tests I am about to describe. What makes them objective is not that they apply to each and every adequate moral perspective but that whether a moral perspective passes the tests is independent of what anyone believes about passing them. Their objectivity depends on whether people and lives shaped by moral perspectives do or fail to possess certain characteristics.

The first such test is whether we possess to a sufficient extent the character traits required for successful self-direction. These character traits are the moral modes of objectivity, breadth, depth, and reflection. If we do possess them, our lives are much more likely to be good than otherwise. The possession of these character traits is a matter of degree. This test requires that we should have them to such a degree as to make them significant features of our characters. One criterion of sufficient possession is that any full description of their possessors would be seriously inadequate unless it gave central place to them.

If we pass this test, we are objective because we do not allow selfishness or fantasy to corrupt our judgments about complex moral situations. We perceive the facts as they are, not in the light they cast on us, nor as we would wish them to be or as we fear they might be. We have enough breadth to be aware of the moral possibilities suggested by other moral traditions and by the possibilities of our own tradition. Our judgments, then, are informed by these possibilities, because we know the options open to us, and we can articulate them in terms of the moral idioms of our tradition. This knowledge and capacity are at once liberating, by giving scope to our judgments and subsequent actions, and limiting, by excluding options as prohibited by or alien to our moral tradition. We also have sufficient depth, so that our judgments are made from the moral perspectives we have constructed out of the possibilities our moral tradition provides. These perspectives, formed of the hierarchical structure of our commitments, provide the distinctions between what is important and unimportant, necessary and contingent, serious and trivial, from our moral point of view. But the construction of individual perspectives is a complex and very difficult process, for it requires balancing the wants we have and the goods we seek over against the possibilities and limitations of the conventions of our moral tradition. The task of moral reflection is to achieve and maintain this balance and, thus, to find a fit between individuals and their tradition.

If we possess these character traits to a sufficient extent and our conduct is informed by them, we have fine characters. Thus, we are capable of good lives. Such characters enable us to avoid obstacles or to surmount them if we must, which may prevent those who lack them from living good lives. Cataclysmic events may still deprive us of good lives, but lesser adversity will not. And I should add the reminder that fine characters are not self-centered. If people possessing them are indeed reflective, they know that conformity to social morality and intimate personal relationships are necessary for good lives. So they will care about decency and love, not only because they make their own lives better, although, of course, they do, but because they are among their commitments. Yet we cannot conclude that if we have fine characters, we shall live good lives, provided nothing cataclysmic happens, for there remains a question about moral perspectives.

This question does not hinge on the adequacy of moral perspectives, for I am assuming that fine characters are enlisted in living according to adequate moral perspectives. The question arises because there are alternative, equally adequate moral perspectives. Suppose that our situation is that we live according to an adequate moral perspective that satisfies the three conditions and the previous test, our circumstances are favorable, and our lives are unfolding as we wish. We may still have doubts left. We may say to ourselves that our lives are going well but not as well as they might. We are living the life, say, of a scholar, but we could also have been lawyers or artists; we have married the person we loved, and we have a good life together, but there are other people, other kinds of marriages, and perhaps, there is something to be said for remaining single. These are not idle doubts but serious questions about self-direction. The question is not whether we have succeeded or failed; I am assuming that we have succeeded. Rather, the question is whether having succeeded at this life is as good as it would have been to succeed at other lives we could have lived. What would remove these doubts?

The second test would. I shall make use of Nietzsche's redolent notion of eternal recurrence, but I do not claim to be faithful in my interpretation.[2] The idea is that the test of whether a life is free from the doubts I have just described is that we would wish it to go on without essential changes. Not even if our lives lasted for a very long time would we wish to alter them in any significant way. And, if we were asked to perform a Faustian thought-experiment, in which we could start again and do things differently, we would make the same important decisions we had made before. Passing the test set by this thought-experiment suggests that the life that has thus proved itself is free from serious doubts. Of course, reflective people cannot help wondering about their lives in this way. But having passed this test, the wonderings are introspective musings, not serious doubts.

The third test makes it possible to explain what it is in lives that makes us wish for their continuation without significant changes. The explanation is that we possess the external and internal goods we seek. These goods, it will be remembered, are internal, if they are produced by activities appropriate to our moral perspectives. External goods accrue to us from the recognition we get from others for what they regard as our achievements. One good reason, then, for regarding our lives as good, and for wanting them to go on as they have been, is that they provide the anticipated internal and external goods, and so we are satisfied with them. If the internal goods are missing, our lives will not seem good, for we do not find satisfaction in doing what we have committed ourselves to doing. Our activities cannot but seem drudgery to us. If we receive external goods, the drudgery may appear less oppressive, but the hollowness at the center, created by the absence of internal goods, cannot be compensated for by undeserved rewards. The relief provided by unjustly gained external goods is bound to be infrequent, and our unenjoyable lives must go on. Monotonous work, hypocritically pursued professions,

[2] My reading of Nietzsche is influenced by Nehamas, *Nietzsche: Life as Literature*, chapter 5, and by the earlier version of the chapter "The Eternal Recurrence."

intimate personal relationships based only on contract or duty are some examples of the joyless lives from which internal goods are absent.

The condition to aim at, then, is a life rich in internal goods and one that has a just share of external goods. We deserve internal goods and justly given external goods if we have earned them by successful self-direction. We have developed fine characters, and we have adequate moral perspectives. Thus, we live lives both we and others find good, and so we can reasonably wish them to go on and on.

If a moral perspective meets the three conditions and the life lived according to it passes the three tests, its goodness has been objectively justified. But I have not claimed that if a life does not pass the tests, it cannot be objectively justified. Meeting the three conditions is necessary for good lives; but passing the three tests is not. There may be good lives that do not conform to the eudaimonistic conception. This possibility is important, for it reminds us that there is no reason to think that available options exhaust the variety of good lives human beings can live. Moral traditions preserve and transmit these options, but they should not stand in the way of other moral traditions. Furthermore, trying to live according to new and untested moral perspectives are much-needed, although risky, experiments in living. The importance of these experiments is that they test the limits of human possibilities and thus introduce greater freedom and variety into our lives. Thus, they enlarge our moral possibilities and save the moral tradition from rigidifying into an orthodoxy.

I have chosen a passage from Iris Murdoch as the epigraph of this chapter because it expresses so well what I have tried to do. She thinks that moral philosophy is the examination of the most important of all human activities. And, in agreement with her, I think that living a good life is this activity. She thinks that the examination of this activity should be realistic, in taking due account of human nature, and that it should commend a worthy ideal. I think that the eudaimonistic conception of good lives is such an ideal and that it is based on a realistic view of human nature. Thus, I commend this ideal to readers who have persisted thus far.

CHAPTER TWELVE

The Integrity and Purity of Good Lives

> 'To thine own self be true'—with what promise the phrase
> sings in our ears! Each one of us is the subject of the
> imperative and we think of the many difficulties and doubts
> which would be settled if only we obeyed it.
>
> —Lionel Trilling[1]

INTEGRITY AND MORAL PERSPECTIVES

Integrity is a complex notion. In one of its senses, it is principled action; in another, it is wholeness. We show integrity in the first sense if we have made a commitment and act according to it. But there is more to it, because our actions deserve to be taken as signs of integrity only if it is difficult to act in accordance with our commitments. Thus, integrity, in the first sense, is revealed only in the face of challenge. If we habitually act according to our commitments, even and especially when it is difficult to do so, then we have integrity in the first sense.

Yet we may not have it in the second sense, because principled people may punctiliously adhere to shifting commitments or they may try to live up to incompatible commitments. The second sense of integrity, wholeness, can be ascribed only to people whose commitments form a coherent hierarchical structure enduring through time. As we have seen, such a structure is a moral perspective. To have integrity, in the second sense, then, is to be true to our moral perspectives, and this is my subject in the present chapter.

Moral perspectives are essential components of our identity, for they form a central part of the evaluative dimension of our lives. We judge the goodness of our lives from our moral perspectives, and so integrity, being true to our moral perspectives, is necessary for good lives. Both integrity and the goodness of lives are matters of degree. One of the factors determining how good our lives are is the degree of integrity we possess. For the moral perspectives to which we adhere through more or less integrity are constituted of commitments; these commitments are to satisfying our wants; and good lives de-

---

[1] Trilling, *Sincerity and Authenticity*, 4.

pend on the satisfaction of important wants. Reasonable people, wishing to live good lives, therefore, will also wish to have integrity.

Living according to our moral perspectives is the project of self-direction: we aim to change our present selves into better future selves, in order to approximate more closely the requirements of our moral perspectives. But as our self-direction proceeds, and we grow in objectivity, breadth, depth, and reflection, as our judgments improve and we come to a better appreciation of the significance of the moral idioms of our moral tradition, so also change our moral perspectives. These changes in our selves, brought about by changes in our moral perspectives, are not changes of identity but a growing appreciation of what our identities involve. They lead us to articulate our inchoate feelings, to understand our inexplicit assumptions and commitments, to become alive to the significance of the intimations of our moral perspectives. Self-direction, if it goes well, is in the direction of increased clarity and moral sensitivity.

As our moral perspectives, and consequently our selves, develop in this desirable direction, so develops with them our integrity. Part of the complexity of the notion of integrity consists in prompting us to be true to changing things. This is why the relation between the two senses of integrity is not simply that integrity, in the sense of wholeness, is the disposition constituted of episodes of acting according to our commitments when it is difficult to do so. For integrity may well involve violating some of the commitments of our present selves in order to acquire selves we regard as better. Thus, integrity in honoring our present commitments may actually conflict with integrity in the sense of wholeness.[2]

If we think of creating our better selves in terms of integrity, then the process may appear paradoxical, for it involves both adhering to and weakening our present commitments. The appearance of a paradox is created by the failure to distinguish between the two senses of integrity. Integrity is to be true to ourselves. But the selves may be the present selves we have undertaken to improve or the future selves we aspire to having. Integrity in the first sense, as principled action, involves being true to our present selves; integrity in the second sense, my own, involves being true to the selves toward which our moral perspectives direct us.

These two selves may partly coincide, but they are unlikely to do so completely, since few of us have achieved the better selves we want to have. Nevertheless, the two senses of integrity remain connected, for

[2] The first sense of integrity is close to what has been called shallow sincerity; see Fingarette, *Self-Deception*, 51–52.

both involve habitually honoring our commitments when it is difficult to do so. Thus, it is frequently a matter of indifference whether an action is said to exemplify the first or the second sense of integrity. For my purposes, however, the distinction is important, because good lives are intimately connected with integrity in the second sense, while their connection with integrity in the first sense is only loose.[3]

Let us now consider an act of integrity. In his life of Alexander, Plutarch tells us about Callisthenes, nephew of Aristotle, a philosopher himself, who accompanied Alexander on the campaign to Persia: "[I]n the matter of obeisance he behaved like a true philosopher, not only in his sturdy refusal to perform it, but also in being the only man to express in public the resentment which all the oldest and best Macedonians felt in private. By persuading the king not to insist on this tribute, he delivered the Greeks from a great disgrace and Alexander from even a greater one."[4]

Obeisance was a serious matter, involving prostrating oneself on the ground. For the Greeks, it was a religious gesture that they owed only to some of their gods, and Alexander was a man. For the Persians, on the other hand, obeisance was a social act routinely performed to kings. Alexander's demand that the Greeks should pay obeisance to him, as the conquered Persians did, was thus doubly offensive. It was sacrilegious, and it reduced the Greeks to the status of barbarians. This was behind Callisthenes' protest.

Yet kings were not to be trifled with. Not only was obedience to them a duty, it was also a matter of self-interest, because the king guaranteed the cohesion of the group. In a foreign country, in the midst of conquered enemies, the authority of the king was essential to the unity and the security of the Greeks. Furthermore, obedience was also backed by the king's absolute power over the lives, wealth, and citizenship of his subjects. Callisthenes risked losing all by his public refusal of obeisance.

Callisthenes' conduct exemplified integrity because, although it was difficult, he adhered to his moral perspective. Callisthenes shared with his fellow Greeks in Persia, and elsewhere, substantial parts of this perspective. They shared much of their conceptions of good lives, many of their judgments about good and evil, and a sense of the importance of many of their joint commitments. Alexander, being a Greek, shared it also. Yet, although he ought to have been protecting his subjects' moral perspectives, as well as his own, he was

---

[3] For an illuminating discussion of the two senses of integrity, closely parallel to my own, see Taylor, *Pride, Shame, and Guilt*, chapter 5.

[4] Plutarch, *The Age of Alexander*, 312.

endangering them by his demand of obeisance from the Greeks. Callisthenes' act of integrity was a reaffirmation for himself and a reminder to Alexander and to the other Greeks of what they were about. As a man of integrity should, Callisthenes defended the moral perspectives, the key to the good lives for all of them, against Alexander's ill-conceived challenge.

Essential to understanding integrity, and Callisthenes' exemplification of it, is that it is an attitude adopted in the face of difficulties. Integrity is called for because our moral perspectives conflict with something else. It may be some authority, our own pleasure or security, the temptations of wealth, power, or status, or the inherent difficulties of adhering to our moral perspectives. Integrity is the refusal to be swayed from our moral perspectives in the face of this conflict.

But the moral perspectives integrity protects differ from person to person, and, therefore, so do the forms integrity takes. I do not merely mean that different people remain true to different moral perspectives but also that remaining true to them takes quite different attitudes. For Callisthenes, integrity involved disobedience; but for Clarendon, integrity was to obey the frivolous Charles II and accept his own ignominious dismissal after a lifetime of loyal service. Montaigne acted with integrity when he retired from public service to private life. But for Charles de Gaulle, integrity was, first, to seek public office, then to leave it, and then to accept it again when France was prepared to abide by his principles, only to resign it forever when anarchy, once again, got the better of his countrymen. So the attitude involved in integrity is not to prefer the private to the public, nor to refuse to alter our conduct, nor is it to disobey legitimate authority. What is it then? I shall move toward an answer by considering first a mistaken analysis of integrity: Kierkegaard's.

INTEGRITY AND PURITY: KIERKEGAARD'S MISTAKE

Kierkegaard identified the morally required attitude toward integrity as purity of heart, or, briefly, purity. His *Purity of Heart*[5] is an extended meditation on a biblical passage: "Draw nigh to God and he will draw nigh to you. Cleanse your hands, ye sinners; and purify your hearts, ye double minded."[6] Drawing near to God is to draw near to the good; to stop being double-minded by purifying one's heart. And "purity of heart is to will one thing" (53).

Kierkegaard would have interpreted Callisthenes' conduct as an in-

---

[5] Kierkegaard, *Purity of Heart*; page references are given in parentheses.
[6] James 4:8, AV.

dication of purity. Callisthenes had a conception of the good; he did not allow himself to be deterred from it; he willed only it. Thus, he was not double-minded, and therein consisted his integrity. What would it have been for Callisthenes to be deterred? If he had willed the good because of hope of reward or fear of punishment, he would, then, have willed the good not for its own sake, as purity dictates, but for the sake of something else. "To will the Good for the sake of reward is double-mindedness. To will one thing, therefore, is to will the good without considering the reward" (72). And "willing the Good only out of fear of punishment . . . is the same as to will the Good for the sake of reward, to the extent that avoiding an evil is an advantage of the same sort as that of attaining a benefit" (79). Callisthenes did not behave as he did for reward; in fact, he risked great injury to himself. So he was not double-minded. But why should we think that if we are not double-minded, if we really will only one thing, then we shall will the good?

Because "[g]enuinely to will one thing, a man must in truth will the Good" (121–22). And why should this be so? Because if we are pure, without double-mindedness, then our souls will be allowed to speak clearly, and they will speak for the good. For "[t]he person who wills one thing that is not the Good, he does not truly will one thing. . . . For in his innermost being he is, he is bound to be, double-minded" (55). And conversely, "if . . . a man should in truth will only one thing, then this thing must, in the truth of his innermost being, be one thing" (66). One more step will bring us to the core of Kierkegaard's thinking.

Purity is bound to lead to the good, because our innermost being, the soul, is attuned to the objective good, God, which exists outside of ourselves. The pure uncorrupted soul, in freedom from double-mindedness, will necessarily aim for the good, because evil is simply interference with the natural processes of the soul, reflected by the various forms of double-mindedness. Purity, therefore, leads to the good, and double-mindedness to evil, because purity is to be in harmony with the cosmic order that is good, while double-mindedness is to be separated from it. In this view, integrity is to listen attentively to one's soul and to resolve conflicts between its promptings and worldly rewards and punishments in favor of the soul. This, Kierkegaard would have said, is what Callisthenes had done.

One objection to Kierkegaard's view is that there is no convincing reason for accepting the metaphysical theory presupposed by it. This has been argued many times by critics of Christianity, and I shall not repeat the old case. An additional reason for not doing so is that the moral portion of Kierkegaard's view can be held without the metaphysics; Rousseau, for instance, had done so. I shall, therefore, argue against the moral view independently of its supposed metaphysical underpinnings.

Did Callisthenes will only one thing? Superficially, it seems so. For what he meant to do by his public refusal of obeisance was to adhere to his moral perspective. And since it was shared to a considerable extent by his fellow Greeks, he was also defending their moral perspectives, including Alexander's, against whom the defense was needed. But this is superficial, because the shared portions of their moral perspectives were a complicated structure of conventions, commitments, and wants of external and internal goods. It was thought to be good; the *it*, however, was not one thing, but many. Callisthenes' defense was like protecting one's house from deterioration: a matter of having to do many things. His integrity was pure, in the sense of not being motivated by personal gain; but it was not pure in the sense Kierkegaard needs of wanting only one thing.

Kierkegaard's reason for thinking that we will the good if we will only one thing was his belief in a benign and love-impregnated cosmic order. But what reason is there for thinking that there is the good, the *summum bonum*, without the metaphysics? Lacking a supernatural grounding, we must observe human nature and history. And what we can conclude from that is that, while there are some universal and necessary conditions without which human lives cannot be good, namely those grounded on the facts of the body, self, and social life, when these conditions are met, lives reflect many different conceptions of goodness. There are different conceptions of external and internal goods in the Homeric tradition, in Aristotle, in monasticism, in the Protestant Ethic, in Byronic romanticism, in the lives of Victorian gentlemen, and in the long tradition running from Plato, through Jesus and Kant, to Kierkegaard. As I have argued repeatedly, there is no good reason to think that all good lives will take one of these forms in civilized conditions when we are willing the good without thinking of reward and punishment. And there are excellent reasons, provided by personal experience, history, literature, and anthropology, for thinking that good lives take many different forms. So Kierkegaard was mistaken in thinking both that purity will lead us to will one thing, because the moral perspectives in the background are complicated, and that they will lead different people to will the same thing, since there are many different and yet adequate moral perspectives. But he was also mistaken in thinking that having the kind of purity he valued is good without qualification and being, what he called, double-minded is an obstacle to moral goodness. I think that purity may lead to vicious fanaticism, and, in one sense, double-mindedness is part of being a reflective moral agent.

Kierkegaard supposed that moral progress was from double-mindedness to purity. In this progression, we engage in deeper and deeper self-examination, and, in the course of it, we gradually free ourselves from the corrupting desire for the external goods the human world can offer; thus we get rid of double-mindedness. One reason for rejecting this view, as we have seen, is that external goods are necessary for good lives. Another reason is that the supposition that goodness is bound to await us at the end of self-examination is mistaken. Why should we believe that once the desire for external goods is removed, only benign and loving sentiments will be left? What happens to such equally basic impulses as aggression, hostility, suspicion, jealousy, pride, envy, and so on? On this point, Kierkegaard is opposed, not only by those who reject his metaphysics, but also by many defenders of the Christian tradition. Salvation, according to them, is not in human hands precisely because human nature is unavoidably tainted by evil; good and evil exist in us side by side. Only with the help of divine grace can we overcome evil. The secular equivalent of this realistic appraisal of human nature, if not of its improvement, is the apt observation that "[t]o say that altruism and morality are possible in virtue of something basic to human nature is not to say that men are basically good. Men are basically complicated; how good they are depends on whether certain conceptions and ways of thinking have achieved dominance."[7] Kierkegaard failed to see that the result of vigorous and honest self-examination may be the sort of discovery Kurtz made at the end of his journey, in Conrad's *The Heart of Darkness*: that in his innermost self lay "The horror! The horror!" Great purity is compatible with great evil. To will one thing is to be single-minded, but whether it is good to be single-minded depends on what is willed.

What counts against single-mindedness, counts for double-mindedness. Now, the enterprise of defending double-mindedness must seem perverse, for the word suggests duplicity, and nobody can be seriously defending that. But, of course, it is not duplicity but a healthy dose of moral care that I think we should have. To be double-minded, in my sense, is to interpose reflection between what we want and what we do. It is to refrain from acting spontaneously because we know that such action may be evil. It is a necessary condition of self-direction, for it consists in the kind of monitoring ourselves that complex moral situations require. If we were not double-minded in

[7] Nagel, *The Possibility of Altruism*, 146.

this way, we could not have objectivity, breadth, and depth, we would lack good judgment, and we could not decide about the relative importance of our commitments. Consequently, we could not have adequate moral perspectives.

Callisthenes was admirable in his integrity because he risked everything in defense of his moral perspective. But it is not for his purity that we should honor Callisthenes; he wanted many external goods, including, no doubt, rewards, and it would be amazing if he had not wanted to avoid punishment. In the reflections of reasonable people, external goods, rewards, and punishments have an important role. They are, after all, connected with living good lives. This may or may not be corrupting, and in Callisthenes' case it was not. He was true to his moral perspective, and he was willing to risk his life for it, because he saw it endangered by Alexander. The risk was reasonable because he believed that good lives for him, and for his fellow Greeks, were possible only through the jeopardized moral perspective. Integrity and good lives were connected for Callisthenes, and they should be connected for all reasonable people.

Kierkegaard's praise for single-mindedness and his condemnation of double-mindedness both stem from his belief in the intrinsic goodness of human beings. My suspicion of single-mindedness and advocacy of double-mindedness also have a common root: the belief that we, as well as most situations we face in personal morality, are intrinsically complicated. This is cause for optimism, because there is good in us; and it is cause for pessimism, because there is evil in us.

Our previous discussion of external and internal goods makes it possible to understand Kierkegaard's mistake. Underlying his identification of integrity and purity is a deep suspicion of external goods. This suspicion has long historical roots. It can be found in Plato; it was a cornerstone of Stoicism; Christian moralists placed external goods firmly among the glittering objects in the City of Man that turned out to be other than gold; and various champions of authenticity suspected those who wanted them of bad faith. The source of this suspicion is the accurate observation that the possession of external goods is a contingent matter, and if we seek them, we should be prepared for frustration. But, as we have seen, it does not follow that external goods are not good. The mistake of Kierkegaard and of the antiworldly tradition to which he belongs is to try to make the contingency of external goods easier to bear by denying that they are good. This denial seems untenable to me.

The deep truth in this antiworldly tradition is that we are responsible for self-direction and the primary satisfactions of that process come from our inner lives. But inner satisfactions are not the only satisfactions. Our judgments of ourselves are connected in countless ways with how others judge us. We share with others our moral idioms, we learn from some and teach others, we cooperate and compete with our friends and colleagues, we join with them in exercising judgment; the opinions of others unavoidably reflect on ourselves. External goods are the currency, the symbolic forms of these opinions. These opinions are fallible, but so are our own. To trust only one is to make judgments about how we should live even less reliable than they need to be. Of course, well-considered personal judgment should take precedence over public opinion, especially in complex moral situations. But if personal judgment and public opinion coincide, they are more likely to be correct, and if they diverge, there should be good reasons for coming down on the side of personal judgment. Kierkegaard's antiworldliness led him to rule public opinion out of court.

The sources of the antiwordly view are *hubris* and hypocrisy. It is *hubris* if it is thought that, if we reflect deeply, then we are bound to reflect well. Even our best-considered judgments are fallible, and we all benefit from the discipline of subjecting them to public scrutiny. Or, the antiworldly attitude may be due to the hypocritical pretense that we do not live in the world and care about its opinion. There may be a few people who genuinely do not care about external goods and whose judgments need no improvement, but I see no reason why they should serve as models for most of us who do care and are fallible.

It is best, I think, to take Kierkegaard's position as a warning against a certain kind of corruption. We may care too much for external goods. The musician who measures success by the length of applause; the athlete who is in it for the money; the philosopher whose satisfactions come from delivering crushing public rejoinders; the politicians for whom accomplishment means popularity are all corrupt in this way. If by purity we mean resistance to this kind of corruption, then we should all be in favor of it. However, what purity, in this sense, requires is not rejecting external goods but maintaining a proper balance between them and internal goods. Montaigne can teach us something about that.

LIVING IN THE WORLD: MONTAIGNE'S SOLUTION

Montaigne saw himself as living in the "sick age" of sixteenth-century France, of whose "worm-eaten and maggoty body" even the "justest party is still a member" (759).[8] He was a minor aristocrat, possessing moderate wealth, status, and prestige. These were connected with public service, and Montaigne was engaged in it for thirteen years as a counselor attached to the parliament of Bordeaux. He found the laws he was administering unjust, and he retired to private life. As he noted: "In this year of Christ 1571, at the age of thirty-eight, on the last day of February, his birthday, Michel de Montaigne, long weary of the servitude of the court and of public employments, while still entire, retired to the bosom of the learned virgin [his library], where in calm and freedom from cares he will spend what little remains of his life, now more than half run out. If the fates permit, he will complete this abode" (ix). Montaigne intended to write and to reflect, and it was for this that he needed "freedom, tranquility, and leisure" (x). But the fates did not permit it. He was obliged to be mayor of Bordeaux for two terms and to mediate between the warring Protestants and Catholics. Why did he do it? Because "in such a [worm-eaten and maggoty] body the least diseased member is called healthy; and quite rightly, since our qualities have no titles except by comparison. Civic innocence is measured according to the places and the times" (760).

Montaigne faced a fundamental conflict between public and private life. The internal goods of his way of life were connected with both. But there was a tension between them because public life was soiling; it conflicted with Montaigne's trying to live what he regarded as a good life. He saw this, as well as the necessity of being soiled: "[I]n every government there are some offices which are . . . vicious. Vices find their place in it and are employed for sewing society together, as are poisons for the preservation of our health. . . . The public welfare requires that a man may betray and lie and massacre" (600). Montaigne's conflict is known to us as the problem of dirty hands.

Kierkegaard would have said that to see this as a conflict is already to be corrupt: Montaigne was double-minded. When public life is seen as a source of internal goods, there lurks behind this perception a corrupt want for the wrong things: power and prestige are false gods. The error is to think of external goods as if they were internal. Purity calls for retreat into ourselves, because no genuine internal good can come from involvement with the world. Thus, Kierkegaard would have said that Montaigne was right to retire, and he was wrong to come out of retirement and expose himself to inevitable soil by being a mayor and a go-between.

But it was Kierkegaard who had been wrong about this: seeking

---

[8] Numbers in parentheses refer to the pages of *The Complete Essays of Montaigne*.

internal goods through public life can be corrupting, but it need not be. Montaigne's life and the *Essays*, "a book consubstantial with its author" (504), are great partly because we can learn from them how to see corruption for what it is and yet to avoid it. Montaigne's way of life required both living in the world and withstanding its corruption. How could he do both?

"The mayor and Montaigne," said Montaigne, "have always been two, with a very clear separation" (774). What was this separation? On the one hand, "[a]n honest man is not accountable for the vice and stupidity of his trade, and should not therefore refuse to practice it: it is the custom of his country, and there is profit in it. We must live in the world and make the most of it such as we find it" (744). On the other hand, "I have been able to take part in public office without departing one nail's breadth from myself, and to give myself to others without taking myself from myself" (770). But how is this possible? How can we remain true to ourselves, have integrity, and, at the same time, engage in vicious and stupid practices? Montaigne's answer was to offer only "limited and conditional services. There is no remedy. I frankly tell them my limits" (603). He will soil himself up to a point but not beyond it. What is this point?

Montaigne gave no general answer because he was thinking mainly of his own case. We know what his limits were in some cases but not why. However, we can give a clearer answer by recalling the hierarchical structure of commitments that compose moral perspectives. In chapter 9 I distinguished between unconditional, defeasible, and loose commitments. Unconditional commitments include our allegiances to deep conventions; defeasible commitments are usually to the variable conventions of our social morality; while loose commitments are to the forms in which more basic commitments are expressed. All these commitments are to supposed external and internal goods. And we seek these goods because we believe that they will make our lives better.

Montaigne and Kierkegaard would have agreed that our unconditional commitments must be to internal goods. Beyond this, however, their disagreement begins. Kierkegaard thought that the good life cannot include any commitment to external goods. Even if our unconditional commitments are to internal goods and only our defeasible and loose commitments are to external goods, we are still double-minded. We, then, do not will the goods only for their own sake but also for the sake of the rewards public life holds out. Montaigne thought that there were many different good lives, and they included both external and internal goods. There was, in his view, nothing wrong with defeasible and loose commitments to external goods. "We must live in the world and make the most of it as we find it" (774). Montaigne would have agreed with Kierkegaard that living in the world can be corrupting. But it did not corrupt Montaigne, and it need not corrupt others. What must be done is to make only "limited and conditional" (603) commitments to external goods; the right attitude is, "I frankly tell them my limits" (603). The limits are the unconditional commitments to internal goods; they must not be compromised by defeasible or loose commitments to external goods.

So the answer we can extract from Montaigne to the question of what is the proper balance between external and internal goods is that internal goods are primary and that we may do what our conceptions of good lives call for in seeking external goods, just so long as we do not violate unconditional commitments to internal goods. In this way Montaigne can live in the world "without departing one nail's breadth from myself, and to give myself to others without taking myself from myself" (770).

Integrity is to adhere, in the face of difficulties, to the pattern of hierarchically organized commitments that compose our moral perspectives. Moral perspectives lead to good lives because they include satisfactions derived from what we do and from being publicly recognized for it. If there is no genuine satisfaction involved in living according to our moral perspectives, not even plentiful enjoyment of external goods can change the fact that our lives and activities fail to please us. External goods cannot compensate for the lack of internal ones. Those who think otherwise are corrupt. The way to avoid this corruption is, not by denying that external goods are satisfying, but by not allowing the desire for external goods to interfere with unconditional commitments to internal goods. Part of integrity is to maintain their proper balance by remaining true to the moral perspective composed of the hierarchy of our commitments.

INTEGRITY IN EFFORT AND ADVERSITY

There is yet another way in which the distinction between external and internal goods leads to a better understanding of integrity. Integrity is shown in the presence of difficulty, and it has two forms depending on whether the difficulty concerns external or internal goods. The difficulty in the way of internal goods may be that our characters are insufficiently developed; we lack the objectivity, breadth, depth, or good judgment required by our moral perspectives. Thus, we fail to get the internal goods because of our shortcomings. Integrity here consists in continuing with the hard and often discouraging process of self-direction, so that we would become able and willing to honor our commitments. This is the integrity of effort: remaining true to our better selves, while recognizing how far short our actual selves fall. Integrity of effort is shown, positively, by doing what we can to improve in the desired way and, negatively, by not giving in to the temptations of powerlessness, self-deception, or immediate gratification.

The other form of integrity is needed when we are living as our moral perspectives prescribe, but, through no fault of our own, we are unjustly deprived of the external goods we deserve. Here, integrity comes to not allowing this misfortune to disrupt our lives and activities. This is integrity in adversity, and it too consists in remaining true to our moral perspectives; the difficulty, however, is not due to our shortcomings but to the injustice surrounding us. Integrity in adversity is also shown, positively, by trying to improve the corrupt institutions and, negatively, by not allowing rage, envy, jealousy, resentment, shame, or misplaced guilt to interfere with continued self-direction. In the course of a normal lifetime, most people need both forms of integrity.

The alternative to responding to difficulties with integrity is to allow our allegiance to our moral perspectives to weaken. But since the good lives we want can be achieved only by adhering to our moral perspectives, lack of integrity will lead to frustrated lives. If we lack integrity in adversity, in the face of being deprived of deserved external goods, we diminish the chances of enjoying such internal goods as we may have. And if we have no integrity of effort, we are unlikely to be successfully self-directed, hence, we shall be incapable of achieving internal goods and, thus, remove ourselves from the ranks of candidates who deserve external goods.

Callisthenes, then, showed that he had integrity in adversity in the face of the difficulty created by Alexander's injustice. Alexander represented the institution responsible for the distribution of external goods. These goods were honor and respect. Alexander was unjust because he did not give the Greeks the honor and respect they deserved and he demanded from them honor and respect he himself did not deserve. Callisthenes' integrity consisted in trying to remedy the injustice that jeopardized the moral perspectives of the Greeks in Persia.

PREREFLECTIVE AND REFLECTIVE PURITY

If there is a proper balance between external and internal goods in our lives, and if we are not deterred by difficulties from living according to our moral perspectives, then we have integrity. And if we have integrity, we are uncorrupted. But it is natural to suppose that uncorrupted people are pure. So it seems that integrity and purity are connected after all. Yet I rejected Kierkegaard's attempt to establish the connection between them. What, then, is their connection?

I shall answer by reflecting on something Wittgenstein wrote: "Now as to Moore—I don't really understand Moore, &, therefore, what I'll say may be quite wrong. But this is what I'm inclined to say: —That Moore is in some ways extraordinarily childlike is obvious, & the remark you quoted (about vanity) is certainly an example of that childishness. There is also a *certain* innocence about Moore; he is, e.g. completely unvain. As to it's being to his '*credit*' to be childlike—I can't understand that; unless it's also to a child's credit. For you aren't talking of the innocence a man has fought for, but of an innocence that comes from the natural absence of temptation."[9] The quality Wittgenstein ascribed to Moore is purity. We can learn from this passage to distinguish between prereflective purity, which is "a natural absence of temptation," and reflective purity, which "a man has fought for." I do not know which Moore had. My interest is in the distinction and in proposing a way of drawing it.

We can approach the notion of prereflective purity by recalling the Aristotelian scheme for practical reasoning, discussed in chapter 5. I distinguished there between simple moral situations, typical of social morality, and complex ones, usually to be found in personal morality. Prereflective purity has its home in simple moral situations. When people know the conventions of their social morality and spontaneously act according to them over a long period of time, they have prereflective purity. Such people experience no moral struggle, they do not have to resist temptation, they know what morality calls for, and they simply do it.

Prereflective purity should be distinguished from moral innocence. The morally innocent are untouched by morality; their activities are spontaneous, but they are not led by moral considerations. Morally innocent actions may be kind or cruel, altruistic or selfish. They come from the heart, but it is an uninformed heart. When the child says to the fat guest, "You are fat," he is acting with moral innocence. Prereflective purity also comes from the heart, but it is informed by morality. The spontaneity of moral innocence is pre-moral; the spontaneity of prereflective purity is the result of well-learned moral lessons. If prereflective purity is immoral, it is because the moral tradition with which the agent has so completely identified is immoral.

[9] From a letter of Wittgenstein, quoted by Malcolm, *Ludwig Wittgenstein*, 80.

Prereflective purity reflects total immersion in a moral tradition. Moral innocence comes from the absence of moral education.

Prereflectively pure people have great and unintended moral force. They embody and exemplify an ideal of which the vast majority in their tradition falls short. They are not showing off; they do not aim to be didactic; they make no heroic efforts—they just simply and naturally ring true. We, who share their tradition, may respond to them with admiration or with the suspicion that they are too good to be true; they may provoke us to test just how good they really are, or we may half contemptuously regard them as not having been really tried. But we cannot ignore them. We have to adopt an attitude, or a confused mixture of attitudes, toward them because they represent an ideal, our ideal, and we all know how far we, ourselves, are from achieving it. They challenge us, without meaning to, by being what we feel we ought to be. Melville's Billy Budd, Dostoyevsky's Prince Myshkin and Alyosha Karamazov are such prereflectively pure people.[10]

No matter how attractive prereflective purity is, it is impossible to maintain it in complex moral situations, because the natural, spontaneous, intuitive responses have become impossible. We may want to do very much what morality requires, yet we cannot just do it in typical complex moral situations, because we are often unsure what it is. If we are to do the right thing, we must first judge what it is. And this judgment requires an adequate moral perspective, based on objectivity, breadth, and depth that only much reflection can give us. So morally good conduct in complex moral situations requires good judgment and excludes prereflective purity, while in simple situations the requirement is the reverse.

Another reason why prereflective purity is misplaced outside of simple moral situations is that it requires an incredible degree of obliviousness to our social setting. It would require us to live in the world and not to be aware of the considerations that influence others in their responses to us and of their expectation that our conduct toward them will be guided by similar considerations. Prereflective purity in complex moral situations would lead us to live constantly at cross-purposes with others. If we understand that external goods matter to others, then our prereflective purity has already begun to fade, because we must see ourselves as a source of external goods, for we are among the distributors of status, prestige, rank, and respect.

[10] For some philosophical considerations of them, see Hartmann, *Ethics*, especially volume 2, chapter 18; Myrna, "Purity in Morals," is a good critical discussion of Hartmann; and Kolenda, *Philosophy in Literature*, chapters 3–4, treats illuminatingly Dostoyevsky's and Melville's characters.

If we do not understand that external goods matter to others, we are fools. "Stupidity pushed to a certain point *is* . . . immorality."[11] Admittedly, such fools may be the holy fools of Dostoyevsky and Melville. I wonder, however, what they would have said, not to some ineffectual weakling like Ivan Karamazov, but to Montaigne or John Stuart Mill, for instance, in a long conversation about the facts of social life. In any case, for the rest of humanity, apart from holy fools, prereflective purity is lost forever. Its loss is part of the price we pay for self-direction and personal morality.

I think that those who regret its loss do so, not because they fail to see the need for self-direction, good judgment, and the reflection that must go with them, but because they miss the simplicity and spontaneity that accompany prereflective purity. The constant reflective scrutiny of ourselves is burdensome. We yearn to do as we please without having to seek the nod of the censor we ourselves have appointed, but who is a censor nevertheless.

But must it be like this? Is it necessary that good judgment and reflection should be experienced as burdens? I do not think so. Imagine people whose moral perspectives have become their second nature. They are quite clear about their conceptions of good lives, and they are living according to them. They have chosen a beneficial way of life, and they are successful at it; they enjoy reciprocated loving relationships with other people, and they harmoniously coexist with strangers and acquaintances they casually encounter in daily life. Of course, things have not always gone as well as this. They have reached their present state of moral development only after much struggle, trial and error, hard work, discipline, and self-examination. But all this is now behind them. They have succeeded in transforming themselves into the person they wanted to be. Complex situations still confront them, but clarity, sensitivity, past reflection, and a lot of experience enable them to find the right interpretations without much difficulty. The result of their thorough identification with their moral perspectives and of the good judgment they have gained is that complex moral situations appear to them as simple ones do to most of us. As grandmasters of chess know at a glance what an average player may take hours to figure out, as architects quickly envision a two-dimensional plan in three-dimensional spatial terms, a process with which laymen may endlessly struggle, so do complex moral situations appear simple to some moral agents. Their perspectives have become natural to them, and their judgments follow easily and spontaneously. They are not tempted by false options any more; they have

[11] James, *The Golden Bowl*, 62.

their contrary urges firmly in control; they are not plagued by doubts; they no longer have to think laboriously through the steps leading to the right interpretation. They have regained purity. It is not prereflective purity but reflective purity gained by long moral struggle. It is the purity of undistorted vision, deep understanding of the world, uncorrupted judgment, a balanced view of external and internal goods, and the result of past reflection. It is the fruit of having achieved objectivity, breadth, and depth in morality.[12]

Thus, integrity and purity are connected. Kierkegaard saw something important, although he mistook its nature. As Wittgenstein suggests, purity is not the natural absence of temptation but the result of having worked our way through the temptations of external goods, self-deception, and compromise and having reached a stage of moral development where they cease to be temptations. It is to have reached Montaigne's attitude: "We must live in the world and make the most of it as we find it," but to do so by offering only "limited and conditional services," by knowing and frankly stating our limits.

---

[12] I feel obliged to note that, while I have no sympathy whatever for it, there is a groping in the German romantic tradition for the same conclusion as I have reached. See Heller, "The Taking Back of the Ninth Symphony."

Works Cited

Adkins, Arthur W. H. *Merit and Responsibility*. Oxford: Clarendon Press, 1960.

Annas, Julia. "Personal Love and Kantian Ethics in *Effi Briest*." *Philosophy and Literature* 8(1984): 15–31.

Aristotle. *Eudemian Ethics*. Translated by J. Solomon. In *The Complete Works of Aristotle*, edited by Jonathan Barnes. Princeton: Princeton University Press, 1984.

———. *Nicomachean Ethics*. Translated by William David Ross and revised by John O. Urmson. In *The Complete Works of Aristotle*, edited by Jonathan Barnes. Princeton: Princeton University Press, 1984.

———. *Poetics*. Translated by Ingram Bywater. In *The Complete Works of Aristotle*, edited by Jonathan Barnes. Princeton: Princeton University Press, 1984.

———. *Politics*. Translated by Benjamin Jowett. In *The Complete Works of Aristotle*, edited by Jonathan Barnes. Princeton: Princeton University Press, 1984.

———. *Rhetoric*. Translated by W. Rhys Roberts. In *The Complete Works of Aristotle*, edited by Jonathan Barnes. Princeton: Princeton University Press, 1984.

Austen, Jane. *Sense and Sensibility*. Harmondsworth: Penguin, 1969.

Baier, Annette. *Postures of the Mind*. Minneapolis: University of Minnesota Press, 1985.

Beiner, Ronald. *Political Judgment*. Chicago: University of Chicago Press, 1983.

Berlin, Isaiah. *Four Essays on Liberty*. Oxford: Oxford University Press, 1969.

———. *Concepts and Categories*. Edited by Henry Hardy with an introduction by Bernard Williams. London: Hogarth, 1978.

Bolt, Robert. *A Man for All Seasons*. New York: Random House, 1965.

Brogan, Dennis W. *The American Character*. New York: Knopf, 1944.

Brookner, Anita. *Look at Me*. London: Cape, 1983.

Brown, James. "Moral Theory and the Ought-Can Principle." *Mind* 86(1977): 206–23.

Bruford, William H. *The German Tradition of Self-Cultivation*. Cambridge: Cambridge University Press, 1975.

Cioffari, Vincenzo. "Fortune, Fate, and Chance." In *Dictionary of the History of Ideas*, edited by Philip P. Wiener. New York: Scribner's, 1973.

Cooper, John M. "Aristotle on Friendship." In *Essays on Aristotle's Ethics*, edited by Amelie Rorty. Berkeley: University of California Press, 1980.

———. "Aristotle on the Forms of Friendship." *Review of Metaphysics* 30(1977): 619–48.

Cooper, John M. "Aristotle on the Goods of Fortune." *Philosophical Review* 94(1985): 173–96.

———. *Reason and the Human Good in Aristotle.* Cambridge: Harvard University Press, 1975.

Conrad, Joseph. *Heart of Darkness.* In *Great Short Works of Joseph Conrad.* New York: Harper & Row, 1967.

Devlin, Patrick. *The Enforcement of Morals.* London: Oxford University Press, 1968.

Dodds, Eric Robertson. "On Misunderstanding *Oedipus Rex,*" *Greece and Rome* 13(1966): 37–49.

Douglas, Mary. *Natural Symbols.* London: Barrie & Jenkins, 1978.

Drabble, Margaret. *The Needle's Eye.* New York: Popular Library, 1972.

Falk, W. David. "Morality, Self, and Others." In *Ethics,* edited by Judith J. Thomson and Gerald Dworkin. New York: Harper & Row, 1968.

Fingarette, Herbert. *Self-Deception.* London: Routledge, 1977.

Fontane, Theodor. *Effi Briest.* Translated by Douglas Parmee. Harmondsworth: Penguin, 1967.

Foot, Philippa. *Virtues and Vices.* Berkeley: University of California Press, 1978.

Gallie, William B. *Philosophy and the Historical Understanding.* London: Chatto & Windus, 1964.

Gert, Bernard. *The Moral Rules.* New York: Harper & Row, 1973.

Goffman, Erving. *Interaction Ritual.* New York: Pantheon, 1967.

———. *The Presentation of Self in Everyday Life.* New York: Doubleday, 1959.

Gowans, Christopher G., ed. *Moral Dilemmas.* New York: Oxford University Press, 1987.

Hampshire, Stuart. *Morality and Conflict.* Oxford: Blackwell, 1983.

———. *Two Theories of Morality.* Oxford: Oxford University Press, 1977.

Hardie, William F. R. *Aristotle's Ethical Theory.* Oxford: Clarendon Press, 1980.

Hart, Herbert L. A. *Law, Liberty, and Morality.* Stanford: Stanford University Press, 1953.

———. "Social Solidarity and the Enforcement of Morals." *University of Chicago Law Review* 55(1967): 1–13.

Hartmann, Nicolai. *Ethics.* Translated by S. Coit. London: Allen & Unwin, 1932.

Heller, Erich. "The Taking Back of the Ninth Symphony." In Erich Heller's *In the Age of Prose.* Cambridge: Cambridge University Press, 1984.

Hume, David. *An Enquiry Concerning the Principles of Morals.* Edited by L. A. Selby-Bigge. Oxford: Clarendon Press, 1961.

———. *A Treatise of Human Nature.* Edited by L. A. Selby-Bigge. Oxford: Clarendon Press, 1960.

Ibsen, Henrik. *The Master Builder.* Translated by Eva Le Galliene. New York: New York University Press, 1955.

Irwin, Terrence H. "Reason and Responsibility in Aristotle." In *Essays on Ar-*

istotle's Ethics, edited by Amelie Rorty. Berkeley: University of California Press, 1980.

James, Henry. *The Ambassadors*. Harmondsworth: Penguin, 1973.

———. *The Golden Bowl*. London: Methuen, 1956.

Kant, Immanuel. *Critique of Pure Reason*. Translated by Norman Kemp Smith. London: Macmillan, 1953.

———. *Foundations of the Metaphysics of Morals*. Translated by Lewis White Beck. Indianapolis: Bobbs-Merrill, 1969.

Kekes, John. *The Nature of Philosophy*. Oxford: Blackwell, 1980.

Kierkegaard, Søren. *Purity of Heart*. Translated by Douglas V. Steere. New York: Harper & Row, 1948.

Knox, Bernard M. W. *Oedipus at Thebes*. New Haven: Yale University Press, 1957.

Kolenda, Konstantin. *Philosophy in Literature*. Totowa, N.J.: Barnes & Noble, 1982.

Lawrence, David Herbert. *Selected Essays*. Harmondsworth: Penguin, 1950.

Lloyd-Jones, Hugh. *The Justice of Zeus*. Berkeley: University of California Press, 1983.

MacIntyre, Alasdair. *After Virtue*. Notre Dame: University of Notre Dame Press, 1981.

———, ed. *Revisions*. Notre Dame: University of Notre Dame Press, 1983.

Mackie, John L. *Hume's Moral Theory*. London: Routledge, 1980.

Malcolm, Norman. *Ludwig Wittgenstein: A Memoir*. London: Oxford University Press, 1958.

Mercer, Philip. *Sympathy and Ethics*. Oxford: Clarendon Press, 1972.

Mill, John Stuart. *On Liberty*. Edited by Currin V. Shields. Indianapolis: Bobbs-Merrill, 1956.

Miller, David. *Philosophy and Ideology in Hume's Political Thought*. Oxford: Clarendon Press, 1981.

Mitchell, Basil. *Law, Morality, Religion in a Secular Society*. London: Oxford University Press, 1970.

Montaigne, Michel. *The Complete Essays of Montaigne*. Translated and edited by Donald M. Frame. Stanford: Stanford University Press, 1958.

Murdoch, Iris. *The Black Prince*. New York: Viking, 1973.

———. *The Good Apprentice*. London: Chatto & Windus, 1985.

———. *The Nice and the Good*. London: Chatto & Windus, 1968.

———. *The Sovereignty of Good*. London: Routledge, 1970.

Myrna, Frances. "Purity in Morals." *Monist* 66(1983): 283–97.

Nagel, Thomas. "The Fragmentation of Values." In Thomas Nagel's *Mortal Questions*. Cambridge: Cambridge University Press, 1979.

———. "Moral Luck." *Aristotelian Society Proceedings* supplementary volume 50(1976): 137–51.

———. *The Possibility of Altruism*. Oxford: Clarendon Press, 1970.

Nehamas, Alexander. "The Eternal Recurrence." *Philosophical Review* 89(1980): 331–56.

Nehamas, Alexander. *Nietzsche: Life as Literature*. Cambridge: Harvard University Press, 1985.

Neu, Jerome. "What is Wrong with Incest?" *Inquiry* 19(1976): 27–39.

Nietzsche, Friedrich. *The Genealogy of Morals*. Translated by Walter Kaufmann. In *Basic Writings of Nietzsche*, edited by Walter Kaufmann. New York: Random House, 1966.

———. *Thus Spoke Zarathustra*. Translated by Walter Kaufmann. In *The Portable Nietzsche*, edited by Walter Kaufmann. Harmondsworth: Penguin, 1976.

Norton, David L. *Personal Destinies*. Princeton: Princeton University Press, 1976.

Nussbaum, Martha Craven. *The Fragility of Goodness: Luck and Ethics in Greek Tragedy and Philosophy*. Cambridge: Cambridge University Press, 1986.

Oakeshott, Michael. *Rationalism in Politics*. London: Methuen, 1962.

Passmore, John. *The Perfectibility of Man*. London: Duckworth, 1970.

Phillips, Dewi Z. "Allegiance and Change in Morality." In Dewi Z. Phillips's *Through a Darkening Glass*. Notre Dame: University of Notre Dame Press, 1982.

Pincoffs, Edmund L. *Quandaries and Virtues*. Lawrence, KS: University of Kansas Press, 1986.

Plato. *The Republic*. Translated by Benjamin Jowett. In *The Dialogues of Plato*. New York: Random House, 1937.

———. *Symposium*. Translated by Benjamin Jowett. In *The Dialogues of Plato*. New York: Random House, 1937.

Plutarch. *The Age of Alexander*. Translated by Ian Scott-Kilvert. Harmondsworth: Penguin, 1973.

Popper, Karl Raimund. *Objective Knowledge*. Oxford: Clarendon Press, 1972.

Rescher, Nicholas. *Ethical Idealism*. Berkeley: University of California Press, 1987.

Ross, William David. *Foundations of Ethics*. Oxford: Clarendon Press, 1939.

———. *The Right and the Good*. Oxford: Clarendon Press, 1930.

Smart, John J. C., and Williams, Bernard. *Utilitarianism: For and Against*. Cambridge: Cambridge University Press, 1973.

Sophocles. *Oedipus the King* and *Antigone*. Translated by Robert Fagles. In *The Three Theban Plays*, introduced and with notes by Bernard M. W. Knox. New York: Viking, 1982.

Stevenson, Robert Louis. *Dr. Jekyll and Mr. Hyde*. London: Folio Society, 1948.

Strawson, Peter F. *Individuals*. New York: Doubleday, 1963.

Styron, William. *Sophie's Choice*. New York: Random House, 1979.

Taylor, Charles. "Responsibility for Self." In *The Identities of Persons*, edited by Amelie Rorty. Berkeley: University of California Press, 1976.

Taylor, Gabrielle. *Pride, Shame, and Guilt: Emotions of Self-Assessment*. Oxford: Clarendon Press, 1985.

Tolstoy, Leo. *The Death of Ivan Ilych and Other Stories*. Translated by A. Maude. New York: Signet, 1960.

Trilling, Lionel. *Sincerity and Authenticity*. Cambridge: Harvard University Press, 1972.

Twain, Mark. *The Adventures of Huckleberry Finn*. Harmondsworth: Penguin, 1966.

Vlastos, Gregory. "Justice and Equality." In *Social Justice*, edited by Richard B. Brandt. Englewood Cliffs, NJ: Prentice-Hall, 1962.

Wharton, Edith. *The Age of Innocence*. New York: Scribner's, 1920.

Williams, Bernard. "Conflicts of Values." In Bernard Williams's *Moral Luck*. Cambridge: Cambridge University Press, 1981.

———. *Ethics and the Limits of Philosophy*. London: Fontana, 1985.

———. "Introduction." In *Concepts and Categories*, by Isaiah Berlin, edited by Henry Hardy. London: Hogarth, 1978.

———. "Moral Luck." *Aristotelian Society Proceedings* supplementary volume 50(1976): 115–35.

Wollheim, Richard. *The Thread of Life*. Cambridge: Harvard University Press, 1984.

Woolf, Virginia. *Moments of Being*. Edited by Jeanne Schulkind. Sussex: Sussex University Press, 1976.

Index